THE ACADEMY COLLECTION
QUICK REFERENCE GUIDES FOR FAMILY PHYSICIANS

CHALLENGING DIAGNOSES

D0743775

THE ACADEMY COLLECTION
QUICK REFERENCE GUIDES FOR FAMILY PHYSICIANS

CHALLENGING DIAGNOSES

MARGARET E. McCAHILL, MD

*Director, Combined Family Medicine-Psychiatry
    Residency Program
Associate Director, Family Medicine Residency Program
University of California, San Diego
San Diego, California*

ERIK LINDBLOOM, MD

*Academic Fellow and Clinical Instructor
Department of Family and Community Medicine
University of Missouri-Columbia
Columbia, Missouri*

Series Medical Editor
RICHARD SADOVSKY, MD, MS

*Associate Professor of Family Medicine
State University of New York Health Science Center
Brooklyn, New York*

Williams & Wilkins
A WAVERLY COMPANY

BALTIMORE • PHILADELPHIA • LONDON • PARIS • BANGKOK
BUENOS AIRES • HONG KONG • MUNICH • SYDNEY • TOKYO • WROCLAW

HEAL
.08629900

Editor: Jonathan W. Pine, Jr.
Development Editor: Robert Newman, Co Medica, Inc
Project Manager, AAFP: Leigh McKinney
Managing Editor: Molly L. Mullen
Marketing Manager: Daniell Griffin
Project Editor: Ulita Lushnycky
Design Coordinator: Mario Fernandez

351 West Camden Street
Baltimore, Maryland 21201-2436 USA

Rose Tree Corporate Center
1400 North Providence Road
Building II, Suite 5025
Media, Pennsylvania 19063-2043 USA

Printed in the United States of America

Library of Congress Cataloging-in-Publication Data

McCahill, Margaret E.
    Challenging diagnoses / Margaret E. McCahill, Erik Lindbloom.
      p.   cm. — (The Academy collection—quick reference guides for
family physicians)
    Includes bibliographical references and index.
    ISBN 0-683-30423-2
    1. Mental illness—Diagnosis—Handbooks, manuals, etc. 2. Syndromes—Diagnosis—Handbooks, manuals, etc. 3. Systemic lupus erythematosus—Diagnosis—Handbooks, manuals, etc. 4. Developmental disabilities—Diagnosis—Handbooks, manuals, etc. 5. Headache—Diagnosis—Handbooks, manuals, etc. 6. Family medicine—Handbooks, manuals, etc. I. Lindbloom, Erik. II. Title. III. Series.
    [DNLM: 1. Mental Disorders—diagnosis handbooks. 2. Neurologic Manifestations handbooks. 3. Diagnosis, Differential handbooks. 4. Family Practice—methods handbooks. WM 34 M478c 1998]
RC469.M38   1998
616.8′ 0475—dc21
DNLM/DLC
for Library of Congress
                                        98-22561
                                            CIP

To purchase additional copies of this book, call our customer service department at **(800) 638-0672** or fax orders to **(800) 447-8438.** For other book services, including chapter reprints and large quantity sales, ask for the Special Sales department.

Canadian customers should call **(800) 665-1148,** or fax **(800) 665-0103.** For all other calls originating outside of the United States, please call **(410) 528-4223** or fax us at **(410) 528-8550.**
Visit Williams & Wilkins on the Internet: **http://www.wwilkins.com** or contact our customer service department at **custserv@wwilkins.com.** Williams & Wilkins customer service representatives are available from 8:30 am to 6:00 pm, EST, Monday through Friday, for telephone access.

                                   99 00 01 02 03
                              1 2 3 4 5 6 7 8 9 10

Krul

To our mothers, Margaret Mary Cahill and Trish Altman, who first modeled patience, persistence, and caring inquiry into all of life's challenges.

And to Dr. Theodore E. Woodward, Professor Emeritus of Medicine at the University of Maryland School of Medicine, who dedicated his life to teaching many generations of physicians that the only way to meet all diagnostic challenges in medicine is to LISTEN to the patient and take a thorough history, observe and examine the patient personally, CARE for the patient, with emphasis upon observation, care, and instruction at the bedside. Despite all of our remarkable technical advances in medicine, Dr. Woodward's principles remain the essential core of the practice of clinical medicine.

SERIES INTRODUCTION

Family practice is a unique clinical specialty encompassing a philosophy of care rather than a modality of care provided to a specific segment of the population. This philosophy of providing longitudinal care for persons of all ages in the complete context of their physical, emotional, and social environments was modeled by general practitioners, the parents of our modern specialty. To provide this kind of care, the family physician needs a broad knowledge base, appropriate evaluation tools, effective interventions, and patient education.

The knowledge base needed by a family physician is extraordinarily large. The American Academy of Family Physicians and other organizations provide clinical education through conferences and journals. Individual family physicians have written journal articles about a specific clinical topic or have tried to cover the broad knowledge base of family medicine in a single volume. The former are helpful, but may cover only a narrow segment of medicine, while the latter may not provide the depth needed to be useful in actual patient care.

The Academy Collection: Quick Reference Guides for Family Physicians is a series of books designed to assist family physicians with the broad knowledge base unique to our specialty. The books in this series have all been written by practicing family physicians who have special interest in the topics, and the chapters have been formatted to provide easy access to information needed at varying stages in the physician-patient encounter. Each volume is unique because each author has personalized the volume and provided a unique family physician perspective.

This series is not meant to be a final reference for the family physician who seeks a comprehensive text. The series also does not cover every topic that may be encountered by the family physician. The series does offer, in a depth determined appropriate by the authors, the information needed by the physician to handle the majority of patient encounters. The series also provides information to make patient care a combined doctor-patient effort. Specific patient education materials have been included where appropriate. Readers can contact the American Academy of Family Physicians Foundation for other resources.

The topics selected for The Academy Collection were chosen based on what family physicians said they needed. The first group of books covers office procedures, conditions of aging, and some of the most challenging diagnoses seen in family practice. Future books in the series will address musculoskeletal problems, skin conditions, environmental medicine, children's health, and gastrointestinal problems.

I welcome your comments. Please contact me at the American Academy of Family Physicians with your suggestions (Rick Sadovsky, MD, Series Editor, The Academy Collection, c/o AAFP, 8880 Ward Parkway, Kansas City, MO 64116; e-mail: academycollection@aafp.org). This collection is meant to be useful to you and your patients.

Richard Sadovsky, MD, MS
Series Editor

CONTENTS

Dedication   v

Series Introduction   vii

Diagnostic Charts   xiii

Introduction to Challenging Diagnoses   *xxxiii*

CHAPTER 1
Anxiety Disorders   1
　　Margaret E. McCahill

CHAPTER 2
Attention-Deficit Hyperactivity Disorder   19
　　Erik Lindbloom

CHAPTER 3
Chronic Fatigue Syndrome   29
　　Margaret E. McCahill

CHAPTER 4
Depressive Disorders   37
　　Margaret E. McCahill

CHAPTER 5
Developmental Delay   63
　　Erik Lindbloom

CHAPTER 6
Fibromyalgia Syndrome   73
　　Margaret E. McCahill

CHAPTER 7
Headache   81
　　Margaret E. McCahill

CHAPTER 8
Insomnia   95
　　Margaret E. McCahill

CHAPTER 9
Memory Concerns   107
Erik Lindbloom

CHAPTER 10
*Somatoform Disorders, Factitious Disorders,
and Malingering   119*
Margaret E. McCahill

CHAPTER 11
Substance Use Disorders   141
Margaret E. McCahill

CHAPTER 12
Systemic Lupus Erythematosus   161
Erik Lindbloom

APPENDICES

APPENDIX A
Criteria for Panic Attack   175

APPENDIX B
*Diagnostic Criteria for Panic Disorder (300.01 Panic Disorder
Without Agoraphobia; 300.21 Panic Disorder With
Agoraphobia)   176*

APPENDIX C
Diagnostic Criteria for 308.3 Acute Stress Disorder   177

APPENDIX D
*Diagnostic Criteria for 309.81 Post-traumatic
Stress Disorder   179*

APPENDIX E
*Diagnostic Criteria for 300.3 Obsessive-Compulsive
Disorder   181*

APPENDIX F
*Diagnostic Criteria for 300.02 Generalized Anxiety
Disorder   183*

APPENDIX G
*Diagnostic Criteria for 309.21 Separation Anxiety
Disorder   184*

APPENDIX H
A Comparison of Selected Benzodiazepines   185

APPENDIX I
The Basic Mental Status Examination 186

APPENDIX J
Folstein's Mini-Mental State Examination 188

APPENDIX K
Diagnostic Criteria for a Major Depressive Episode 191

APPENDIX L
Diagnostic Criteria for 300.4 Dysthymic Disorder 194

APPENDIX M
Diagnostic Criteria for the Adjustment Disorders 196

APPENDIX N
Diagnostic Criteria for 301.83 Borderline Personality Disorder 197

APPENDIX O
Overview of Treatment for Depression 198

APPENDIX P
Antidepressants Commonly Used in Primary Care 199

APPENDIX Q
Clinical Guidelines from AHCPR 200

APPENDIX R
Diagnostic Criteria for 300.81 Somatization Disorder 208

APPENDIX S
Diagnostic Criteria for Pain Disorder 209

APPENDIX T
Diagnostic Criteria for 300.7 Hypochondriasis 210

APPENDIX U
Diagnostic Criteria for 300.11 Conversion Disorder 211

APPENDIX V
Diagnostic Criteria for Factitious Disorder 212

Recommended Reading 213

Index 217

Diagnostic Charts

Clinical Manifestations	Concurrent Finding	Diagnosis Considerations
Anxiety/worry	"Hand-wringer" with diffuse global anxiety that causes significant distress or impairs life functions	• Generalized anxiety disorder (p. 1)
	Anxiety in excess of normal in a child about separation from caregiver; may take form of nightmares, physical complaints, etc	• Separation anxiety of childhood/adolescence (p.1)
	History of medical problem such as chronic obstructive pulmonary disease (COPD), asthma, myocardial infarction (MI), etc	• Anxiety disorder due to medical condition (p. 1)
	Intoxication or withdrawal from precipitating medications (see p. 000)	• Substance-induced anxiety disorder (p. 1)
	Months or more after a trauma, physical symptoms, numbing of emotional response, increased arousal, avoidance of reminders of trauma, reexperiencing the trauma	• Post-traumatic stress disorder (p. 1)
	Multiple panic attacks with persistent concern about recurrence; attempts to alter life to avoid attacks	• Panic disorder (p. 1)
	Persistent, recurring, irrational fear and active avoidance of a specific thing or situation, causing distress and impaired life functions	• Phobia (p. 1)
	Recurrent and persistent thoughts or behaviors that occupy more than 1 hr/day, cause distress, or significantly impair life functions	• Obsessive-compulsive disorder (p. 1)
	Shortness of breath, fatigue	• Pulmonary embolism • COPD

continued

Diagnostic Charts *continued*

Clinical Manifestations	Concurrent Finding	Diagnosis Considerations
		• Congestive heart failure (CHF) • Pulmonary edema • Pulmonary hypertension • Arrhythmia
	Sudden chest pain radiating to the arm or jaw or both	• MI
	Sudden intense fear or discomfort, with palpitations, chest pain, fear of losing control, etc	• Panic attack
	Weight loss, restlessness, increased appetite, tremor	• Hyperthyroidism
	Within 4 weeks of a trauma, physical symptoms, numbing of emotional response, increased arousal, avoidance of reminders of the trauma, reexperiencing the trauma	• Acute stress disorder (p. 1)
Developmental delay in children	Impaired social relationships	• Autism • Physical or sexual abuse • Substance abuse (p. 141) • Sensory abnormalities • Behavioral disorder
	Poor weight gain or growth	• Environmental or psychosocial factors • Chronic infection or inflammation • Immunodeficiency • Gastrointestinal (GI) malabsorption • Congenital syndromes • Thyroid disease • Chromosomal or inborn errors • Renal disease • Cardiopulmonary abnormalities
	Seizures	• Cerebral palsy • Toxin exposure • Post-traumatic • Vascular/ischemic etiology

continued

Diagnostic Charts *continued*

Clinical Manifestations	Concurrent Finding	Diagnosis Considerations
Diffuse complaints	Goiter, weight gain, fatigue	• Hypothyroidism
	Joint pains	• Rheumatologic disorder • Collagen disease
	Multiple or atypical infections	• HIV disease
	No objective or sufficient findings	• Somatoform disorder (p. 119) • Major depressive disorder (p. 37) • Anxiety disorder (p. 1) • Factitious disorder (p. 119) • Malingering (p. 119)
	Elevated erythrocyte sedimentation rate (ESR) or positive antinuclear antibody (ANA) test result	• Lupus (SLE) (p. 161) or other connective tissue disease
Diffuse muscle pains	Fatigue	• Fibromyalgia (p. 73) • Chronic fatigue syndrome (p. 29) • Myositis • Somatoform disorder (p. 119)
	Muscle wasting	• Osteoarthritis • Peripheral neuropathies
	Numbness and tingling	• Peripheral neuropathies • Anxiety disorders (p. 1)
	Progressive bone pain	• Multiple myeloma
	Tenderness at specific sites	• Fibromyalgia (p. 73)
	Fever	• Influenza • Chronic fatigue syndrome (p. 29) • Acute hepatitis • Viral syndromes • Rheumatologic disorders • Inflammatory conditions
	Inconsistent findings	• Somatoform disorders (p. 119)
	Referred pain at nearby site from pressure over trigger point	• Myofascial pain
	Elevated ESR	• Myositis

continued

Diagnostic Charts *continued*

Clinical Manifestations	Concurrent Finding	Diagnosis Considerations
		• Arthritis • Connective tissue diseases
	Elevated muscle enzymes	• Myositis
	Normal lab test results	• Fibromyalgia (p. 73) • Somatoform disorder (p. 119) • Anxiety or depressive disorder (p. 1, 37)
Positive ANA		• Collagen vascular disease • Fibromyalgia syndrome (p. 73) • SLE (p. 161)
Fatigue or generalized weakness	Behavioral changes	• Substance abuse (p. 141) • Anxiety disorder (p. 1) • Major depressive disorder (p. 37) • Metabolic disorder • Dementia (p. 107) • HIV disease • Other mental disorders • Somatoform disorder (p. 119) • Chronic fatigue syndrome (p. 29)
	Coordination problems, balance problems, tremors	• Parkinson's disease
	Dyspnea	• CHF • Coronary artery disease • COPD • Cardiomyopathy
	Focal muscle weakness	• Multiple sclerosis • Neurologic disorder • Myasthenia gravis • Myositis
	Irritability, breathlessness and numerous somatic complaints	• Anxiety disorder (p. 1)
	Most severe in the morning	• Psychological cause
	Multiple medications	• Polypharmacy
	Nocturia	• Benign prostatic hypertrophy (BPH) or other urethral obstruction • Urinary tract infection (UTI)

continued

Diagnostic Charts *continued*

Clinical Manifestations	Concurrent Finding	Diagnosis Considerations
		• Diabetes mellitus or insipidus • CHF • Renal insufficiency • Cirrhosis with ascites
	Precipitated by psychosocial factors	• Chronic anxiety or stress (p. 1) • Adjustment disorders (p. 37)
	Sleep disturbance/insomnia	• Major depressive disorder (p. 37) • Anxiety disorder (p. 1) • Sleep apnea (p. 95) • Insomnia (p. 95)
	Sleeping excessively during day	• Narcolepsy (p. 95) • Sleep apnea (p. 95)
	Swelling in ankles and around eyes	• Nephrotic syndrome
	Unintended weight loss	• HIV disease • Major depressive disorder (p. 37) • Malignancy • Dietary factors • Hyperthyroidism
	Use of antihistamines, tranquillizers, antihypertensives	• Medicine-induced fatigue
	Edema or pulmonary rales or both	• CHF • Renal insufficiency
	Fever	• Viral or bacterial infection • Rheumatologic condition • Chronic fatigue syndrome (p. 29)
	Generalized musculoskeletal aching or stiffness, with specific tender sites, but normal joint/muscle exam and normal lab test results	• Fibromyalgia (p. 73) • Fibrositis
	Hepatic tenderness	• Hepatitis
	Hepatosplenomegaly	• Infectious mononucleosis • Cancer
	Midsystolic click or late systolic murmur	• Mitral valve prolapse

continued

Diagnostic Charts *continued*

Clinical Manifestations	Concurrent Finding	Diagnosis Considerations
	Patient appears depressed	• Major depressive disorder (p. 37) • Hypothyroidism • Dietary factors
	Decreased hematocrit, pallor	• Anemia
	Decreased thyroid-stimulating hormone (TSH)	• Hyperthyroidism
	Elevated ESR or positive ANA	• SLE (p. 161) or other connective tissue disease
	Icterus, elevated liver function tests	• Hepatitis • Cirrhosis
	Increased TSH	• Hypothyroidism
Fever	Chills	• Malaria • Bacteremia • UTI • Salmonella • Abscess
	Chronic fatigue, generalized malaise, restlessness or sadness	• Chronic fatigue syndrome (p. 29)
	Cough, shortness of breath	• Acute bronchitis • Lung infection • Atelectasis • Pericarditis • Tuberculosis • Pleuritis • Pulmonary embolism • Sarcoidosis
	Diarrhea	• Intestinal parasites • Food poisoning • Viral intestinal disorders • Crohn's disease • Megacolon
	Dizziness	• Otitis media • Otitis externa • Acute labyrinthitis

continued

Diagnostic Charts *continued*

Clinical Manifestations	Concurrent Finding	Diagnosis Considerations
	Frequent or painful urination	• Bladder cancer • Kidney infection • Prostatitis • Urethritis • UTI
	Medication use	• Drug interaction/drug fever
	Nausea and vomiting	• Brain abscess • Encephalitis • Brain hemorrhage • Food poisoning (e.g., Salmonella) • Acute hepatitis • Meningitis • Peritonitis • Parasite infection • Appendicitis • Cholecystitis or other acute abdominal conditions • Viral syndrome
	No other symptoms or signs	• Occupational exposure, drug ingestion • Tuberculosis • Parasite infection • Occult carcinoma • Factitious fever • Typhoid fever
	Low-grade fever	• Viral syndrome (e.g., infectious mononucleosis) • Pancreatitis • Pelvic inflammatory disease • Collagen vascular disease • Sinusitis • Hepatitis, acute or chronic • Tuberculosis • Lymphoma • Carcinoma • Drugs • Thyroiditis • Subacute infective carditis

continued

Diagnostic Charts *continued*

Clinical Manifestations	Concurrent Finding	Diagnosis Considerations
		• Typhoid fever • Benign tumors • Connective tissue diseases
	Lymphadenopathy	• Infection • Chronic fatigue syndrome (p. 29) • Leukemia • Lymphoma • Sarcoidosis
	Rash	• Lyme disease • Infectious arthritis • Viral syndromes • Rheumatic fever • Rocky Mountain spotted fever • Drug reactions • Streptococcal infections • Staphylococcal infections
	Slow heart rate	• Typhoid fever • Some viral infections
	Elevated serum, alkaline phosphatase	• Hepatic infection • Disseminated tuberculosis • Lymphoma • Hepatic neoplasm • Infectious mononucleosis • Cytomegalovirus infection
	ESR > 100 mm/hr	• Tuberculosis • Neoplasm • Connective tissue diseases • Viral infections
Forgetfulness/ memory complaints	Chronic fatigue with musculoskeletal symptoms and sleep disturbance	• Chronic fatigue syndrome (p. 29)
	Drug or toxin exposure, dietary deficiency	• Alcohol dementia • Narcotic or toxin poisoning • Thiamin B_1 deficiency • Vitamin B_{12} deficiency • Korsakoff's syndrome (p. 111)

continued

Diagnostic Charts *continued*

Clinical Manifestations	Concurrent Finding	Diagnosis Considerations
	Elderly patient	• Benign senescent forgetfulness (p. 107) • Alzheimer's disease (p. 107) • Pick's disease (p. 107) • Lewy body variant dementia (p. 107) • Frontal lobe degeneration
	Fatigue, weight gain	• Hypothyroidism • Major depressive disorder (p. 37) • Addison's disease
	Hallucinations	• Substance abuse (p. 141) • Lewy body variant dementia (p. 107) • Psychosis
	Movement disorder/gait disturbance	• Parkinson's disease • Huntington's chorea • Lewy body variant dementia (p. 107) • Creutzfeldt-Jakob disease • Hydrocephalus
	Progressive decrease in cognitive skills	• Alzheimer's disease (p. 107) • Multi-infarct dementia (p. 107) • Other progressive dementing processes (p. 107)
	Sadness	• Major depressive disorder (p. 37)
	Severe headache, nausea and vomiting	• Brain tumors (p. 80) • Increased intracranial pressure
	Sudden onset	• Other intracranial pathology, metabolic abnormalities, substance abuse
	Sudden onset of weakness, speech abnormality	• Cerebrovascular accident
	Use of benzodiazepines, hypnotic or other psychotropics	• Medication-induced forgetfulness (p. 107)

continued

Diagnostic Charts *continued*

Clinical Manifestations	Concurrent Finding	Diagnosis Considerations
	Evidence of infection	• HIV disease • Syphilis • Granulomatous disease • Other viral/fungal/protozoan etiology
	Evidence of vascular disease	• Multi-infarct dementia (p. 107) • Vasculitis • Subcortical dementia (p. 107)
	Hepatitis, Kaiser-Fleischer rings, psychiatric symptoms	• Wilson's disease
	Normal exam and lab test results	• Major depressive disorder (p. 37) • Anxiety disorder (p. 1)
Headache	Acute, "worst headache ever"	• Meningitis (p. 80) • Subarachnoid hemorrhage (p. 80)
	Aggravated by coughing, sneezing	• Vascular headache (p. 80) • Increased intracranial pressure (p. 80) • Cough headache (p. 80)
	Aura, unilateral (often), throbbing, nausea	• Migraine headache (p. 80)
	Band-like, bilateral, associated with stress/fatigue	• Muscle contraction headache (p. 80)
	Blurred vision	• Increased intracranial pressure (p. 80)
	Burning scalp pain or tenderness	• Giant cell arteritis (p. 80)
	Chronic nature, vertigo, tinnitus, after trauma	• Post-traumatic stress disorder (p.1)
	Deep-seated aching, recurrent, worse with activity, projectile vomiting	• Brain tumor (p. 80)
	Diffuse myalgias, upper respiratory infection/GI symptoms	• Viral syndrome
	Dull, persistent, constricting pain	• Tension headache (p. 80)
	Eye pain, seeing halos	• Glaucoma

continued

Diagnostic Charts *continued*

Clinical Manifestations	Concurrent Finding	Diagnosis Considerations
	Fatigue, weakness	• Anemia
	Generalized, sudden onset during/ immediately after coitus	• Coital headache (p. 80)
	Loud snoring	• Sleep apnea (p. 95)
	Maxillary/mandibular tenderness	• Trigeminal neuralgia • Temporomandibular joint syndrome • Temporal arteritis (p. 80)
	Morning headache	• Tension headache (p. 80) • Bruxism (p. 95)
	Multiple other symptoms with no objective findings	• Somatoform disorder • Major depressive disorder (p. 37) • Anxiety disorder (p. 1) • Viral syndrome
	Muscle aches, pains, stiffness	• Fibromyalgia (p. 73) • Influenza
	Nocturnal, unilateral, orbital pain with lacrimation, rhinorrhea	• Cluster headache (p. 80)
	Chronic occipital or nuchal headache with stiff neck in older adult	• Cervical arthritis
	Occurrence with computer use or after reading	• Eye pain due to facial muscle strain
	Patient sees halos	• Glaucoma
	Sinus/ocular tenderness, purulent rhinorrhea	• Sinusitis (p. 80)
	Vomiting, coordination problems, decreased appetite	• Hydrocephalus
	Fever	• Brain hemorrhage (p. 80) • Encephalitis • Temporal arteritis (p. 80) • Chronic fatigue syndrome (p. 29) • Viral syndrome

continued

Diagnostic Charts *continued*

Clinical Manifestations	Concurrent Finding	Diagnosis Considerations
		• Sinusitis (p. 80) • Meningitis
	Temporal artery tenderness, age > 50, elevated ESR, visual symptoms, unilateral	• Temporal arteritis (p. 80)
Impaired memory	Appearance and remittance of seemingly unrelated neurologic symptoms	• Multiple sclerosis
	Dietary deficiency	• B_{12} deficiency
	Gradual development to disorientation with mood and personality changes	• Alzheimer's disease (p. 107) • Multi-infarct dementia (p. 107) • Pseudodementia of depression (p. 107)
	Headaches, nausea and vomiting; paralysis	• Brain tumor (p. 80) • Subdural hematoma (p. 80) • Stroke
	Minimal memory loss in otherwise healthy person	• Age-associated memory impairment (p. 107)
	Sadness	• Major depressive disorder (p. 37) • Bereavement (p. 37)
	Severe fatigue	• Chronic fatigue syndrome (p. 29) • Hypothyroidism
	Sudden loss of memory	• Acute trauma • Cerebrovascular accident • Intracranial hemorrhage (p. 80) • Brain lesions • Substance abuse (p. 141) • Alcohol use (p. 141) • Medications
	Use of medications or other drugs	• Substance abuse (p. 141) • Drug reactions
	Fever	• Chronic fatigue syndrome (p. 29) • Encephalitis

continued

Diagnostic Charts *continued*

Clinical Manifestations	Concurrent Finding	Diagnosis Considerations
		• Meningitis • Infection
	Involuntary movements	• Seizure disorder • Huntington's chorea
	Resting tremor, bradykinesia	• Parkinson's disease
	Sudden onset of weakness, speech abnormalities	• Cerebrovascular accident
Insomnia	Early morning wakening, depressed mood, anhedonia, diminished energy, concentration, and appetite	• Major depressive disorder (p. 37) • Thyroid disease
	Frequent awakening	• Sleep apnea (p. 95) • Major depressive disorder (p. 37) • Anxiety disorder (p. 1)
	Loud snoring	• Hypothyroidism • Sleep apnea (p. 95) • Obesity/pickwickian syndrome
	Nocturia	• BPH or other urethral obstruction • Diabetes mellitus or insipidus • CHF • Renal insufficiency • Cirrhosis with ascites
	Palpitations	• Hyperthyroidism • Mitral valve prolapse • Anxiety disorder (p. 1) • Tachyarrhythmias
	Poor sleep quality	• Caffeine use • Medications, such as psychotropics, β-blockers, sympathomimetics, diuretics, hypnotics • Painful, uncomfortable conditions and changes in sleep habits of older adults • Nocturnal myoclonus (p. 95) • Restless legs syndrome (p. 95)
	Somatic complaints	• Anxiety disorder (p. 1) • Organic disease

continued

Diagnostic Charts *continued*

Clinical Manifestations	Concurrent Finding	Diagnosis Considerations
		• Somatoform disorder (p. 107, 119) • Major depressive disorder (p. 37)
	Substance or chronic medication use	• Drug/alcohol dependent insomnia (p. 95) • Tolerance to sleep medications • Caffeine consumption
Lymphadenopathy	Tender	• Acute leukemia • Infection
	Axillary adenopathy	• Hodgkin's disease • Non-Hodgkin's lymphoma • Carcinoma • Infections • Insect bites • Trauma
	Cervical adenopathy	• Carcinoma • Rubella • Toxoplasmosis • Infectious mononucleosis • Tuberculosis • Sarcoidosis • Lymphoma • Lymphoreticular neoplasms
	Epitrochlear adenopathy	• Infections • Sarcoidosis • Secondary syphilis • Non-Hodgkin's lymphoma
	Generalized (more than 2 separate lymph node groups)	• Carcinoma • HIV disease • Lymphoma • Leukemia • Infectious mononucleosis • Cytomegalovirus • Tuberculosis • Viral hepatitis • Secondary syphilis • Toxoplasmosis

continued

Diagnostic Charts *continued*

Clinical Manifestations	Concurrent Finding	Diagnosis Considerations
		• Histoplasmosis • Drug allergy • Autoimmune disorders • Skin rashes
	Inguinal adenopathy	• Carcinoma • Venereal infections • Lower extremity infections • Lower extremity trauma
	Nontender, firm, large, rubbery	• Lymphoma
	Nontender, hard, fixed	• Solid tumor metastases
	Intra-abdominal or retroperitoneal nodes	• Tuberculosis • Malignant carcinoma
	Intrathoracic adenopathy (mediastinal and hilar adenopathy)	• Lymphoma • Lung diseases • Infectious mononucleosis • Sarcoidosis • Fungal infections • Tuberculosis • Lung cancer • Metastatic carcinoma
Poor school performance in children	Disruptive behavior	• Attention-deficit hyperactivity disorder (p. 19) • Conduct disorder • Oppositional defiant disorder • Schizophrenia • Personality disorder • Obsessive compulsive disorder (OCD) (p. 1)
	Fear	• School phobia • Separation anxiety disorder (p. 1) • Post-traumatic stress disorder (p. 1) • Stranger anxiety • Schizophrenia
	Social withdrawal	• Autism • Substance abuse (p. 141) • Affective disorders (p. 37)

continued

Diagnostic Charts *continued*

Clinical Manifestations	Concurrent Finding	Diagnosis Considerations
		• Anxiety disorders • Sensory abnormalities • Eating disorder
Sadness, feeling blue	Comorbid condition	• General medical condition with depression (p. 41–42)
	Death of loved one	• Bereavement (p. 37)
	Disturbance in normal daily activities, sleep disturbance	• Major depressive disorder (p. 37)
	Fatigue	• Hepatitis • Depression (p. 37)
	With nausea	• Pancreatic cancer
	With weight gain, constipation	• Hypothyroidism
	Identifiable stressful event or serious medical condition	• Adjustment disorder (p. 37)
	Mania	• Bipolar disorder (p. 37)
	Medication use	• Medication-induced depression (p. 37)
	More mild depression for 2 years or more	• Dysthmic disorder (p. 37)
	Multiple somatic complaints	• Mood or anxiety disorder (p. 1)
	Postpartum	• "Baby blues" or postpartum depression (p. 37)
	Recent loss of a loved one	• Grief reaction (p. 37)
	Resting tremors, stiffness and weakness	• Parkinson's disease
	Seasonal pattern	• Major depressive disorder (p. 37)
	"Stable instability" and intense reaction to perceived rejection	• Borderline personality disorder (p. 37)
	Substance/alcohol abuse or dependence	• Depression secondary to substance abuse (p. 37)

continued

Diagnostic Charts *continued*

Clinical Manifestations	Concurrent Finding	Diagnosis Considerations
Sensory neuropathies	Diminished position sense and deep tendon reflexes, imbalance, possible motor dysfunction	• Large-fiber neuropathies
	Exposure to heavy metals	• Toxic neuropathy
	Fatigue	• Anemia • Diabetes mellitus • Multiple sclerosis
	Intermittent	• Anxiety disorder (p. 1) • Hyperventilation
	Lymphadenopathy, muscle aches, fever	• Sarcoidosis
	Multifocal	• Diabetes mellitus • Alcohol or drug use (p. 141) • Polyarteritis nodosa • Dietary deficiencies • Guillain-Barré syndrome • Multiple sclerosis • Rheumatoid arthritis • Amyloidosis • Malnutrition • Medications • Hereditary • Infection
	Muscle weakness	• Spinal stenosis, tumors, or injury • Anemia • Brain tumors (p. 80) • Disk herniation • Peripheral neuropathy • Spondylosis • Transient ischemic attack
	Symptoms wax and wane	• Multiple sclerosis
	Unifocal extremity involvement	• Medial/ulnar nerve entrapment • Meralgia paresthetica • Sleeping position

continued

Diagnostic Charts *continued*

Clinical Manifestations	Concurrent Finding	Diagnosis Considerations
	Burning, painful dysesthesias, decreased pinprick and temperature sensation	• Small-fiber neuropathies
	Dermatomal distribution of pain, skin eruption	• Herpes zoster
	Diffuse complaints with no objective findings	• Somatization disorder (p. 119)
	"Restless" or twitching legs	• Nocturnal myoclonus (p. 95) • Restless legs syndrome (p. 95)
	Arousal during REM (rapid eye movement)	• Nightmares
	Daytime sleeping	• Change in sleep habits
	Difficulty falling asleep or anxious feeling	• Anxiety disorder (p. 1) • Thyroid disease • Inactivity during day • Transient situational insomnia (p. 95) • Exercise/caffeine intake close to bedtime (p. 95) • Chronic pain (e.g., HA, GI, arthritis)
Tremor	Antecedent dementia	• Alzheimer's disease (p. 107)
	Involuntary tremor worsening with emotional stress, may be familial	• Essential tremor
	Sudden onset of fear and panic, palpitations	• Anxiety disorder (p. 1)
	Weight loss with increased appetite, restlessness	• Hyperthyroidism
	Worsened by coffee, drugs, nicotine, fatigue	• Enhanced physiologic tremor • Hyperthyroidism • Hypoglycemia • Substance withdrawal (p. 141)
	Appear, then disappear, weakness in extremities	• Multiple sclerosis

continued

Diagnostic Charts *continued*

Clinical Manifestations	Concurrent Finding	Diagnosis Considerations
	Movement disorders looking like tremors	• Asterixis • Myoclonus • Fasciculations
	Occurs with intentional movement	• Cerebellar disease • Wilson's disease • Multiple sclerosis
	Proximal tremor with liver disease	• Wilson's disease
	Tremor at rest, stiffness, fixed expression	• Parkinson's disease
Weight loss	Abdominal pain	• Intestinal parasites • Colitis • Cancer • Crohn's disease • Leukemia • Pancreatitis • Ulcer
	Anorexia	• Poor dentition • Dementia (p. 37) • Major depression • Anxiety disorders (p. 1) • Metabolic disorders • Drugs (p. 141) • Substance abuse (p. 141) • Anorexia nervosa • Carcinoma • Infection
	Chronic cough	• Tuberculosis • CHF • Lung cancer
	Fatigue, weakness	• CHF • Anemia • Any of the above
	Increased appetite	• Diabetes mellitus • AIDS • Hyperthyroidism • Intestinal absorption abnormalities

continued

Diagnostic Charts *continued*

Clinical Manifestations	Concurrent Finding	Diagnosis Considerations
	Joint swelling, pain and stiffness	• Rheumatoid arthritis • Collagen vascular disease (e.g., SLE [p. 161])
	None, younger person	• Psychogenic disorders
	Normal appetite	• Socioeconomic factors
	Recurrent infections	• Immunodeficiency disease • Gammopathy (e.g., multiple myeloma)
	Lymphadenopathy	• Carcinoma • Lymphoma • Infection • Sarcoidosis • Tuberculosis • HIV disease
	Swollen legs	• CHF • Nephrotic syndrome • Cirrhosis • Carcinoma
	Anemia, low serum albumin	• Malnourishment • Liver disease

NTRODUCTION

This volume focuses on the patients who provide family physicians with the greatest opportunity both to exercise their skills as clinical detectives and diagnosticians and to practice the art of medicine—and whose problems and symptoms make up at least 60% of what a family physician encounters in a day. It also addresses the diagnostic entities that can merge or imitate other diagnoses—that can look exactly like one illness at one point in time yet turn out to be something entirely different. This volume is about the disorders that cause most busy physicians to stop and say, "hmm. . . . " It is about the things that even experienced family physicians may not feel "absolutely sure" about in their practice.

We often hear in our training years, "common things present commonly." Common things are not always obvious, however. Most family physicians feel comfortable making a diagnosis of depression, and they know that this is a common problem. Yet, a very large percentage of major depressive disorders go unrecognized. Anxiety disorders are the most common mental illness, and patients who have anxiety (especially panic disorder) typically present to the family physician with multiple physiologic complaints.

Disorders on the somatoform spectrum are extremely common, making up at least 25% of family physicians' practices and consuming more than 50% of their time. Somatizers generally hop from one physician to another, seeking costly, counterproductive, and sometimes risky procedures to diagnose and treat their perceived problems. Parents present with concerns about their children's behavior. A patient wonders about some memory problems: Is it normal aging? Is it Alzheimer's disease? At least one third of adults in the United States have some disturbance of sleep; nearly everyone has headaches. Patients with systemic lupus erythematosus (SLE) can present with any symptom, which may mimic any other illness.

Common things present commonly, but there are many chameleons, metamorphosing illnesses, and many symptoms so subtle when considered separately that even the most common diagnoses can be overlooked. Common things do present commonly, but recognizing them in all their diverse presentations and sorting out the subtypes to arrive at the proper treatment present a challenge to every physician.

What are the consequences if a family physician does not recognize the substance or the subtype of depression, anxiety disorder, or somatoform disorder accurately? We know that approximately 75% of prescriptions for antidepressants in the United States are written by nonpsychiatrists. Do we know the different types of common depressive disorders and the treatment nuances of each? Antianxiety medications are among the most frequently prescribed drugs each year in the United States, and 80% of these prescriptions are written by primary care physicians. Do we know which of the anxiety disorders improve with these medications and what the proper alternatives are for patients who do not improve with antianxiety drugs?

An estimated 25% of patients in a primary care waiting room have fatigue as a major problem, and about 60% of these will be found to have fatigue of no known cause. Do we know how to evaluate this ubiquitous symptom and help even those whose fatigue has no known cause to achieve their best health and functioning status? If we do not see these medical illnesses in our patients, we are likely to perform unnecessary tests and procedures. The patient will continue to suffer the consequences of the undiagnosed problem, and the heath care costs for the patient will continue to rise.

Managed care adds to the need to make an accurate diagnosis quickly. Under fee-for-service medicine, the physician and patient had the luxury of more time to establish the correct diagnosis and treatment. It is usually most cost-effective to do the right thing for the patient as soon as it is reasonably possible to do so. This requires prompt and accurate diagnosis of even the most subtle presentations of these common problems.

The organization of this volume is similar in some ways to that of a classic thesaurus—items are organized according to similarity of ideas and relationships among the different entities covered, rather than according to an alphabetical dictionary format. The physician may look in the diagnostic charts in the front of the book to find a particular symptom, then follow the chart to some of the common clinical problems that have this symptom as an important feature.

Moreover, in a chapter about a particular diagnosis or diagnostic category, there are nearby entities that are in the differential diagnosis of the first diagnosis researched. For example, the physician may suspect that the patient is depressed, and the chapter of depressive disorders describes the differential diagnostic features of the various types of depressive syndromes commonly seen in primary care. It makes reference to overlapping symptoms with the anxiety and substance use disorders. After the diagnosis is sorted out, the treatment options for each type of depression are described. The depth of discussion of the medical problems in the text is intended to be both *more* than is found in other quick reference books that many of us use in the turmoil of a busy clinic and *less* than is found in a comprehensive textbook. This book is intended to address the needs of medical specialists in family practice, who have a need for a broad base of information on the topic at hand. It is written for family physicians by other family physicians.

It is hoped that this text will assist the family physician as he or she sorts through the most strictly cognitive aspects of medical thinking and judgment. Many of the medical problems covered in this text have no objective physical findings and no diagnostic laboratory tests. Discerning the correct diagnosis and treatment plan relies entirely on the physician's diagnostic and analytical skills and clinical judgment. Although advances in medical science and technology have helped to establish many medical diagnoses (e.g., many cancers) earlier and with more certainty, this has not been the case for the medical problems and presenting patient complaints that make up the overwhelming majority of what we deal with in a day. To handle these problems, one must still be an astute clinician; an attentive listener; and an unhurried, empathic physician in the very traditional sense. We hope that all physicians will recognize that it is still essential to retain the art of medicine—as well as the science—and we hope that this volume will assist them as they blend those skills into the repertoire of an accomplished clinician.

Margaret E. McCahill

CHAPTER 1

Margaret E. McCahill

Anxiety Disorders

> *Anxiety: a state of being troubled or uneasy in mind about some
> uncertain event: Being in painful or disturbing suspense; concerned,
> solicitous, fraught with trouble . . . worrying . . .*
> — The Oxford English Dictionary

Anxiety is a feature of modern life and is certainly familiar to any graduate of medical training. Up to a point, anxiety itself is a good motivator. It moves us from apathy to action. However, when anxiety is excessive, it becomes disabling; the point when anxiety becomes disabling is unique for each individual.

Physicians should not allow the commonplace nature of anxiety to blind them to the severity and variety of anxiety disorders. Patients with anxiety disorders—notably those with panic disorder—may be more impaired in their life function than patients with chronic diseases, such as congestive heart failure and diabetes (1,2). Many forms of anxiety disorders exist. The following are the most common anxiety disorders encountered in primary care:

- Panic attack
- Panic disorder
- Acute stress disorder
- Post-traumatic stress disorder
- Obsessive-compulsive disorder
- Anxiety disorder due to a medical condition
- Substance-induced anxiety disorder
- Generalized anxiety disorder
- Specific phobias
- Separation anxiety disorder of childhood/adolescence

CHIEF COMPLAINT

Nervousness, worry, fear, irritability, inability to concentrate, and insomnia are common chief complaints of anxiety disorders. Anxious patients may also complain of physical symptoms and often of multiple unexplained symptoms. The specific chief complaints for each diagnosis are described in the following text.

1

EPIDEMIOLOGIC CONSIDERATIONS

Anxiety disorders are the most common of all mental disorders. Lifetime prevalence for anxiety disorders is 30.5% for women and 19.2% for men (2). Female gender and low economic and educational status increase a person's risk for anxiety disorders.

Children of anxious parents are seven times more likely to have an anxiety disorder than are children of normal parents (3). Anxiety disorders are common in children, but the incidence is uncertain. Nevertheless, it is estimated that less than 20% of children with anxiety disorders receive treatment (3). Children with anxiety disorders tend to retain an anxiety syndrome or mood disorder over time, although the specific anxiety disorder may change (3).

Several studies show that patients with anxiety disorders have a rate of approximately 30% current and 60% lifetime comorbid depression (2). Patients with major depression and an anxiety disorder have more severe symptoms, more functional impairment, a poorer treatment prognosis, and a higher suicide risk than those with anxiety disorders and no major depression (2).

HISTORY

Typical symptoms of anxiety disorders are listed in Table 1.1.

Panic Attack

The patient with panic attack characteristically presents with a pattern of symptoms together with a sense of fear and doom. Confirmation of that pattern and exclusion of other medical illnesses establishes the diagnosis. The diagnostic criteria for a panic attack are listed in Appendix A.

Onset of panic attack is usually sudden, and symptoms may peak in less than 10 minutes and resolve within 20 to 30 minutes. Symptoms may be very intense and give the patient a sense of impending doom, losing control, or "going crazy." Symptoms of panic attack may include the following:

- Palpitations
- Sweating
- Trembling
- Shortness of breath
- Choking sensation
- Chest pain
- Abdominal distress
- Dizziness
- Light-headedness
- Fear of losing control
- Fear of dying
- Chills or hot flashes

- Paresthesias
- Derealization
- Fatigue and need to sleep after the attack

TABLE 1.1.   Features Suggestive of Anxiety Disorders in the Patient History

Feature	Possible Diagnosis
Sudden intense fear or discomfort with palpitations, chest pain, fear of losing control, etc.	Panic attack (p. 2)
Multiple panic attacks with persistent concern about recurrence; attempts to alter life to avoid attacks	Panic disorder (p. 4)
Within 4 weeks of a trauma, physical symptoms, numbing of emotional response, increased arousal, avoidance of reminders of the trauma, reexperiencing the trauma lasts from 2–28 days.	Acute stress disorder (p. 5)
One month or more after a trauma, physical symptoms, numbing of emotional response, increased arousal, avoidance of reminders of trauma, reexperiencing the trauma	Post-traumatic stress disorder (p. 6)
Recurrent and persistent thoughts or behaviors that occupy more than 1 hr/day, cause distress, or significantly impair life functions	Obsessive-compulsive disorder (p. 6)
History of medical problem, such as chronic obstructive pulmonary disease, asthma, myocardial infarction	Anxiety disorder due to medical condition (p. 8)
Intoxication or withdrawal from precipitating medications (see p. 8)	Substance-induced anxiety disorder (p. 8)
"Hand-wringing" with diffuse global anxiety that causes significant distress or impairs life functions	Generalized anxiety disorder (p. 9)
Persistent, recurring, irrational fear and active avoidance of specific objects, causing distress and impaired life functions	Phobia (p. 9)
Anxiety in excess of normal about separation from caregiver; may take form of nightmares, physical complaints, and other conditions	Separation anxiety of childhood/adolescence (p. 9)

Note: A person who experiences one or a few panic attacks in a lifetime may not have a panic disorder or other mental disorder, and panic attacks in a person with depression or any other mental disorder may not justify a separate diagnosis of panic attack (4).

Panic Disorder

Patients with panic disorder (PD) experience recurrent, unexpected panic attacks followed by at least 1 month of persistent concern about having additional panic attacks or about the significance or complications of the panic attacks (4,5). The diagnostic criteria for PD are listed in Appendix B. The diagnosis is largely one of exclusion. (Table 1.2 lists some of the medical conditions to be excluded.)

Patients with PD may alter their lives in many ways to avoid perceived precipitants to panic attacks. For example, a patient may stop driving after experiencing panic attacks while behind the wheel. Thus, it is important to ask the patient about the impact of anxiety symptoms on life functioning.

Patients may interpret their experience as a threat to their health in different ways and may have a history of presenting to various specialists with their concerns. For example, patients visiting the emergency department with atypical chest pain have a high incidence of PD. In the neurology clinic, patients with dizziness often have PD (6).

Lifetime prevalence of PD is 5.0% for women and 2.0% for men (2). PD sometimes improves during pregnancy, and it tends to worsen postpartum.

Agoraphobia

Agoraphobia may occur alone, but it most often occurs with PD. The formal diagnosis of PD is listed as "with" or "without" agoraphobia. Agoraphobia is the presence of anxiety about (or avoidance of) places or situations from which escape might be difficult or embarrassing or in which help may not be available in the event of having a panic attack or panic-like symptoms.

PROVOCATIVE CHEMICALS AND PANIC ATTACKS

In vulnerable subjects, panic attack can be provoked in the laboratory by certain compounds. This provocation can be blocked by the medications used in treatment of PD (4,7). Some of these provocative chemicals include the following:
- Lactate infusion
- Carbon dioxide
- Sodium bicarbonate
- Yohimbine
- Isoproterenol
- Fenfluramine (Pondimin)

TABLE 1.2. Selected Medical Conditions in the Differential Diagnosis of Panic Disorder and Other Anxiety Disorders

CARDIOVASCULAR
Anemia, arrhythmia, angina, heart attack, heart failure, mitral valve prolapse

PULMONARY
Asthma, pulmonary embolism

ENDOCRINE
Hyper- or hypothyroidism, adrenal and parathyroid disorders, hypoglycemia

NEUROLOGIC
Cerebrovascular disease, transient ischemic attack, seizure, vestibular dysfunction, Meniere's disease, migraine, infection, dementia

DRUGS
Amphetamines, cocaine, hallucinogens, marijuana, anticholinergics, nicotine, bronchodilators, alcohol withdrawal, opiate and sedative-hypnotic withdrawal, caffeine, antidepressant use, nicotine withdrawal, nonsteroidal analgesics

MISCELLANEOUS
Electrolyte disturbance, anaphylaxis, vitamin B_{12} deficiency, systemic lupus erythematosus, temporal arteritis, uremia, infections including HIV infection, influenza, encephalitis, pneumonia

Adapted from Lydiard RB, Brawman-Mintzer O. Panic disorder across the life span: a differential diagnostic approach to treatment resistance. Bull Menninger Clin 1997;61(2 suppl. A):A66–A94.

Patients with agoraphobia nearly always attempt to alter their lives to avoid their fear. Common behaviors feared by patients with agoraphobia include the following:

• Shopping alone
• Riding a bus
• Driving a car
• Any behavior perceived as a source of embarrassment or danger

In severe cases of agoraphobia, patients may become completely home-bound; in fact, the family may present the history to the physician and request a home visit to initiate treatment.

Acute Stress Disorder

The patient with acute stress disorder (ASD) presents with a history of a diffuse pattern of symptoms, as listed in Appendix C. Key findings include the following:

- The distressing symptoms typically began soon after a significant and traumatic event.
- Symptoms typically arise and resolve within 4 weeks of the trauma (unlike in post-traumatic stress disorder, which lasts for one month or longer).

Temporal proximity helps to clarify the link between the traumatic event and the symptoms of ASD for the patient, family, and physician.

Post-traumatic Stress Disorder

The diagnostic criteria for post-traumatic stress disorder (PTSD) are listed in Appendix D. The clinical presentation of a patient with PTSD may include the following:

- Physical symptoms
- Constricted affect (lack of full range of affect)
- Numbing of emotional responsiveness
- Increased arousal (hypervigilance)

The diagnosis of PTSD can be difficult to establish initially when the patient presents with physiologic or psychological symptoms that are responses to reminders of the traumatic event but has subdued recall of the actual event. In this case, it is helpful to obtain a history from family members. Patients may present a clear history of symptoms that include the recurrence or recollection of dreams of an identifiable traumatic event.

Several factors affect the development and severity of PTSD (7):

- The nature of the trauma
- The duration of the trauma
- The degree to which the individual's life has been affected
- The extent to which the person perceived human malevolence to be behind the trauma
- The person's social isolation
- The person's pretrauma emotional health and resilience

Diagnosis is established as "acute" if the history of symptoms of PTSD is less than 3 months' duration, as "chronic" if symptoms are more than 3 months' duration, and as "delayed" if symptoms began more than 6 months' after the stressor.

Obsessive-Compulsive Disorder

It is common for people to have idiosyncratic habits and rituals; these do not necessarily constitute a disorder. To qualify as obsessive-compulsive disorder (OCD), symptoms must meet the following criteria (7):

DEATH OF A LONG-TERM PARTNER

Elderly people who lose a person with whom they have spent most of their lives have an increased risk of developing a reaction to the loss that is unique to this traumatic separation. This symptom cluster has features of both PTSD and separation anxiety disorder. This experience of bereavement as a "traumatic separation" is associated with negative outcomes, both mental and physical. The family physician should be vigilant for symptoms of PTSD and separation anxiety (discussed in the text that follows) and should offer treatment and support (2).

- Occupy more than an hour per day
- Cause personal distress
- Significantly interfere with occupational and life function

The diagnostic criteria for OCD are listed in Appendix E. Patients with OCD rarely come to the physician and volunteer their concerns. Typically, the physician learns of the patient's OCD symptoms either from family members or school reports or from patients themselves after they have gotten to know the physician over time. Patients with OCD are distressed by their consuming symptoms and are often embarrassed about them. The approach to obtaining a history from a patient with OCD requires considerable patience and tact from the physician.

Some patients have both obsessions and compulsions, and some have only one or the other. The patient experiences increasing anxiety while he or she experiences the obsession. That anxiety may be temporarily diminished if the compulsion is carried out. For example, a patient may have an obsession that he or she is not certain whether the burner on the stove is turned off and a fire may result. This thought is pervasive, and he or she cannot conduct other life business until going to the stove to check again that the burner is turned off.

Although adults with OCD are aware that their obsessions and compulsions are excessive and unreasonable, children may not have this insight. When asked, the adult patient may be able to recall rituals from childhood. For example, an adult presenting for the first time for treatment may recall that she was always the last one to board the school bus when she was 7 years old because she had to count from 1 to 7 seven times before she felt it was safe to board the bus.

OCD usually begins in adolescence or young adulthood, with approximately 65% of patients having onset before age 25 (7). OCD may begin or worsen during pregnancy or the postpartum period (2). Most OCD patients have an episodic course with periods of incomplete remissions, and 10% show a chronic unremitting course (7).

Anxiety Disorder Due to a Medical Condition

Patients with serious or chronic medical illnesses commonly report anxiety symptoms, and these complaints should be sought when obtaining the medical history of these patients. Anxiety symptoms in patients with medical conditions should not be discounted as an appropriate response to the gravity of their condition. Any form of anxiety disorder may occur in these patients, including panic attacks, obsessions, or compulsions or both, or generalized anxiety, nervousness, and worry. Medical conditions often associated with anxiety and panic symptoms include the following:

* Chronic obstructive pulmonary disease
* Asthma
* Acute myocardial infarction
* Postcoronary artery bypass surgery status

Substance-Induced Anxiety Disorder

The symptoms of patients with substance-induced anxiety disorder (SIAD) result from the direct physiologic effect of a drug of abuse, medication, or toxic substance (5). Anxiety symptoms, such as panic attacks, OCDs, phobias, and generalized anxiety, may be seen in both intoxication and withdrawal. The diagnosis of SIAD (in addition to that of intoxication or withdrawal) is made when the symptoms are so severe that they command attention.

A substance use history is essential in establishing the diagnosis of SIAD (Table 1.3). (Obtaining an accurate substance use history is sometimes challenging, but in severe withdrawal it can be lifesaving.) Patients are sometimes reluctant to report substance use, especially with illegal substances but on occasion with prescription medication abuse as well.

When obtaining the history, pay particular attention to recently discon-

TABLE 1.3.   Medications That May Induce Anxiety Disorders

Intoxication With	Withdrawal From
Alcohol	Alcohol
Amphetamines and other stimulants	Cocaine
Caffeine	Anxiolytics
Cannabis	Hypnotics
Cocaine	Sedatives
Hallucinogens	Other substances of abuse
Inhalants	
Phencyclidine	
Other substances of abuse	

Adapted from American Psychiatric Association. Diagnostic and statistical manual of mental disorders. 4th ed. Washington, DC: American Psychiatric Association, 1994.

tinued agents. Benzodiazepines, especially those with a long half-life (e.g., diazepam, flurazepam), may precipitate withdrawal anxiety symptoms 3 to 4 weeks after stopping them.

Generalized Anxiety Disorder

Generalized anxiety disorder (GAD) should be considered in a patient who is a "hand-wringer" with diffuse, global anxiousness that doesn't fit the specific patterns of symptoms seen in PD, OCD, PTSD, or phobias. GAD also includes what was formerly called "overanxious disorder of childhood." The symptoms and diagnostic criteria for GAD are listed in Appendix F.

GAD must be differentiated from reasonable anxiety that arises in response to genuine problems and threats in the patient's life. If the anxiety is appropriate to the situation, the patient may have an adjustment disorder with anxious features.

Specific Phobias

Phobias are persistently recurring, irrational, severe anxiety states precipitated by specific objects, activities, places, or situations. Patients actively avoid the situations associated with their phobia. Phobias are common (e.g., fear of spiders, snakes), and not all are considered disorders. Phobias represent a disorder only when the fear or avoidance behavior is distressing to the patient or causes occupational or life function impairment (7). Some examples of common phobias include the following:

- Agoraphobia
- Social phobias
- Fear of public speaking
- Inability to urinate in a public rest room
- Anxiety about eating in a public place
- Fear of heights (acrophobia)
- Fear of closed spaces (claustrophobia)

Patients often cope with phobias in silence and do not volunteer the history unless asked for it by a person whom they trust and unless the phobia is causing considerable distress and impairment.

Separation Anxiety Disorder of Childhood/Adolescence

The key symptom of separation anxiety disorder is excessive anxiety (inappropriate for age) about actual or anticipated separation from the caretaker. The diagnostic criteria are listed in Appendix G. Separation anxiety initially occurs in a child or adolescent younger than 18 years of age, but symptoms may persist into adulthood.

The history for a child with separation anxiety is almost invariably presented by the parents or caretaker. It is essential to distinguish normal anxiety

TABLE 1.4.   Common Normal Childhood Fears[a]

INFANCY/TODDLERHOOD
Loud noises
Being dropped
Being startled
Loss of support
Separation from mother
Strangers

BY 4TH YEAR
Imaginary creatures
Small animals
Darkness

BY 5TH AND 6TH YEARS
Social fears

SIX YEARS TO ADOLESCENCE
Being hit by a car
Not being able to breathe
Getting burned by fire
Death or dead people
Bombing attacks/being invaded
Getting poor grades
Parental arguments
Being sent to the principal
A burglar breaking into their house
Falling from a high place

Adapted from Craske MG. Fear and anxiety in children and adolescents. Bull Menninger Clin 1997;61(2 suppl. A):A4–A36.
[a]Certain fears may be adaptive in children as they learn to avoid life's dangers.

from excessive anxiety. A history of normal childhood fears (Table 1.4) does not constitute an anxiety disorder unless there are accompanying persistent symptoms that are disturbing or disruptive to the child. For example, it is normal for children to display clinging behavior for the first few days when taken to school. However, children with separation anxiety may exhibit *persistent* clinging when taken to school. Other examples may include the following:

• Refusal to sleep in his or her own bed and wandering into the parents' bed or sibling's bed during the night
• Recurrent nightmares of family members experiencing fire, murder, or other catastrophe (5)

- Physical symptoms (e.g., abdominal pain, nausea, and headache) to avoid going to a babysitter, summer camp, or school, or flat refusal to go to such locations

When the diagnosis of separation anxiety disorder is suspected, it is important to inquire about whether the child has recently experienced some life stress—or simply perceives that such a stress has occurred or will occur. Such stresses may include a death in the family, the death of a pet, a recent move to a new city, immigration to a new country, and an illness of a relative or friend.

PHYSICAL EXAMINATION

A thorough physical examination should be conducted in all patients with anxiety disorders, with emphasis on the cardiac, respiratory, neurologic, and mental status examinations. The physical examination will be normal for all the anxiety disorders except for findings pertaining to any other comorbid medical conditions. However, if a patient is being examined during a panic attack, he or she may have the following signs and symptoms:

- Extremely frightened appearance
- Certainty that death is imminent
- Sinus tachycardia of less than 120 bpm
- Tachypnea
- Mild to moderately elevated blood pressure
- Trembling, shaking, and sweating
- Distant or confused appearance (with depersonalization)

DIAGNOSTIC TESTING

The patient's medical history is the most important diagnostic tool. After a thorough medical history and physical examination, the physician should consider the differential diagnosis and should order the diagnostic test data that are needed to eliminate those disorders in the differential with the anxiety disorders. (Table 1.5)

In the case of PD, Table 1.2 lists some of the medical disorders for which patients can present with anxiety; a review of this table will prompt consideration of some testing that may be indicated by a given patient's medical history and physical examination.

WHEN TO REFER

Patients with anxiety disorders often benefit from referral to a psychotherapist, because the anxiety disorders can be improved to varying degrees with therapy. Referral should also be considered in the following situations:

- When diagnosis is unclear
- When the patient's condition does not respond to appropriate management
- When the patient has suicidal ideation (requires emergent referral to a psychiatrist)

MANAGEMENT

Panic Attack

Panic attack may not require treatment as a separate entity. If the patient has had one or only a few such attacks, is not disturbed or impaired by them, has no other mental illness, and has good insight, he or she may need no additional treatment for the rare panic attack other than education, understanding, and support from the family and physician.

Panic Disorder

PD is most effectively treated by a combination of medication and psychotherapy.

Medications

Commonly used medications for patients with PD include the following:

- Tricyclic antidepressants (TCAs)
- Monoamine oxidase (MAO) inhibitors
- Selective serotonin reuptake inhibitors (SSRIs)
- High-potency benzodiazepines (e.g., clonazepam [Klonopin], alprazolam [Xanax])

TABLE 1.5. Initial Laboratory Investigation in Anxiety Disorder

ALL PATIENTS
Complete blood count (CBC) with differential
Erythrocyte sedimentation rate (ESR)
Complete chemistry panel (including electrolytes, calcium, glucose, renal and liver function tests)
Thyroid-stimulating hormone (TSH)
Urinalysis

SELECTED PATIENTS
Pregnancy test
Electrocardiogram (if cardiac symptoms)
Test for human immunodeficiency virus (HIV) (if any risk factors)
Serum vitamin B_{12} level (if older, increased mean corpuscular volume, deficiency suspected)
Urine drug screen (if any risk)

Initiating therapy: The benzodiazepines (Table 1.6) are often used at the beginning of pharmacotherapy for PD, alone or in combination with TCAs or SSRIs (Table 1.7), to calm the patient's panic symptoms immediately and to help prevent the exacerbation of panic symptoms sometimes seen with the initiation of TCAs or SSRIs.

Continuing therapy: After the TCA or SSRI has become effective, the benzodiazepine can often be tapered very slowly and discontinued.

TABLE 1.6. Selected Benzodiazepines[a]

Agent	Dosage	Comments
Alprazolam (Xanax)	Starting: 0.25–0.5 mg tid Titration: 0.25–0.5 mg/day every 2–3 days Maintenance: 2–6 mg in divided doses	Increase dose if necessary and tolerated
Clonazepam (Klonopin)	Starting: 0.25–0.5 mg bid Titration: 0.25–0.5 mg/day every 3–5 days Maintenance: 1–3 mg/day	Less self-escalation of dose and abuse than with alprazolam

Adapted from Fyer AJ, Mannuzza S, Coplan JD. Panic disorders and agoraphobia, In: Kaplan HI, Sadock BJ, eds. Comprehensive textbook of psychiatry/VI. 6th ed. Baltimore: Williams & Wilkins, 1995:1191–1204.

[a]Avoid benzodiazepines, or use them with caution, in patients with a personal or family history of substance abuse because of the risk of dose escalation, dependence and abuse (2).

TABLE 1.7. Selected Antidepressants[a]

Agent	Dosage
Tricyclic antidepressants (TCAs)	Starting: 10mg/day Titration: 10 mg/day every 3–4 days Maintenance: therapeutic dose
Selective serotonin reuptake inhibitors (SSRIs)	
Fluoxetine (Prozac)	2.5 mg/day (1/4 of the contents of a 10-mg capsule)
Sertraline (Zoloft)	25 mg every other day (or 12.5 mg/day)
Paroxetine (Paxil)	10 mg every other day (or 5 mg/day)

[a] Note the TCAs and SSRIs are very effective in the treatment of panic disorder and prophylaxis against panic attacks. However, patients with panic disorder are notoriously sensitive to these drugs. It is important to start with extraordinarily small doses and very gradually increase the dose. Otherwise, the patient will experience repeated and severe panic attacks and will almost always stop the medication. Because onset of therapeutic benefit is typically seen 2 to 4 weeks after the patient has reached a therapeutic daily dose, stabilization of panic symptoms with the TCAs and SSRIs may take 1 to 2 months or more. After this is achieved, patients are generally comfortable with a new confidence that they can proceed through their day without a panic attack. The therapeutic doses, side effects and factors influencing the selection of the TCAs and SSRIs are described in Chapter 4.

Psychotherapy

Cognitive behavioral psychotherapy is very helpful for patients with PD. It may be more effective combined with pharmacotherapy, although both are very effective when used alone (4).

Acute Stress Disorder

The goal of treatment for ASD is to assist the patient with medical, practical, and psychological needs in a caring and supportive manner, which helps restore a sense of normalcy and control to the patient's life. If the trauma can be dealt with as ASD (and the patient functioned well before the trauma), the outlook for preventing or ameliorating PTSD is good.

Therapeutic Debriefing

Family physician management primarily involves helping the patient to get into a treatment modality that allows proximate therapeutic debriefing of the traumatic event (e.g., referring a rape victim to a rape counselor).

Supportive Care

The physician should also provide a thorough medical evaluation and management of any physical sequelae of the traumatic event. It may be helpful to arrange social service assistance for needs such as food, clothing, and shelter after traumatic events that destroy them.

Post-traumatic Stress Disorder

Medications

There is no single medication for PTSD. TCAs, MAO inhibitors, and SSRIs are sometimes helpful (7). When placing a PTSD patient on medication, it is essential to determine which "target symptoms" will be monitored in determining the efficacy of treatment.

Psychotherapy

When possible, group psychotherapy with others who have experienced the same trauma (and, if acceptable to the patient, the same event) is recommended.

Obsessive-Compulsive Disorder

Medications

Medication for OCD is typically very effective.

- Clomipramine (Anafranil)
- Fluvoxamine (Luvox)
- SSRIs (effective doses will often be at the upper range of those used for depression; see Chapter 4)

Therapeutic effects of these medications may not be evident for 6 to 8 weeks. Benzodiazepines are generally not helpful in patients with OCD.

Psychotherapy

Various forms of psychotherapy have been used for patients with OCD with mixed results. Behavioral therapy seems to help patients manage symptoms (7).

Anxiety Disorder Due to a Medical Condition

Treatment for medically induced anxiety disorder has two goals:

- Optimize the treatment of the medical condition.
- Treat the anxiety.

Treating the anxiety may also speed the patient's recovery from the medical condition and greatly increase the patient's comfort in the interim.

Medications

Benzodiazepines are usually used to treat this type of anxiety. Appendix H compares selected benzodiazepines. Medications not helpful for treatment of patients with panic disorder are listed in Table 1.8.

- Lorazepam (Ativan) is especially useful in physically ill patients who may have some compromise of liver and kidney function, because it has a short half-life, lack of active metabolites, and is associated with relatively few drug interactions. Patients with compromised liver function should receive very small doses (e.g., 0.5 mg no closer than every 3 hours) until their ability to metabolize the drug is established and the dose can be increased.
- Oxazepam (Serax) is an alternative benzodiazepine with no known active metabolites.

Substance-Induced Anxiety Disorders

Treatment of patients with SIAD accompanies treatment of the primary substance use problem. Treatment involves the following:

- Discontinuation of the substance
- Possible entry into an inpatient substance abuse treatment program

Benzodiazepines are generally not used. Medications are used only if indicated for comorbid conditions (e.g., major depression, psychiatric disorders, mania).

TABLE 1.8. Medications Not Helpful for Panic Disorder

- Bupropion (Wellbutrin)
- Maprotiline (Ludiomil)
- Trazodone (Desyrel)
- Buspirone (BuSpar)
- Beta-adrenergic blockers such as propranolol (Inderal); may block some of the peripheral symptoms of panic (eg, tachycardia) but do not block the distress of the panic attacks (4)

Generalized Anxiety Disorder

GAD is a heterogeneous diagnosis, and treatment is far less successful in controlling symptoms than is the treatment of PD, for example.

Medications
The following are commonly used medications for GAD.

- Benzodiazepines bring improvement in about 70% of patients. Most patients with GAD respond to a dose equivalent to 15 to 25 mg per day of diazepam (Valium) (8).
- Buspirone (BuSpar) is also effective, but perhaps less so in patients previously acclimated to benzodiazepines (8). The usual effective dose is 30 to 60 mg per day in three divided doses. There is a 2- to 4-week lag time before onset of therapeutic effect, so some patients drop out of therapy.

Antidepressants such as TCAs and SSRIs are also helpful at times with patients with GAD. Doses and treatment issues are the same as with depression (see Chapter 4).

Psychotherapy
Cognitive behavioral therapy and relaxation techniques help the patient to manage GAD symptoms (8).

Inappropriate Self-Treatment
Many patients with GAD treat their symptoms with alcohol. Alcoholism is a potential comorbid condition for patients with GAD who drink at all.

Phobias
Medications
Medications are generally not used in the treatment of phobias, except for the MAO inhibitor, phenelzine (Nardil), for social phobia (9). See Chapter 4 for a discussion of phenelzine's use, contraindications, and interactions.

Desensitization
Treatment for phobia involves systematic desensitization to the feared object or situation. Self-paced exposure therapy is a technique in which patients arrange a hierarchy of situations at their own pace, ultimately leading to exposure to the most intensely feared object or situation.

Separation Anxiety Disorder of Childhood/Adolescence
Discovery and relief of the underlying fear in separation anxiety disorder may promptly relieve the symptoms. Providing age-appropriate explanations for the child's concerns can prevent long-term sequelae.

Medication

If symptoms of separation anxiety cannot be promptly relieved, the child can be referred to a child mental health specialist. Child psychiatrists sometimes use TCAs for children with significant impairment from separation anxiety disorder (3).

Family Therapy

Family therapy has been found to be most effective for separation anxiety disorder and other anxiety disorders of childhood (3). Studies have indicated that parents can make childhood anxiety worse by focusing on the possible negative outcomes of the child's activities or by being frequently critical and negative toward the child (6). With criticism, children develop an internal sense of themselves as fragile and incompetent. This can be somewhat ameliorated by involving the family in teaching good parenting techniques and in family therapy for the anxious child (6).

PATIENT AND FAMILY EDUCATION

Patients should be encouraged to learn as much as possible about their particular disorder. This is especially true with PD, in which compliance depends on the patient's understanding of the disorder and what to expect from pharmacologic therapy. Generally, the more patients and their families know about the nature and treatment of their anxiety disorder, the more control they feel over their lives and the better their sense of well-being.

Many communities have psychoeducational and support groups for people with specific anxiety disorders—particularly for those with panic and phobias. These groups often have excellent written educational materials for their members and have guest speakers who are local experts in the treatment of anxiety disorders. Physicians should become aware of what resources are available in their communities.

Lifestyle Measures

The patient should make the following changes in lifestyle to aid in overcoming anxiety disorders:

- Avoid stimulant drugs (including caffeine and nicotine), because they may cause increased anxiety.
- Avoid sedative drugs (including alcohol), because anxiety will increase when the blood level of the drug subsides.
- Maintain a proper balance of work, rest, and exercise—all in moderation.

FOLLOW-UP

Follow-up visits should be scheduled according to the following criteria.

Patients receiving medication

- Frequent follow-up visits are necessary until the medication dose is stabilized and the patient is tolerating the medication well with a good therapeutic response
- If the symptoms of panic disorder, OCD, PTSD, and GAD are well managed with a stable dose of medication, the patient may return at 2- to 3-month intervals for medication follow-up visits.

Patients receiving psychotherapy

- Follow-up for psychotherapy of the anxiety disorders is usually done by a psychotherapist.

References

1. Hollifield M, Katon W, Skipper B, et al. Panic disorder and the quality of life: variables predictive of functional impairment. Am J Psychiatr 1997;154:766-772.
2. Shear MK, Mammen O. Anxiety disorders in primary care: a life-span perspective. Bull Menninger Clin 1997;61(2 suppl. A):A37-A53.
3. Craske MG. Fear and anxiety in children and adolescents. Bull Menninger Clin 1997;61(2 suppl. A):A4-A36.
4. Fyer AJ, Mannuzza S, Coplan JD. Panic disorders and agoraphobia, In: Kaplan HI, Sadock BJ, eds. Comprehensive textbook of psychiatry/VI. 6th ed. Baltimore: Williams & Wilkins, 1995:1191-1204.
5. American Psychiatric Association. Diagnostic and statistical manual of mental disorders/VI. 4th ed. Washington, DC: American Psychiatric Association, 1994.
6. Ballenger JC. Discussion and overview: what can we learn if we view panic disorder across the life span and across different presentations and contexts? Bull Menninger Clin 1997; 61(2 suppl. A):A95-A103.
7. Britton KT. Anxiety disorders in a medical setting. In: Isselbacher KJ, Braunwald E, Wilson JD, et al, eds. Harrison's textbook of internal medicine. 13th ed. New York: McGraw-Hill, 1994:2409-2413.
8. Papp LA, Gorman JM. Generalized anxiety disorder. In: Kaplan HI, Sadock BJ, eds. Comprehensive textbook of psychiatry/VI. 6th ed. Baltimore: Williams & Wilkins, 1995:1236-1249.
9. Barlow DH, Liebowitz MR. Specific phobia and social phobia. In: Kaplan HI, Sadock BJ, eds. Comprehensive textbook of psychiatry/VI. 6th ed. Baltimore: Williams & Wilkins, 1995:1204-1218.

CHAPTER 2

Erik Lindbloom

Attention-Deficit Hyperactivity Disorder

Wide coverage in the lay press has helped to familiarize the general public with attention-deficit hyperactivity disorder (ADHD). Consequently, parents and educators often suggest the diagnosis to the family physician. The physician then faces a challenge, because most children with ADHD do not exhibit the behavior of concern in the office (1,2) and ADHD produces no definitive abnormalities on physical examination or laboratory testing. Fortunately, behavioral rating scales provide greater objectivity to what must often be a second-hand diagnosis.

CHIEF COMPLAINT

The following reports from parents, guardians, or teachers include the following types of behavior associated with ADHD:

- Inattentiveness
- Hyperactivity
- Impulsivity
- Difficulty staying focused, following directions, and completing tasks.

Symptoms may be observed in different settings (e.g., home and the classroom). Caregivers may be more quick to express concern about ADHD if it has already been diagnosed in another family member.

HISTORY

Because there are no definitive examination findings or laboratory studies to assist with the diagnosis of ADHD, a detailed history is essential. If possible, assess the overall behavioral pattern using firsthand accounts from more than one source in different settings (e.g., home and school). Table 2.1 lists the diagnostic criteria for ADHD.

As with any pediatric history, a thorough review of birth, social, and

T ABLE 2.1.   Diagnostic Criteria for Attention-Deficit Hyperactivity Disorder

A. Either group (1) or group (2)

   (1) Six (or more) of the following symptoms of inattention have persisted for at least 6 months, to a degree that is maladaptive and inconsistent with developmental level:

Inattention

      (a) Often fails to give close attention to details or makes careless mistakes in schoolwork, work or other activities

      (b) Often has difficulty sustaining attention in tasks or play activities

      (c) Often does not seem to listen when spoken to directly

      (d) Often does not follow through on instructions and fails to finish schoolwork, chores, or duties in the workplace (not due to oppositional behavior or failure to understand instructions)

      (e) Often has difficulty organizing tasks and activities

      (f) Often avoids, dislikes, or is reluctant to engage in tasks that require sustained mental effort (such as schoolwork or homework)

      (g) Often loses things necessary for tasks or activities (e.g., toys, school assignments, pencils, books or tools)

      (h) Is often easily distracted by extraneous stimuli

      (i) Is often forgetful in daily activities

   (2) Six (or more) of the following symptoms of hyperactivity-impulsivity have persisted for at least 6 months to a degree that is maladaptive and inconsistent with developmental level:

Hyperactivity

      (a) Often fidgets with hands or feet or squirms in seat

      (b) Often leaves seat in classroom or in other situations in which remaining seated is expected

      (c) Often runs about or climbs excessively in situations in which it is inappropriate (in adolescents or adults, may be limited to subjective feelings of restlessness)

      (d) Often has difficulty playing or engaging in leisure activities quietly

      (e) Is often "on the go" or often acts as if "driven by a motor"

      (f) Often talks excessively impulsively

      (g) Often blurts out answers before questions have been completed

      (h) Often has difficulty awaiting turn during activities

      (i) Often interrupts or intrudes on others (e.g., butts into conversations or games)

B. Some hyperactive-impulsive or inattentive symptoms that caused impairment were present before age 7 years.

C. Some impairment from the symptoms is present in two or more settings (e.g., at school [or work] and at home).

D. There must be clear evidence of clinically significant impairment in social, academic, or occupational functioning.

E. The symptoms do not occur exclusively during the course of a pervasive developmental disorder, schizophrenia or other psychotic disorder and are not better accounted for by another mental disorder (e.g., mood disorder, anxiety disorder, dissociative disorder or a personality disorder).

developmental issues may suggest concurrent medical, neurologic, or psychiatric factors. Possible (but not definitively proven) risk factors for ADHD include the following (3):

- Prenatal and perinatal complications
- Hypoxic or other organic brain injury
- Toxin exposure
- Seizure disorders

It is important to gather as much information as possible regarding the child's home environment, family relationships, socioeconomic considerations, and any recent changes at home or school. Pay particular attention to the following:

- Home environment (activities provided that interest the child)
- Family relationships (emotional lability, presence of resistance to discipline, type of discipline used)
- Socioeconomic considerations
- Any recent changes at home or school (poor performance, poor peer relationships)
- Medications, particularly antipsychotics, bronchodilators, anticonvulsants, theophylline, and prednisone
- Time course of behavioral problems (onset of troublesome behavior after age 7 is inconsistent with ADHD and may instead signal substance abuse or other major psychosocial stressor)

Behavioral Rating Scales

Because history is so important and can be extremely subjective, behavioral rating scales can be valuable. Many scales are available, and the family physician should be familiar with at least one and use it consistently (1,4–6). Conners Abbreviated Parent-Teacher Questionnaire (Table 2.2) is an example of a quick screening tool; schools may use their own measures.

Behavioral rating scales can be based on observations from parents, teachers, or both. Parents may be less objective, but generally have many more years of contact with the child than the teachers. The scales should be complemented with written descriptions of behavior patterns, which facilitate comparison with the DSM-IV criteria (see Table 2.1). Although scales are not the sole determinant in diagnosing ADHD, serial reassessments with the scales can objectively document improvement.

Note that the diagnostic criteria for ADHD must be considered maladaptive and impairing to the child. A child who is rambunctious during play but can stay focused on a task at home and school does not meet the criteria for ADHD.

TABLE 2.2.   Conners Abbreviated Parent-Teacher Questionnaire

Each item is rated on a scale of 0 to 3. Typical score for hyperactivity is 15 or higher.
1. Restlessness in the "squirming" sense
2. Needs demands met immediately
3. Temper outbursts and unpredictable behavior
4. Distractibility of attention span, which is a problem
5. Disturbs other children
6. Pouts and sulks
7. Quick and drastic mood changes
8. Restlessness—always up and on the go
9. Excitable, impulsive
10. Fails to finish things that he/she starts

Adapted from Goyette CH, Conners CK, Ulrich RF. Normative data on revised Conners Parent and Teacher Rating Scales. J Abnorm Child Psychol 1978;6:221.

PHYSICAL EXAMINATION

Although there are no pathognomonic findings for ADHD, the physical examination is important to exclude other possibilities from the differential diagnosis. The complete examination should include the following:

• Screening of visual and auditory functioning. Children who have difficulty seeing or hearing information that is presented to them can easily appear inattentive.
• Detailed neurologic exam. Focal findings may suggest organic brain disease, particularly in patients with a possible history of seizure activity. Tics may indicate Tourette's syndrome, which can affect treatment decisions.
• Dysmorphic features. These features support further investigation for developmental delay.

DIAGNOSTIC TESTING

Except for the behavioral rating scales, no laboratory tests are routinely used to diagnose ADHD. However, it is important to rule out other conditions as indicated by the patient's physical exam and risk factors. Other findings may include the following:

• Chemistry screening may reveal metabolic disturbances such as hyponatremia or hypoglycemia.
• Thyroid function tests may be abnormal; thyroid hormone resistance is associated with ADHD but the clinical significance of this is unknown. Hypothyroidism may cause developmental delay.

- Electroencephalogram (EEG) or neuroimaging is indicated only when there are focal findings.
- A complete blood count (CBC) with differential is recommended before starting methylphenidate (Ritalin), because anemia and leukopenia are side effects.

DIFFERENTIAL DIAGNOSIS

Table 2.3 lists the most common conditions in the differential diagnosis of ADHD.

Normal Variation

The first question in evaluating for ADHD is whether the child's behavior can be considered normal for his or her age. Active and energetic behavior may be normal for a given age; the task is to determine the degree and pervasiveness of the symptoms (7).

Sensory Abnormalities

Difficulty understanding information (e.g., because of vision or hearing impairment) can cause a child to lose interest in a topic, activity, or instruction.

Learning Disabilities

Difficulty processing information may lead to frustrated behavior and inattentiveness. Referral for educational or neuropsychological testing may prove beneficial for children who are perceived as underachievers.

TABLE 2.3.   Conditions That May Mimic ADHD

Sensory deficit (e.g., vision, hearing)
Learning disability
Developmental delay
Autism
Anxiety
Depression
Conduct disorder
Oppositional defiant disorder
Psychosis
Substance abuse
Partial or absence seizures
Metabolic or endocrine abnormalities
Toxins or medications (e.g., lead, theophylline, prednisone, phenobarbital)
Reaction to stressful home or school environment

Developmental Delay or Autism

A thorough review of the child's developmental milestones may reveal that the behavior of concern is not an isolated symptom but a manifestation of a larger developmental abnormality.

Medical Conditions

Medical abnormalities that are associated with developmental delay, such as hypothyroidism or metabolic abnormalities, should be considered if suggested by the history and physical exam.

Toxins or Medications

Hyperirritability can be the earliest symptom of lead poisoning (8). Medications that can cause attention deficits include theophylline, prednisone, and phenobarbital (1,4).

Neurologic Abnormalities

Absence seizures can produce periods of inattentiveness. These are often distinguishable from simple inattentiveness by the inability to gain the child's attention during the seizure.

Toxic, infectious, or hypoxic brain injury can also result in symptoms similar to those of ADHD, but usually also produce other manifestations of global injury, such as developmental delay.

Psychiatric Disorders

Anxiety or fearfulness (e.g., school phobia or separation anxiety disorder) may manifest as hyperactivity and inattentiveness in certain environments. As in adults, depression can markedly impair concentration. Children with conduct disorder or oppositional-defiant disorder express conflict or emotion as physical action (9).

Other psychiatric conditions, such as schizophrenia and schizotypal personality disorder, are rare in younger children but may present as deterioration from a previously higher level of functioning. It is important to keep in mind that substance abuse is occurring in an increasingly younger population.

Social Factors

Stressful environments at home or at school can result in difficulty concentrating in these environments. Physical abuse, sexual abuse, and substance abuse all can be factors leading to behavioral problems in children.

WHEN TO REFER

The primary management of ADHD can be well handled by the family physician. The degree of impairment the child is experiencing will help determine the potential need and urgency of involving additional specialists in this area. Consider referral in the following circumstances:

* Continuing deterioration
* No improvement with traditional therapy and medication

MANAGEMENT

Before attempting treatment with medication, efforts should be made at behavioral therapy, counseling, and restructuring of classroom and physical education time.

* Behavioral therapy can include a combination of cognitive, social, emotional, and behavioral strategies. Cognitive behavioral techniques, in the form of written exercises or regular activities with a behavior therapist, can have some effect on impulsive behavior (10).
* Social skills training, positive reinforcement, and time-outs may also be effective (6).
* Restructuring of classroom and physical education time can provide a structured environment with adequate time to expend the physical energy that is important for most children. This can be especially valuable for children with ADHD.

Medication

Although effective in 90% of cases, medication should not be the sole method of therapy for children with ADHD (1,11). The mainstay of pharmacologic treatment are the stimulants, methylphenidate (Ritalin), pemoline (Cylert), and amphetamines. Table 2.4 summarizes each medication, including starting doses and side effects.

Methylphenidate is the medication most widely used in the United States for those with ADHD. It has been shown to increase attention span and decrease hyperactivity and impulsivity (12). These changes may lead to mood improvement secondary to increased self-control, with the overall goal being enhancement of performance, acceptance, and quality of life. All the medications can have this positive effect (12); a 70% response rate is reported for each; with a 75% to 95% response rate if all three classes are attempted individually in succession (11,13).

Dosing Schedule

All the classes of medications for children with ADHD have relatively short half-lives of 30 to 60 minutes, but sustained-release formulations are available. Sustained-release formulations may obviate schooltime dosing and associated stigma. If a schooltime dosing is needed, it should be given at a set time;

TABLE 2.4   Medications for ADHD

Medication	Dosing	Side Effects
Methylphenidate (Ritalin)	0.3–0.7 mg/kg/dose 2–3 times/day (max. daily: 60 mg)	Insomnia, irritability, rebound phenomenon, anorexia, alopecia, anemia/leukopenia, depression, social withdrawal, motor tics; probably transient effects on growth and blood pressure
Dextroamphetamine (Dexedrine)	0.15–0.5 mg/kg/dose 1–3 times daily (max. daily: 40 mg)	As above, except no alopecia, anemia, or leukopenia
Methamphetamine (Desoxyn)	Average 0.65 mg/kg/dose once or twice daily (max. daily: 40 mg)	As above
Pemoline (Cylert)	0.5–3 mg/kg once daily (max. daily: 112.5 mg)	Similar to methylphenidate, plus hepatitis

vague directions such as "lunchtime dose" may result in variations of 1 to 2 hours a day, depending on the child's schedule.

Therapy is usually initiated 7 days per week; evening and weekend dosing may be adjusted depending on response. Both physician and parents should remember that ADHD is also present in nonschool hours; medication after school and on weekends may help with homework, sports, and interpersonal relationships.

Monitoring During Therapy
Monitoring during therapy should include the following:

• Annual or biannual weight, height, and blood pressure measurements. Transient growth suppression and mild increase in heart rate and blood pressure have been noted, but no long-term adverse effects in these areas have been observed.
• Regular CBCs for anemia and leukopenia for patients receiving methylphenidate or pemoline.
• Regular liver function tests for patients receiving pemoline.

Potential Complications
• Reversible motor tics have been observed in 1% of children taking these stimulant medications, but they appear safe for children with seizure disorders (14).
• Precipitation of Tourette's syndrome may occur in a small percentage of children with a positive family history (15).

Duration of Treatment

Parents, patients, and physicians alike often wonder how long medications will be needed. As long as clear behavioral benefits persist and no serious side effects develop, treatment with medication can continue indefinitely.

Drug holidays may be instituted when convenient (e.g., summer, weekends) and extended if no worsening occurs. About 50% of children who respond to pharmacologic intervention may benefit from medication as adults (16). ADHD itself may not predispose to future substance abuse, but comorbid conditions such as conduct disorder and antisocial behavioral disorder are associated with increased substance use (10).

FOLLOW-UP

Initial monthly visits are recommended for children with ADHD to fine-tune dosing of medication and monitor side effects. Subsequent visits every 6 to 12 months should be sufficient to reassess the effects of therapy and perhaps for trials of medication withdrawal. It is useful to use serial reassessments with behavioral rating scales to objectively document improvement with medical or behavioral therapy.

PATIENT EDUCATION

The family physician should familiarize himself or herself with the community resources available and educate parents about these resources to assist with the care of their child. As the diagnosis of ADHD has gained prominence, many schools have become sophisticated in addressing the needs of children with ADHD. Many active national support groups exist, including the Attention Deficit Disorder Association (ADDA) and Children and Adults

TABLE 2.5. Support Groups for ADHD

Attention Deficit Disorder Association (ADDA)
9930 Johnnycake Ridge Rd.
Suite 3E
Mentor, OH 44060
800–487-2282
www.add.org

Children and Adults with Attention Deficit Disorder (CHADD)
499 Northwest 70th Ave.
Suite 101
Plantation, FL 33317
800–233-4050
www.chadd.org

with Attention Deficit Disorder (CHADD). Addresses and phone numbers for these organizations are listed in Table 2.5.

References

1. Taylor MA. Evaluation and management of attention-deficit hyperactivity disorder. Am Fam Physician 1997;55:887–901.

2. Sleator FK, Ullman RA. Can the physician diagnose hyperactivity in the office? Pediatrics 1988;81:562.

3. Schneider SC, Tan G. Attention-deficit hyperactivity disorder: in pursuit of diagnostic accuracy. Postgrad Med 1997;101:231–240.

4. Kelly DP, Aylward GP. Attention deficits in school-aged children and adolescents. Pediatr Clin North Am 1992;39:487–512.

5. Dworkin PH. Learning and behavior problems in schoolchildren. Philadelphia: WB Saunders Company, 1985:81–82.

6. Barkley RA. Attention deficit hyperactivity disorder: a handbook for diagnosis and treatment. New York: Guilford Press, 1990.

7. Levine MD. Attentional variation and dysfunction. In: Levine MD, Carey WB, Crocker AC, eds. Developmental-behavioral pediatrics. 2nd ed. Philadelphia: WB Saunders Company, 1992.

8. Chisolm JJ. Increased lead absorption and lead poisoning. In: Behrman RE, ed. Nelson textbook of pediatrics. 14th ed. Philadelphia: WB Saunders Company, 1992.

9. Johnson MR. Psychiatric problems in children and adolescents. In: Stockman JA, ed. Difficult diagnosis in pediatrics. Philadelphia: WB Saunders Company, 1990.

10. Kaplan CS, Thompson AE, Searson SM. Cognitive behaviour therapy in children and adolescents. Arch Dis Child 1995;73:472–475.

11. Committee on Children With Disabilities, Committee on Drugs. Medication for children with an attention deficit disorder. Pediatrics 1987;80:758–760.

12. Klein RG. The role of methylphenidate in psychiatry. Arch Gen Psychiatr 1995;52:429–433.

13. Elia J, Borcherding BG, Rapoport JL, Keysor CS. Methylphenidate and dextroamphetamine treatments of hyperactivity: are there true nonresponders? Psychiatr Res 1991;36:141–155.

14. Feldman H, Crumrine P, Handen BL, et al. Methylphenidate in children with seizures and attention-deficit disorder. Am J Dis Child 1989;143:1081–1086.

15. Gadow KD, Sverd J. Stimulants for ADHD in child patients with Tourette's syndrome: the issue of relative risk. J Dev Behav Pediatr 1990;11:269–271.

16. Fargason RE, Ford CV. Attention deficit hyperactivity disorder in adults: diagnosis, treatment, and prognosis. South Med J 1994;87:302–309.

Margaret E. McCahill

Chronic Fatigue Syndrome

The cause of chronic fatigue syndrome (CFS) is not known. Moreover, theories involving multiple viral infections and immune system abnormalities have been advanced but not proved. The precise definition of CFS continues to evolve, and definitive treatment remains elusive. Nevertheless, establishing the diagnosis when appropriate can benefit patients, and helping patients understand and cope with their condition can be a most rewarding experience.

CHIEF COMPLAINT

Patients typically complain of chronic or relapsing fatigue that is disabling in intensity and has lasted for months or longer. Common accompanying complaints may include impaired concentration and short-term memory, sleep disturbances, and musculoskeletal pain.

HISTORY

A thorough medical history must be obtained from a patient who is thought to have CFS, with emphasis on the following:

- Medical and psychosocial circumstances at the onset of the fatigue
- Any history of depression, alcohol, or substance abuse
- Any history of symptoms of other psychiatric disorders
- Use of medications (prescription, over-the-counter drugs, nutritional supplements)
- Any history of other medically unexplained symptoms

Symptoms that support a diagnosis of CFS are listed in Table 3.1.

Because CFS is a diagnosis of exclusion, the history must exclude any condition that would explain the patient's chronic fatigue. Some examples are listed in Table 3.2. Other medical or psychiatric problems that may cause some degree of fatigue but whose presence does not adequately explain CFS or exclude the diagnosis are listed in Table 3.3. Note that depression can coexist with CFS and that depressive symptoms, including fatigue and sleep disturbance, exacerbate the disability from CFS.

EPIDEMIOLOGIC CONSIDERATIONS

Because of imprecise definitions and diagnosis, the true prevalence of CFS is not known. The pool of potential cases is extremely large: Up to 25% of patients in ambulatory clinics report fatigue as a major problem, and up to 64% of those have no known cause for their fatigue (1). Similarly, the exact percentage of symptoms of psychiatric disorders in CFS patients is unknown; estimates range from less than 50% up to 80% of patients (2,3).

TABLE 3.1.   Diagnostic Criteria for CFS

1. The presence of clinically evaluated, unexplained, persistent, or relapsing chronic fatigue of new or definite onset (not lifelong) and of at least 6 months' duration. Fatigue is not the result of ongoing exertion (physical or mental), is not substantially relieved by rest, and results in significant reduction in previous levels of occupational, educational, social, or personal activities.

2. The presence of four or more of the following symptoms, all of which must be of at least 6 months' duration and must not have predated the fatigue:
   a. Self-reported impairment in concentration or short-term memory, severe enough to interfere with daily activities
   b. Sore throat
   c. Tender cervical or axillary lymph nodes
   d. Muscle pain
   e. Multijoint pain without joint swelling or redness
   f. Headaches of a new type, pattern, or severity
   g. Unrefreshing sleep
   h. Postexertional malaise lasting more than 24 hours

Note. When a patient has had chronic fatigue of 6 months' duration but fails to meet the full diagnostic criteria, then that person's condition is classified as "idiopathic chronic fatigue."

Adapted from Fukuda K, Straus SE, Hickie I, et al. The chronic fatigue syndrome: a comprehensive approach to its definition and study. Ann Intern Med 1994;121:953–959

TABLE 3.2.   Conditions That Exclude a Diagnosis of CFS or Unexplained Chronic Fatigue

Untreated hypothyroidism
Sleep apnea or other sleep disturbances
Narcolepsy
Side effects of medication
Previously treated malignancy, for which recurrence must be considered
Severe anemia
Congestive heart failure
Chronic lung disease
Diabetes
HIV infection or other infectious diseases
Unresolved hepatitis B or C infection
Anorexia nervosa or bulimia nervosa
Neurologic disorders
Severe obesity
Past or present diagnosis of any of the following:
• Major depression with psychotic or melancholic features
• Bipolar affective disorder
• Schizophrenia or delusional disorders of any subtype
• Dementia of any type
• Alcohol or other substance abuse from 2 years before the onset of chronic fatigue or thereafter

Note: Any unexplained abnormality on physical examination, laboratory test, or imaging study that might suggest an exclusionary medical condition must be resolved before a diagnosis of CFS or unexplained chronic fatigue can be established.

Adapted from Fukuda K, Straus SE, Hickie I, et al. The chronic fatigue syndrome: a comprehensive approach to its definition and study. Ann Intern Med 1994;121:953–959.

When obtaining the history, it is challenging at times to sort out chronic fatigue of unknown cause from "weakness" (reduced motor capacity), asthenia or malaise (loss of strength, energy, or vitality), neurasthenia (psychic weakness), myasthenia (e.g., the muscle weakness of myasthenia gravis), lassitude and lethargy (often readily explained by overexertion, poor physical conditioning, inadequate rest, stress, and obesity), prolonged fatigue (persisting 1 month or longer), chronic fatigue (persisting 6 months or longer but without the full syndrome), and chronic fatigue syndrome.

PHYSICAL EXAMINATION

A complete physical examination, including a mental status examination (Appendix I), should be done to assist in eliminating diagnoses in which patients can present with fatigue. Because patients complaining of fatigue often have been scheduled for only a brief appointment, you may wish to devote the

TABLE 3.3. Conditions That Do Not Adequately Explain Chronic Fatigue or Exclude a Diagnosis of CFS or Unexplained Chronic Fatigue

Fibromyalgia

Anxiety disorders

Somatoform disorders

Major depression without psychosis or melancholic features

Neurasthenia

Multiple chemical sensitivity

Adequately treated hypothyroidism (normal thyroid-stimulating hormone with treatment)

Adequately treated asthma (normal pulmonary function with treatment)

Infectious diseases, such as Lyme disease or syphilis, which have received a full course of appropriate antibiotic therapy before the development of chronic sequelae

Isolated, unexplained physical findings, abnormal laboratory results, or imaging test abnormalities insufficient for diagnosis of an exclusionary medical condition (e.g., elevation of antinuclear antibody titer inadequate to establish a diagnosis of a connective tissue disorder, isolated mild elevation of erythrocyte sedimentation rate, or isolated mild elevation of alkaline phosphatase)

Adapted from Fukuda K, Straus SE, Hickie I, et al. The chronic fatigue syndrome: a comprehensive approach to its definition and study. Ann Intern Med 1994;21:953–959.

first visit to obtaining the history and some laboratory studies and then schedule a longer second visit for the physical examination. During the mental status exam, give particular attention to the following:

- Mood
- Intellectual function
- Memory
- Personality organization
- Signs or symptoms of depression, anxiety disorder, or other psychiatric disorders
- Thoughts of self-harm

DIAGNOSTIC TESTING

To establish a diagnosis of CFS, there must be no other explanation for the CFS symptoms. Thus, any condition that would explain the patient's chronic fatigue must be excluded. Useful test are listed in Table 3.4.

TABLE 3.4.   Initial Screening Laboratory Tests for Patients With Fatigue

FOR ALL PATIENTS

Complete blood count (CBC) with differential cell count

Erythrocyte sedimentation rate (ESR)

Serum chemistries, including glucose, electrolytes, creatinine, blood urea nitrogen (BUN), calcium, phosphorus, albumin, total protein, globulin, liver function tests (at least alanine transaminase [ALT], alanine aminotransferase), alkaline phosphatase

Thyroid-stimulating hormone (TSH)

Urinalysis

FOR SELECTED PATIENTS (BASED ON HISTORY AND PHYSICAL EXAM)

Tuberculosis screening (PPD)

Syphilis serology (RPR/VDRL)

Vitamin B_{12} deficiency screening

HIV testing

Lyme titer (in high-risk geographic areas)

Some examples of specific tests that are not helpful and not indicated in the routine evaluation and diagnosis of CFS include serologic tests for Epstein-Barr virus, retroviruses, human herpesvirus 6, enteroviruses, and *Candida albicans;* immunologic tests, including cell population and function studies; and imaging studies, including magnetic resonance imaging (MRI) scans and radionuclide scans of the head (1). Such studies should be done only if indicated to substantiate or exclude a specific diagnosis for which there is evidence in the medical history and physical or from the screening tests previously listed.

WHEN TO REFER

You may wish to refer the patient with fatigue for consultation (possibly to a neurologist or rheumatologist) if the diagnosis of CFS is uncertain or if the patient suffers a progressive deterioration despite comprehensive management. You should consider consultation with a mental health specialist if the patient is willing to learn about Cognitive behavioral therapy (discussed in the following text) as a skill in coping with the symptoms of the CFS or if other mental illness is suspected.

MANAGEMENT

Because there is no specific treatment for CFS, management should focus on symptomatic treatment and on assisting the patient with education, lifestyle changes, psychosocial support, and developing coping skills. The typical therapeutic plan might include the following:

- Medication for management of target symptoms (identified by patient and physician) (4)
- Cognitive behavioral therapy to enhance intellectual skills in coping with CFS (5)
- Proper balance of exercise, rest and diet
- Stress management skill development
- Physical therapy (in some cases)
- Regularly scheduled follow-up visits with the family physician to monitor for the development of any new illness or symptom.

Medication for Symptomatic Treatment

No medications have demonstrated clear benefits for patients with CFS (5). Medication management typically focuses on symptom relief. For instance, nonsteroidal anti-inflammatory drugs or acetaminophen are used for headache, fever, and musculoskeletal aches (narcotic analgesics should be avoided), and antihistamines and decongestants are used for allergic rhinitis and sinusitis.

It is important to look for and treat any depressive disorders in patients with CFS because symptoms of major depression, including fatigue and sleep disturbance, exacerbate the disability associated with CFS. Nonsedating antidepressants often provide some symptomatic relief of fatigue in CFS patients with or without major depression. Antidepressants are discussed in Chapter 4.

Cognitive Behavioral therapy

Cognitive behavioral therapy (CBT) has been shown to be of benefit in patients with CFS (5). Through the specific cognitive steps learned in CBT, patients can develop a positive coping strategy for living with CFS. They can overcome the feelings of powerlessness and hopelessness that often slow the progress in the management of CFS and improve their outlook regarding themselves, the world, and the future.

Physical and Environmental Measures

Patients should be advised to avoid extremes of activity and inactivity. Work or exercise to the point of exhaustion is harmful. Total rest is also harmful, leading to further deconditioning, increased fatigue, disturbed sleep patterns, and worsened self-image. Patients should schedule exercise for the time of day when they have the most energy, and rest during periods of fatigue.

Patients should also be advised to eat a balanced diet, avoiding fads and eccentricities (e.g., avoid "protein diet," "grapefruit diet"). Vitamin supplements have no proven benefit and megadoses of vitamins should be avoided, but a multivitamin supplement (1 tablet/day) is permissible if the patient desires. The use of vitamin B_{12} injections has been shown to be of no value in CFS unless this specific deficiency has been documented by blood levels (4).

Patients should also be encouraged to make the following lifestyle modifications:

- Minimal or no alcohol
- No recreational drugs
- No smoking
- Avoidance of caffeine, especially before sleep
- Avoidance of large meals before sleep

Alternative Therapies

Countless anecdotes notwithstanding, no traditional or nontraditional remedies have proved effective for treatment of patients with CFS. If alternative treatments really worked for CFS patients, mainstream medicine would adopt them and they would no longer be alternative. Patients who seek information about CFS via computer should be cautioned that much of the medical information on the internet has not been screened and may not be accurate. Gently and with understanding, guide patients away from alternatives that are toxic, expensive, or unreasonable (4).

PATIENT EDUCATION

Good patient education assists in the development of a solid therapeutic alliance between the patient and physician, which is essential for the establishment of an effective treatment plan. It is important to cover the following areas with patients:

- What is and is not known about CFS
- The course of CFS—chronic and relapsing
- Reassurance that CFS is not known to shorten longevity, despite its chronic nature
- No evidence that CFS is inherited
- Reassurance that patients with CFS are not "crazy"
- Reassurance that you understand and believe the patient's complaints

FAMILY/COMMUNITY SUPPORT

Psychosocial support is extremely valuable for patients with CFS. It is helpful for close family members to learn about what the patient is experiencing and what is *not* true about CFS. Several national organizations distribute

TABLE 3.5. Sources of Information About CFS

National Chronic Fatigue Syndrome and Fibromyalgia Association
3521 Broadway, Suite 222
Kansas City, MO 64111
816-931-4777

Chronic Fatigue & Immune Dysfunction (CFIDS) Association of America
P.O. Box 220398
Charlotte, NC 28222–0398
800-442-3437

Massachusetts Chronic Fatigue and Immune Dysfunction Association, Inc. (Mass CFIDS)
808 Main Street
Waltham, MA 02154
781-893-4415

Adapted from Ruffin MT, Cohen M. Evaluation and management of fatigue. Am Fam Physician 1994; 50:625–634.

information about CFS; three of these are listed in Table 3.5. Some of these agencies may be able to assist the patient in locating a local support group.

FOLLOW-UP

The patient with CFS should be seen at regularly scheduled intervals—every 1 or 2 weeks when the patient's symptoms are severe or every 2 to 3 months when the patient is doing well. The visits generally are brief. The focus is on listening for a change in the symptoms that might indicate that a new or treatable condition is emerging. Some limited physical examination should be done at each visit.

REFERENCES

1. Fukuda K, Straus SE, Hickie I, et al. The chronic fatigue syndrome: a comprehensive approach to its definition and study. Ann Intern Med 1994;121:953-959.
2. McPhee SJ, Schroeder SA. Fatigue. In: Tierney LM, McPhee SJ, Papadakis MA, eds. Current Medical Diagnosis & Treatment 1997. 36th ed. Stamford, CT: Appleton & Lange, 1997:25-26.
3. Plum F. Weakness, asthenia, and fatigue. In: Bennett JC, Plum F, eds. Cecil textbook of medicine. 20th ed. Philadelphia: WB Saunders Company, 1996:2027-2028.
4. Straus SE. Chronic fatigue syndrome. In: Isselbacher KJ, Braunwald E, Wilson JD, et al, eds. Harrison's textbook of internal medicine. 13th ed. New York: McGraw-Hill, 1994:2398-2400.
5. Ruffin MT, Cohen M. Evaluation and management of fatigue. Am Fam Physician 1994;50:625-634.

CHAPTER 4

Margaret E. McCahill

Depressive Disorders

I am now the most miserable man living. . . . If what I feel were equally distributed to the whole human family, there would not be one cheerful face on earth.

Abraham Lincoln, 16th president of the United States, who suffered a depressive disorder

Depression may be due to any one or a combination of five major mental disorders:

- Major depressive disorder or bipolar disorder
- Dysthymic disorder
- Adjustment disorder with depressed mood
- Borderline personality disorder
- Depression secondary to substance abuse or dependence

In addition, the symptoms of bereavement may overlap with those of the depressive disorders, although a normal grief reaction per se is not a mental disorder.

CHIEF COMPLAINT

Patients may complain of depression but more commonly complain of fatigue or any of a number of somatic complaints. Common chief complaints that ultimately prove to be depression include the following:

- Headache
- Gastrointestinal disturbances
- Backache
- Any unexplained pain

HISTORY

A thorough history is essential for determining which depressive disorder is at play. The diagnostic features are presented below for each of the five major depressive disorders (Table 4.1).

TABLE 4.1.   Features Suggestive of Depressive Disorder in the Patient History

Feature	Possible diagnosis
Disturbance in normal daily activities	Major depressive disorder (p. 38)
Mania	Bipolar disorder (p. 39)
Seasonal pattern (seasonal affective disorder)	Major depressive disorder (p. 38)
Depression for 2 years or more, with less impairment than major depression	Dysthymic disorder (p. 39)
Identifiable stressful event or serious medical condition	Adjustment disorder (p. 40)
"Stable instability" and intense reaction to perceived rejection	Borderline personality disorder (p. 40)
Substance/alcohol abuse or dependence	Depression secondary to substance abuse (p. 40)
Recent loss of a loved one	Grief reaction (p. 41)
Medication use (see p. 43 for a list)	Medication-induced depression (p. 42)
Postpartum	"Baby blues" or postpartum depression (p. 42)
Multiple somatic complaints or somatoform disorder	Mood or anxiety disorder (p. 42)

When obtaining a history to establish the diagnosis, it is essential to get a thorough substance use history. It would be counterproductive and possibly dangerous to prescribe antidepressant medications for someone who continues to use amphetamines, cocaine, other stimulants, alcohol, or other drugs. (Substance abuse and dependence are discussed in Chapter 11.)

Major Depressive Disorder

The diagnostic criteria for major depressive disorder (MDD) are listed in Appendix K. In addition to feelings of depression, guilt, hopelessness, and suicidal ideation at times, a distinguishing feature of MDD is the presence of what are sometimes called "neurovegetative signs" of depression. These are disturbances of appetite, sleep, energy, concentration, and libido. There are special types of MDD to be sought in the history. These include the following:

- A seasonal pattern in which MDD occurs, typically during the fall and winter months (usually October through February)
- MDD with psychotic symptoms (e.g., hallucinations and delusions)
- Atypical depression in which the neurovegetative symptoms are the opposite of the classic pattern, characterized by hypersomnia, hyperphagia, weight gain, interpersonal rejection sensitivity, and leaden paralysis (a heavy or leaden feeling in the arms and legs) (1).
- History of mania (Table 4.2)

MDD is seen twice as often in women as in men and may occur at any age. However, the peak age for onset of the first episode is 25 years. The point prevalence of MDD in adults is 5% to 9% for women and 2% to 3% for men and is not related to ethnicity, education, income, or marital status (1). There is a familial pattern, with MDD being 1.5 to 3 times more common in first-degree relatives of patients with MDD than in the general population (1,2).

It is useful to ask patients about previous episodes of depression. Approximately 50% to 60% of patients who have had a single episode of MDD will have a second episode; of those who have had two episodes, about 70% will have a third episode; and of those who have had three, about 90% will have a fourth episode (1).

Dysthymic Disorder

The diagnostic criteria for dysthymic disorder, or dysthymia, are listed in Appendix L. The differences between dysthymia and MDD are principally a matter of degree and duration (Table 4.3).

Although many of the specific symptoms of disturbance of appetite, sleep, energy, self-esteem, and mood seem similar, they are generally milder disturbances in patients with dysthymia than those in patients with MDD and are present consistently for years at a time.

When asked, "How long have you felt depressed?" the dysthymic patient often answers, "All my life, as far back as I can remember." It is possible for a person who has dysthymic disorder to have a superimposed MDD. This is called "double depression" and is often more severe and more refractory to treatment than dysthymia alone.

In adults, women are two times more likely to have dysthymia than men; in children, dysthymia occurs equally in boys and girls (1). The lifetime prevalence of dysthymic disorder is approximately 6%; the point prevalence is

---

T ABLE 4.2. Symptoms Supporting a Diagnosis of Bipolar Disorder

Whenever the medical history suggests major depressive disorder, it is important to exclude a history of mania before establishing the diagnosis and treatment plan. The patient may experience a distinct period of abnormally and persistently elevated, expansive, or irritable mood, lasting 1 week or more (or a shorter time if hospitalization was required), which is severe enough to interfere with normal daily functions. In addition, the patient must have a history of the simultaneous presence of three or more of the following:
- Inflated self-esteem or grandiosity
- Decreased need for sleep
- Pressured speech
- Flight of ideas or feeling that thoughts are racing
- Easy distractibility
- Increase in school, work, or sexual activity or psychomotor agitation
- Excesses in high-risk pleasurable activities, such as spending sprees, sexual indiscretions, or foolish business activities

Adapted from American Psychiatric Association. Diagnostic and statistical manual of mental disorders. 4th ed. Washington, DC: American Psychiatric Association, 1994.

TABLE 4.3. **Distinguishing Dysthymia From Major Depressive Disorder**

Dysthymia	Major Depressive Disorder
Patients continue to function capably, though unhappily.	Patients are more impaired by their illness.
Patients cannot be diagnosed until the dysphoria has continued beyond 2 years, or 1 year for children and adolescents.	Episodes may remit spontaneously within 2 years.

approximately 3%. Dysthymia is more common in first-degree relatives of patients with MDD than in the general population (1).

Adjustment Disorder With Depressed Mood

The diagnostic criteria for adjustment disorder with depressed mood are presented in Appendix M. The patient may present with a history of depressed mood, tearfulness, and feelings of hopelessness, but there is a clearly identifiable stressful event to which the patient's distress reaction can be attributed.

Borderline Personality Disorder

The diagnostic criteria for borderline personality disorder (BPD) are listed in Appendix N. It is rare for a patient with BPD to come to the physician with a complaint of persistent instability in interpersonal relationships, affect, mood, self-image, and impulsivity. Most commonly, BPD patients come to their doctor with the complaint of depression and often are threatening suicide imminently at the time of presentation. The hallmark of BPD is "stable instability" and marked, intense changes in affect when the patient feels any sense of rejection or abandonment.

Patients with BPD sometimes create a strain in the physician's office by recruiting the physician or staff members to do special favors for them (special calls, appointments, medication refills, or other accommodations beyond usual office policies) only to react in an intensively negative fashion when they push the limits too often or too far.

Seventy-five percent of those diagnosed with BPD are women, and the prevalence is estimated at 2% of the general population (1). BPD is about five times more common among first-degree relatives of those with BPD than in the general population (1).

Depression Secondary to Substance Abuse/Dependence

The patient who is abusing or dependent on alcohol or other substances generally does not complain of depression, although depression is a very common consequence of substance abuse and dependence. Patients usually avoid medical intervention, and, if they seek medical attention at all, they have somatic complaints and deny the importance of their substance use.

Family members of the patient with depression resulting from substance abuse may report seeing the patient as "depressed," because they often see the person while he or she is "coming down" from the influence of the substance. This is particularly true when the substance is amphetamines, cocaine, and other stimulants, but it may also be true of alcohol and prescription substance abuse and dependence. Family members may be completely unaware of the substance use disorder.

Bereavement

The grieving person may have many of the same symptoms as those listed in Appendix K for MDD, but these occur in the setting of the recent death of a loved one or some other serious loss, such as divorce or loss of an important relationship. The length of a normal grief reaction varies according to the person's culture. However, symptoms consistent with MDD that persist for more than 2 months suggest that MDD may be complicating the bereavement (Table 4.4).

History of Depression in Special Circumstances
Medical Comorbidity
Patients with significant medical illnesses should be evaluated for major depression. It should not be assumed that what appears to be depression just represents a "natural reaction" to having suffered a stroke or myocardial infarction, or to having cancer, for example (Table 4.5).

Depression has been estimated to occur in 50% of cancer patients, 25% to 30% of stroke patients, 18% to 50% of patients with coronary artery disease, 4% to 70% of those with Parkinson's disease (3), and 8.5% to 27.3% of those with diabetes mellitus (4). Depressive symptoms in these patients may resemble those of patients with MDD (Appendix K) or adjustment disorder (Appendix M).

Depression may increase the mortality risk of patients with comorbid conditions. At 6 months after myocardial infarction, the mortality rate of nonde-

TABLE 4.4. Symptoms That May Indicate More Than a Normal Grief Reaction

- Guilt about things other than issues regarding the patient's actions or inaction around the time of death of their loved one
- Thoughts of death other than thinking that he or she would be better off dead or should have died with the deceased
- Excessive preoccupation with worthlessness
- Marked psychomotor retardation
- Prolonged or marked functional impairment
- Hallucinatory experiences other than feeling that he or she hears, or briefly sees, the deceased

Adapted from American Psychiatric Association. Diagnostic and statistical manual of mental disorders. 4th. ed. Washington, DC: American Psychiatric Association, 1994.

TABLE **4.5.**   Features That Help Distinguish Major Depression From an
Understandable Adjustment Disorder in the Setting of Medical Illness

The presence and persistence of the following symptoms suggest major depression rather than adjustment
disorder in this setting.
• Feelings of guilt
• Sense of failure
• Sense of being punished
• Indecision and psychomotor retardation
• Loss of interest in activities previously considered important
• Persistent suicidal thoughts
• Crying spells

Adapted from McCoy DM. Treatment considerations for depression in patients with significant medical comorbidity. J Fam Pract 1996;43(6suppl):S35–S44.

pressed patients was less than 5%, in contrast to the mortality rate of depressed patients of 17% (5).

Various depression screens have been evaluated for cancer patients. One of the most effective was the simple question: "Are you depressed?"

Medications That May Induce Depressive Symptoms

When obtaining the history in a patient with depression, a careful medication history—including the use of any over-the-counter medications—is important (Table 4.6).

Patients With Chronic Pain

Patients with chronic pain have a lifetime prevalence of MDD of 20% to 70%, and depressed patients perceive their pain as being more severe than that of nondepressed patients (6).

The Postpartum Patient

Up to 85% of new mothers experience some depressed mood after the birth of their child, with most of them having "baby blues." However, 5% to 20% experience a postpartum depression (7). These mothers meet the diagnostic criteria in Appendix K for MDD. New mothers may be reluctant at first to give a history of depression, feeling that they should convey only joy regarding their new motherhood. An especially empathic approach to taking their history may be helpful. A history of postpartum depression with one pregnancy increases the risk for recurrence with subsequent pregnancies.

The Somatizing Patient

When a patient presents with multiple somatic symptoms, one should consider the possibility of depressive disorder or anxiety disorder. Table 4.7 lists the increasing probability of the presence of a mood disorder or anxiety disorder as the number of symptoms increases. The somatoform disorders are addressed in Chapter 10, but depression must first be excluded before the patient is given a somatoform diagnosis and management plan.

PHYSICAL EXAMINATION

Patients with MDD, dysthymic disorder, adjustment disorder with depressed mood, and BPD will have a normal physical examination except for the mental status examination and findings from any other comorbid condition. The mental status examination (Appendices I and J; Table 4.8) will show depressed affect in most instances, although some patients present with more irritability and anger than sadness.

Although no physical findings are specific to a diagnosis of depressive disorder, it is important to perform a thorough physical examination to rule out other medical problems that might present initially with depressive symptoms.

TABLE 4.6. Classes of Medications That Can Cause Depression

Antihypertensives and Cardiac Medications	Stimulants	Other Prescribed Medications	Over-the-Counter Substances
Reserpine, methyldopa (Aldomet), procainamide	Amphetamines, cocaine (rebound depression)	Antineoplastic agents, antiparkinsonian drugs, antipsychotic medications, anticonvulsants, antibiotics, sedatives, tranquillizers and antianxiety drugs, oral contraceptives, corticosteroids	NSAIDs, caffeine, cimetidine (Tagament), rantidine (Zantac)
(Procanbid), digitalis, thiazide diuretics, pravastatin (Pravachol), other antihypertensives			

Adapted from McCoy DM. Treatment considerations for depression in patients with significant medical comorbidity. J Fam Pract 1996;43(6 suppl):S35–S44; and Keshaven MS. Medication-induced depression. Prim Psychiatr 1997;4(4):71–76.

TABLE 4.7. Number of Symptoms and Presence of a Mood or Anxiety Disorder

Number of Physical Symptoms	Prevalence of a Mood Disorder	Prevalence of an Anxiety Disorder
0 to 1	2%	1%
2 to 3	12%	7%
4 to 5	23%	13%
6 to 8	44%	30%
9 or more	60%	48%

Adapted from Kroenke K, Spitzer RL, et al. Physical symptoms in primary care: predictors of psychiatric disorders and functional impairment. Arch Fam Med 1994;3:744–779.

TABLE 4.8. Physical and Mental Status Exam Findings in Patients With Depression

Major Depressive Disorder (MDD)	Dysthymic Disorder	Adjustment Disorder With Depressed Mood	Borderline Personality Disorder (BPD)	Depression Secondary to Substance Abuse/ Dependence
More psychomotor retardation than the patient with dysthymia, adjustment disorder, or BPD May have poor personal hygiene Difficulty concentrating during the visit "Pseudodementia" of depression, tearfulness	Less psychomotor retardation than the patient with MDD; tearfulness	Less psychomotor retardation than the patient with MDD; tearfulness	May have multiple, usually horizontal scars on the anterior wrists and forearms from prior episodes of self-inflicted cutting; often displays intense anger affect; tearfulness	Palmar erythema or other physical stigmata of alcoholism (for alcohol abuse) Presence of puncture sites over veins or ulceration of the nasal septum from inhalation of drugs (for drug abuse); tearfulness

TABLE 4.9. Diagnostic Steps for Excluding Other Medical Problems

Neurologic examination
    Stroke
    Demyelination
    Degenerative and traumatic disorders
Rheumatologic examination
    Lupus erythematosus and other autoimmune disorders
Cardiovascular examination
Screening for endocrine and metabolic disorders
Consideration of malignancy
    Pancreatic cancer
    Lung cancer
    Kidney cancer
    Gastrointestinal cancer
    Brain cancer

DIAGNOSTIC TESTING

No specific laboratory test establishes a diagnosis of MDD. The controversial dexamethasone suppression test (DST) is negative in about 50% of patients with MDD (false-negatives), and the test is frequently falsely positive in patients with alcoholism, malnutrition, obesity, pregnancy, major physical illness, anticonvulsant use, excessive caffeine intake, and age over 65 years of age (2).

One laboratory abnormality that seems to correlate with the depressive state is a decrease in rapid eye movement (REM) latency seen on the polysomnographic recording; that is, there is a shortened duration of the first non-REM period of sleep (1). This is seen in MDD, bipolar depression, and dysthymic disorder and does not help to differentiate among them.

Although no specific laboratory test establishes a diagnosis of depressive disorder, it is important to perform certain tests to screen out other medical problems in patients who present with depressive symptoms (Tables 4.9 and 4.10).

WHEN TO REFER

The family physician should consider referring the patient with a depressive disorder to a mental health professional any time that the diagnosis is in doubt or in the situations listed in Table 4.11. When psychiatric consultation is

TABLE 4.10.   Initial Laboratory Test Screening for Depressed Patients

FOR ALL PATIENTS

Complete blood count (CBC) with erythrocyte sedimentation rate (ESR)—Screens for hematologic disorders and autoimmune and inflammatory disorders. An increase in the red cell size, or mean corpuscular volume (MCV), on the CBC may alert the physician to the possibility of alcoholism or vitamin B_{12} deficiency. Vitamin B_{12} level should be checked whenever an elevated MCV is discovered.

Chemistry panel—Screens for diabetes, kidney, adrenal, and liver disease.

Urine analysis.

Evaluation of thyroid-stimulating hormone (TSH)—Should always be checked in the initial evaluation of depressive disorders.

FOR SELECTED PATIENTS

Pregnancy test—Appropriate for many women before deciding on a treatment plan.

Serologic test for syphilis (VDRL or RPR)—Appropriate for some patients.

HIV or AIDS testing—Because AIDS may initially present with depression, testing should be considered if the patient has any risk factors.

Radiologic studies—Indicated if the medical history and physical examination suggest a need to rule out neurologic lesions or carcinoma.

TABLE 4.11. When to Consider Consultation

Type of Consultant	When
Psychotherapist	If indicated and desired by the patient and if the family physician does not have the skill, time, or interest to provide this therapy
Psychiatrist (emergently)	If suicidal ideation is present If psychosis is present If hospitalization may be indicated
Psychiatrist (nonemergently)	For patients with major depressive disorder (MDD) during pregnancy For patients with "double depression" For patients with a depressive disorder complicated by the presence of an additional psychiatric illness
Psychiatrist skilled in electroconvulsive therapy (ECT)	For patients with severe MDD; ECT is a very safe procedure and the most rapidly effective treatment for MDD.

indicated, the family physician often works together with the psychiatrist in the management of the patient.

MANAGEMENT

Risk of Suicide

Suicide can be a very real risk in any patient who suffers depressive symptoms, regardless of the specific diagnosis established or epidemiologic factors. Approximately 15% of patients with recurrent MDD will die by suicide, and the lifetime suicide attempt rate is nearly the same for MDD and dysthymic disorder (2). Eight to 10% of patients with BPD die by suicide (8), and many more attempt it. Approximately 70% of suicide victims had one of two psychiatric disorders: depression and alcoholism (9). These are particularly worrisome in combination.

The physician should never hesitate to ask the patient directly about suicidal ideation and plans (Table 4.12). Asking the patient about suicide does not suggest it to the patient and does not increase its likelihood. Asking about suicide could be a very great relief to the patient, giving him or her the opportunity to talk openly to someone about a very burdensome feeling. It could save the patient's life.

Management Approach

Appendix O is an algorithm of a general approach to the treatment of depression. Management of the patient with depressive syndrome varies according to the diagnosis (or combination of diagnoses) established.

Major Depressive Disorder

The most effective approach to the treatment of MDD is an integrated plan that includes education of the patient and family regarding the nature of MDD, supportive therapy by the physician, encouraging the development of coping skills, vigilance regarding suicide potential, and, in most instances, antidepressant medication.

Dysthymic Disorder

Historically, the treatment of dysthymic disorder was limited to interpersonal psychotherapy or long-term psychoanalytic psychotherapy, and medications were felt to be of little benefit. This view has gradually changed, with dysthymia now considered part of the depressive disorder continuum and treated in a manner more similar to major depression. When antidepressant medication is indicated, the prescribed time before a therapeutic response is seen may be much longer than that seen with major depression.

Adjustment Disorder

The patient with an adjustment disorder with depressed mood may benefit greatly from supportive visits with the physician and psychotherapy. These should be tried initially, and medication considered later if specific target symptoms (listed in Appendix K) suggestive of depression persist.

Borderline Personality Disorder

The patient with BPD requires an understanding by the physician and staff that there will be sudden, intense affects and demanding, recurrent crises in the care of the patient. The physician and staff need to maintain professional boundaries and set appropriate limits for the patient. It is by the repeated process of crisis-meets-limit-setting (without abandonment) over 5 or more

TABLE 4.12.   Factors That Increase the Risk of Suicide

- Middle age or elderly
- Male
- White
- Unmarried (widowed or divorced have even higher risk)
- Unemployed
- Socially isolated
- Alcoholic
- Medically ill
- Access to guns
- Family history of suicide

Adapted from Roy A. Suicide. In: Kaplan HI, Sadock BJ, eds. Comprehensive textbook of psychiatry/IV. 6th ed. Baltimore: Williams & Wilkins, 1995:1739–1751.

years that the patient with BPD improves somewhat, experiencing fewer crises of less intensity, but rarely a cure.

Patients with BPD benefit from psychotherapy. Although psychotherapy can help greatly, it will not eliminate the need for the understanding of crisis management by the family physician and staff. A book by Kreisman and Straus for the lay public can help those close to BPD patients to better understand the illness (see reference 10). Medication is sometimes indicated for patients with BPD, but psychiatric consultation is recommended when this is the case.

Depression Secondary to Substance Abuse/Dependence

The patient with depression secondary to substance abuse and dependence must be persuaded to stop all substance use and to enter a substance abuse treatment program. Most depression that is secondary to substance use resolves within 6 to 8 weeks of discontinuation of the substance. If depressive symptoms persist or if they are severe, treatment for depression may be needed in addition to a substance abuse treatment program.

Bereavement-Related Depression

The bereaved person needs to process the grief and reorganize his or her life without the physical presence of the deceased person. This requires time and the close support of relatives, friends, and the clergy as appropriate to the patient's beliefs. Supportive visits with the family physician are helpful. In some instances of difficulty or complications in grieving, it may be helpful to consult a psychotherapist. Medication is usually not indicated, although the prescription of a sleeping aid for a few days at the time of the death and funeral is often seen in practice.

Antidepressant Medications

The decision to prescribe an antidepressant medication is in many ways one of the most complex aspects of the practice of medicine (Table 4.13). Appendix P compares some of the commonly prescribed medications. All antidepressant medications—there are more than 20—are equally efficacious (Table 4.14). Studies of the efficacy of antidepressants vary, with the most conservative estimates being 66% probability of successfully treating the symptoms of MDD (11,12). This places the probability of successful treatment of MDD with medication alone in a category similar to many other medical conditions treated by the family physician. See Appendix Q for clinical guidelines of the Agency for Health Care Policy and Research for the various depressive disorders.

Selection, and whether to prescribe at all, must be based on a thorough knowledge of the patient's medical condition. A medical history and physical examination (with particular attention to blood pressure and weight monitoring throughout treatment) must therefore be done first. Certain baseline

TABLE 4.13. Points to Consider When Assessing the Patient's Medical Condition

- Potential drug interactions between the antidepressant and any other medications that the patient must take.
- Integrity of the patient's cardiovascular system, hepatic, and renal function, and neurologic system
- Presence or absence of glaucoma, vision difficulties, and urinary outlet problems (e.g., prostatic hypertrophy)

TABLE 4.14. Features Common to All Antidepressants

- Delay in onset of clinical response (7–28 days typically, but longer for the elderly and for patients with dysthymia)
- Risk of precipitating mania or hypomania (the tricyclic agents probably present a greater risk than the other choices)
- Potential side effects

laboratory data must be obtained and interpreted, as previously described; when tricyclic antidepressants (TCAs) are used in children or in adults over age 40 years, an electrocardiogram (ECG) should be performed and evaluated before use of TCAs. If all these parameters are normal, then the choice of agent focuses on several practical points:

1. If the patient has used an antidepressant in the past with success, that antidepressant should be considered as the first choice in a recurrent episode.
2. If the patient has a first-degree relative with MDD and that person has used an antidepressant with success, that medication should be considered first, if all other factors agree with that choice.
3. If the patient is taking other medications, potential drug interactions dictate the potential choices of antidepressants.
4. If the patient has other medical conditions, care must be taken to ensure that the antidepressant chosen does not exacerbate the other illnesses. For example, if a patient has congestive heart failure, TCAs with a negative inotropic effect (which includes all TCAs except nortriptyline) should be avoided. If a patient has a medical condition that might not tolerate an accidental hypertensive crisis with the use of the monoamine oxidase (MAO) inhibitors, these medications should be avoided.
5. Side effects should be used to advantage, if possible. For example, if the patient is having trouble getting to sleep, a sedating antidepressant may be helpful. Similar examples can be made for hypersomnia, appetite and weight gain, and bowel habits.
6. Safety in overdose should be considered. The TCAs and MAO inhibitors (often taken with other drugs in a suicide attempt) are much more dan-

gerous in overdose than the selective serotonin reuptake inhibitors (SS-RIs), for example.

7. Patient compliance factors (especially number of doses per day) must be considered.
8. Cost factors should always be considered, and sometimes limited managed care formularies dictate which medication will be used. In any case, the physician should learn all the medical issues involved in the use of a limited number of medications with which he or she can become comfortable prescribing on a regular basis.
9. Identifying specific "target symptoms" at the outset of treatment and following these symptoms with each visit help the patient and physician assess efficacy for a given patient. For example, insomnia, fatigue, poor concentration, feelings of hopelessness and irritability, and crying spells might be the target symptoms followed for a particular patient, with the patient and physician understanding that it is relief of these symptoms that medication offers. This helps the patient understand that antidepressant medications are not "happiness pills."

Sometimes we are fortunate enough to be able to start a patient on an antidepressant and have excellent clinical results with minimal or no apparent side effects. It seems more common, however, to start a patient on medication and find some nuance that needs further medical intervention, whether that be a change to a different antidepressant or the change of some other medication to eliminate drug interactions or the medical management of side effects to enable the continuation of an antidepressant that is working well. These steps in the prescribing of antidepressant medication challenge the physician to use all the skills of the practice of medicine.

With the latter general principles in mind, in addition to the drug-specific information that follows and the review of Appendix P, the physician will be able to select an initial antidepressant for most patients. What follows are several points of interest regarding some specific medications and some special clinical situations.

Selective Serotonin Reuptake Inhibitors

SSRIs constitute a class of antidepressants generally considered the agents of first choice for the treatment of MDD in primary care (Table 4.15). They are highly effective, are safer in overdose, and have fewer and milder side effects.

Side Effects. All the medications in this class can commonly cause nausea, loose stools, and headache. If the patient can tolerate these symptoms for the first 7 to 10 days, they often remit with time. Fluoxetine and sertraline can cause insomnia, and paroxetine may be somewhat sedating. One side effect that occurs in about 30% of patients taking SSRIs is delayed orgasm or anorgasmia. This resolves with time in the minority of those affected. "Drug hol-

TABLE 4.1 5. SSRI Profile

Fluoxetine (Prozac)
   Effective and well tolerated but can cause a troublesome restlessness. The very long half-life of its active metabolites makes drug interactions a consideration, and changing to alternate antidepressants can be more complex than some other antidepressants.

Fluvoxamine (Luvox)
   Marketed only for the treatment of obsessive-compulsive disorder (OCD) in the United States. This medication is used in much of the rest of the world for major depressive disorder (MDD) and might be a good choice for the patient with both MDD and OCD.

Sertraline (Zoloft)
   May cause less agitation and insomnia than fluoxetine and less potential memory impairment in the elderly (4) and therefore may be a good choice for depression in the patient with Alzheimer's disease. It is also useful for the treatment of MDD with comorbid anxiety disorders.

Paroxetine (Paxil)
   A good first-line antidepressant for many patients, including the elderly. It is also used for MDD with anxiety disorders and OCD.

idays" can be tried for those on paroxetine (this does not work for those on fluoxetine because of its very long half-life). If this is not helpful, the patient may try cyproheptadine (4 to 8 mg) taken 1 to 2 hours before sexual activity. If none if these methods improves the anorgasmia, the patient can be switched to another SSRI or to another class of drug, such as nefazodone (13). There are many less common side effects of the SSRIs listed in the *Physicians' Desk Reference*.

   Drug Interactions. The 1997 edition of the *Medical Letter Handbook of Adverse Drug Interactions* (14) lists 46 different significant drug interactions for the SSRIs—some with potentially life-threatening significance (Table 4.16). The physician should review all of the patient's medications for potential drug interactions before prescribing an SSRI. Use of an up-to-date drug interaction compendium is suggested.

Tricyclic Antidepressants

Side Effects. All the TCAs have some degree of sedation and anticholinergic side effects, such as dry mouth, constipation, potential for blurred vision, urinary retention, and nausea (Table 4.17). In addition, the TCAs are quinidine-like drugs and can cause cardiac arrhythmias, especially in patients with long QT intervals on electrocardiogram (ECG) at baseline or in patients with other conduction defects. TCAs can cause postural hypotension, tachycardia,

TABLE 4.16. Some of the Most Serious SSRI Drug Interactions

Monoamine oxidase (MAO) inhibitors
  May produce a syndrome of various cardiovascular, gastrointestinal, neurologic, and psychiatric symptoms and can be life-threatening. If a patient has been on an MAO inhibitor, at least 2 weeks of drug-free interval should pass before starting an SSRI. If a patient has been on an SSRI, particularly fluoxetine (Prozac), he or she should be drug-free at least 5 to 6 weeks before an MAO inhibitor could be started.

Type 1C antiarrhythmic agents
  Potential interaction with fluoxetine, sertraline, and paroxetine.

Tricyclic antidepressants (TCAs)
  Potentially dangerous interaction with elevated TCA blood levels. Occasionally, a psychiatrist adds a low-dose TCA to treatment with an SSRI, but the dosage of the TCA is generally very small (e.g., desipramine, 10–25 mg/day).

Carbamazepine (Tegretol), lithium, nifedipine (Adalat, Procardia), phenytoin (Dilantin), verapamil (Calan, Isoptin), and valproate (Depakote, Depakene)
  Possible toxicity when combined with fluoxetine. Levels should therefore be monitored carefully.

Warfarin (Coumadin)
  May interact with SSRIs to lead to increased coagulation times. Bleeding occurred with warfarin and paroxetine without increase in coagulation time (14).

SSRI = selective serotonin reuptake inhibitor.

dizziness, ataxia, tremor, leukopenia, syndrome of inappropriate ADH secretion, sexual dysfunction, and obstructive jaundice.

Drug Interactions. There are 52 potential drug interactions listed for TCAs in the 1997 edition of the *Medical Letter Handbook of Adverse Drug Interactions* (Table 4.18) (14). The physician should carefully review all the patient's medications with an up-to-date drug interaction compendium before prescribing TCAs.

Monoamine Oxidase Inhibitors

The MAO inhibitors, phenelzine (Nardil) and tranylcypromine (Parnate), available in the United States, are useful in atypical depression, panic disorder, agoraphobia, and depression resistant to first-line agents, such as SSRIs and TCAs. The patient on MAO inhibitors must be able to understand and follow special dietary precautions to avoid tyramine-containing foods and beverages. A patient who is frail and not likely to survive the hypertensive crisis that could arise with accidental ingestion of tyramine-containing foods or who lives at such a distance that delay in receiving medical help with such a crisis would put the patient's life at risk should not be prescribed MAO inhibitors. These potential problems and the seriousness of potential drug interactions have made MAO inhibitors second-choice medications, after SSRIs and TCAs.

TABLE 4.17. Profile of Tricyclic Antidepressants (TCAs)

Amitriptyline (Elavil)
   One of the oldest TCAs and no longer a drug of choice for most patients. It is a prominent cause of falls in the elderly and of anticholinergic delirium. Because it has the highest side-effect profile of any antidepressant, most other drugs are a better choice. Amitriptyline is prescribed only if the patient has had excellent results in the past with it and is still young enough to tolerate it safely.

Amoxapine (Asendin)
   A TCA that is really a neuroleptic in disguise. The active metabolite is 7-hydroxyamoxapine, a neuroleptic agent, which can cause tardive dyskinesia, extrapyramidal side effects, and parkinsonism (2). Psychotic symptoms must be present for a neuroleptic prescription to be justified, so amoxapine should be used only for major depressive disorder (MDD) with psychotic features. A better choice for MDD with psychotic features would be to prescribe an antidepressant and a separate antipsychotic medication. Then, when the patient improves and the psychosis resolves, the antipsychotic/neuroleptic can be stopped and the antidepressant can be continued. With this as a superior treatment plan, there is no first-line application for amoxapine in primary care.

Clomipramine (Anafranil)
   A TCA used mainly for obsessive-compulsive disorder. It is very sedating and has sexual dysfunction as a side effect in most patients (13).

Desipramine (Norpramin)
   One of the least sedating, least anticholinergic TCA. It is believed to work primarily in the norepinephrine system, in contrast to the SSRIs.

Doxepin (Sinequan)
   Very sedating.

Imipramine (Tofranil)
   Somewhat sedating and anticholinergic but better tolerated than amitriptyline. Imipramine is the TCA standard to which newer antidepressants are often compared.

Nortriptyline (Pamelor)
   Somewhat anticholinergic and sedating, but less so than most of the TCAs (except desipramine). Nortriptyline has established therapeutic drug levels above or below which it does not generally work well. The ability to monitor drug levels is an advantage whenever drug interactions are a potential problem. Nortriptyline is also believed to have less negative inotropic effect on the heart—and therefore less potential—to decrease cardiac output, compared to other TCAs. Nortriptyline has a lower therapeutic dosage range (40–150 mg/day) compared with most TCAs (75–300 mg/day).

TCAs = tricyclic antidepressants; SSRIs = selective serotonin reuptake inhibitors.

TABLE 4.18. Some of the Most Serious TCA Drug Interactions

Cimetidine (Tagamet)—Possible toxicity with antidepressant

Estrogens or oral contraceptives—Possible toxicity with antidepressant
Diltiazem (Cardizem), verapamil—Possible toxicity with imipramine
Monoamine oxidase (MAO) inhibitors—Delirium, coma, hyperrexia, convulsions, and serotonin syndrome

Phenytoin (Dilantin)—With imipramine, can lead to toxicity with phenytoin

Quinidine—Possible toxicity with TCA

Sympathomimetic amines—Possible hypertension, hypertensive crisis, cognitive mood disturbances

Selective serotonin reuptake inhibitors (SSRIs)—see Table 4.16

Adapted from Goodnick PJ. Practical considerations in the treatment of depression in the diabetic patient. Prim Psychiatr 1997;4:37–40.

TABLE 4.19. Some of the Most Serious Monoamine Oxidase (MAO) Inhibitors Drug Interactions

• All other antidepressants—Serotonin syndrome, delirium, coma, hyperpyrexia, convulsions, mania, and varied cardiovascular, gastrointestinal, neurologic, and psychiatric symptoms
• Sympathomimetic amines—Severe hypertension and possible crisis.
• Amantadine (Symmetrel), buspirone (BuSpar), guanadrel (Hylorel), levodopa (Carbidopa, Sinemet)—Possible hypertension and crisis
• Insulin, oral hypoglycemics, phenformin—Possible increased hypoglycemic effect
• Meperidine (Demerol)—Severe encephalopathy

Adapted from Goodnick PJ. Practical considerations in the treatment of depression in the diabetic patient. Prim Psychiatr 1997;4:37–40.

Drug Interactions. The 1997 edition of the *Medical Letter Handbook of Adverse Drug Interactions* lists 30 potential adverse interactions with MAO inhibitors (Table 4.19) (14). The physician should carefully review all of the patient's medications with an up-to-date drug interaction compendium before prescribing MAO inhibitors.

Atypical Antidepressants
Several antidepressants fall into unique categories, and they are generally second- or third-line choices in the treatment of depression (Table 4.20).

Management With Medication in Special Circumstances (Table 4.21)
The Diabetic Patient
Treatment with antidepressants has been reported to cause fluctuations in blood glucose. In some instances, alleviation of depression may improve patient compliance with diabetes management. In other instances, there has been the suggestion that some antidepressants (especially nefazodone,

TABLE 4.20. Atypical Antidepressants Profile

Bupropion (Wellbutrin)
An effective antidepressant alternative. Its usefulness has been limited by the tendency to lower seizure threshold. The newer, sustained-release forms of the medication should help reduce this risk.

Maprotiline (Ludiomil)
An effective antidepressant that may have fewer anticholinergic side effects than the tricyclic antidepressants. Its usefulness is limited by an increased incidence of seizures and reports of blood dyscrasias (2).

Mirtazapine (Remeron)
A very new antidepressant. It should be considered a second-line agent until more is known of its long-term use.

Nefazodone (Serzone)
A newer generation of antidepressant of the trazodone class. It is somewhat sedating but has a low incidence of other side effects. Nefazodone is often substituted when sexual dysfunction and anorgasmia are problems with the selective serotonin reuptake inhibitors (SSRIs), because it is not known to cause these side effects (13).

Trazodone (Desyrel)
Controversy regarding whether or not trazodone is effective in the treatment of depression (2). It is sometimes used as a treatment for insomnia. Priapism is a rare side effect that needs immediate urologic intervention to prevent impotence as a sequela.

Venlafaxine (Effexor)
May have fewer drug interactions than many of the other antidepressants and has been helpful in treatment-resistant depression. Blood pressure may increase somewhat and must be monitored.

trazodone, and venlafaxine) enhance insulin sensitivity, and hypoglycemia has occasionally occurred when these agents are prescribed to diabetic patients taking insulin or other glucose-lowering agents (4). Careful glucose monitoring is advised when the diabetic patient is started on an antidepressant, and the patient may need lower doses of insulin or other agents used for the treatment of diabetes.

The Pregnant or Lactating Patient
Although depression is a very common disorder, relatively little is known about the effects of antidepressant medications during pregnancy. Potential concerns involve fetal malformations, problems during the perinatal period, and long-term neurobehavioral effects on the infant. If possible, depression during the first trimester should be treated only with psychotherapy and supportive measures (16). If the patient is severely ill with incapacitating depression, suicidality, or psychosis, hospitalization should be considered first-choice treatment, with medication reserved for instances in which hospitalization alone fails. Antidepressants may be needed in the second and third

SEROTONIN SYNDROME

Serotonin syndrome is a potentially life-threatening, iatrogenic disorder and a potential complication of psychopharmacotherapy. Because the symptoms may be nonspecific, the diagnosis of serotonin syndrome may be easily missed. The serotonin syndrome most commonly occurs when two or more serotonergic drugs are given concurrently. Symptoms may begin within hours of an increase in medication dosage or the addition of another medication. Symptoms include the following:

- Cognitive-behavioral changes, such as confusion, disorientation, agitation, irritability, coma, unresponsiveness, and hypomania
- Autonomic nervous system symptoms, such as hyperthermia, diaphoresis, tachycardia, hypertension, pupil dilation, and flushing
- Neuromuscular symptoms, such as myoclonus, hyperreflexia, muscle rigidity, restlessness, hyperactivity, tremor, ataxia, incoordination, clonus, and bilateral Babinski's sign

There is no specific laboratory test to make the diagnosis of serotonin syndrome, and it is important to suspect it clinically and intervene early to prevent mortality which occurs in 11% of patients with serotonin syndrome (15).

Management consists of the following:

- Stopping all serotonergic medications
- Supportive care
- Possible use of antiserotonergic medications such as cyproheptadine (Periactin) or methysergide (Sansert), as second-choice agent. Careful adjustments should be made in medication before resuming psychopharmacologic treatment (15).

---

trimesters if the patient and the physician providing maternity care agree that they are worth the risk. If an antidepressant is to be used during pregnancy, the current *Physicians' Desk Reference* or similar current source should be consulted to seek an antidepressant that is listed as FDA Category A or B. There are no antidepressants in category A at this time.

Some physicians have advised stopping antidepressant therapy approximately 2 weeks before delivery to try to prevent hyperactivity, seizures, or a withdrawal syndrome in the newborn. However, there is no evidence that the withdrawal syndrome experienced by the infant in utero is any safer than the one he or she experiences after delivery, and so recent recommendations have shifted to continuing the antidepressant treatment and managing the withdrawal symptoms in the infant after delivery, as appropriate (16).

All antidepressant medications are secreted in breast milk, and the long-term effect of neurotransmitter stimulation of the newborn is not known. It is recommended that mothers who need antidepressant therapy not breast-feed their infants (16). This is a very sensitive matter for the mothers, but with support, they can be helped to see that a formula-fed baby whose mother is not depressed and is therefore alert, loving, and attentive is better off than a breast-fed infant whose mother is too ill to care appropriately for him or her.

Length of Antidepressant Medication Treatment
First Episode
An antidepressant is started and the dose increased gradually until a good remission of symptoms occurs. This may take up to 2 to 8 weeks. After MDD symptoms are in remission, antidepressant medication is continued at full dose for 4 to 6 months and then gradually tapered (e.g., 25% dose reduction per week) over 1 to 5 months.

Second Episode
The patient may require full-dose antidepressant treatment for 2 to 4 years before gradual tapering of medication to prevent relapse of symptoms.

TABLE 4.21. The Patient With a Comorbid Medical Condition

Comorbid Condition	Good Medication Choices	Medications to Avoid
Parkinson's disease	Bupropion, venlafaxine	TCAs, MAO inhibitors, SSRIs (if selegiline is used)
Stroke	SSRIs, possibly desipramine, nortriptyline	Other TCAs, MAO inhibitors, bupropion
Alzheimer's disease	SSRIs, nefazodone, venlafaxine	TCAs, bupropion, and fluoxetine if agitation is a factor
Cancer patients with pain using opiates	TCAs (constipation risk)	MAO inhibitors
Cachexia	Sertraline, paroxetine, nefazodone, TCAs, venlafaxine	Fluoxetine
Nausea		Bupropion, SSRIs, venlafaxine
Cardiac disease	SSRIs, bupropion, nefazodone	TCAs, venlafaxine (if hypertension is a consideration); SSRIs if type 1C antiarrhythmics are used
Patients taking medications for allergy	Most are OK, except for potential drug interactions	SSRIs, nefazodone, or fluvoxamine because of potential cardiac arrhythmia with terfenadine (Seldane)[a] or astemizole (Hismanal)

Adapted from McCoy DM. Treatment considerations for depression in patients with significant medical comorbidity. J Fam Pract 1996;43(6 suppl):S35–S44.

TCA= tricyclic antidepressants; MAO = monoamine oxidase; SSRI= selective serotonin reuptake inhibitors.

[a]Terfenadine is no longer available in the United States.

TABLE 4.22. Characteristics of Patients Requiring Long-Term Maintenance Therapy

- History of 3 or more episodes of major depressive disorder (MDD)
- History of 2 or more rapidly recurring episodes
- Preexisting dysthymia (double depression)
- Late age of onset
- Prolonged or severe episodes of MDD
- Family history of depressive disorder
- Seasonal pattern of depression
- Coexisting anxiety disorder or substance abuse
- Poor initial response to antidepressant treatment

Adapted from Hirschfeld RM, Schatzberg AF. Long-term management of depression. Am J Med 1994;97(6A): 33S–38S.

Third Episode
Antidepressant medication may need continuation indefinitely to prevent recurrence.

Long-term Maintenance
Some patients may require long-term maintenance therapy with antidepressants after remission is established. Characteristics of such patients are listed in Table 4.22 (17).

Psychotherapy
The most common psychotherapeutic approaches used by family physicians are supportive therapy and cognitive therapy, or a blend of both, as appropriate to the patient's needs. A widely read approach to psychotherapy in the primary care setting is provided in *The Fifteen Minute Hour: Applied Psychotherapy for the Primary Care Physician,* by Stuart and Lieberman (18).

When the patient comes to the physician seeking short-term psychotherapeutic assistance, particularly concerning a specific life event, it is helpful for the patient to work on clarifying his or her options in the situation through the use of an approach such as that presented in *The Fifteen Minute Hour.* Family physicians can help patients learn the difference between thoughts, feelings, and behavior, and that a difficult situation can be dealt with by considering three questions and four options:

QUESTIONS	OPTIONS
1. What are you feeling?	1. Leave it.
2. What do you want?	2. Change it.
3. What can you do about it?	3. Accept it as it is.
	4. Reframe it (learned in therapy).

Adapted from Gunderson JG, Phillips KA. Personality disorders. In: Kaplan HI, Sadock BJ, eds. Comprehensive textbook of psychiatry/IV, 6th ed. Baltimore: Williams & Wilkins, 1995:1441.

Learning basic psychotherapeutic techniques, like any other skill, requires considerable study, and it requires clinical practice under the supervision and proctoring of an experienced therapist. This is best done during the residency training years. For those who have completed this training, here are a few reminders for those who would provide basic supportive care in a primary care office:

1. Maintain a therapeutic approach.
   - Be empathetic.
   - Explore options.
   - Encourage new (constructive) behaviors.
   - Provide explanations (occasionally).
   - Give anticipatory guidance, but only when it is in your area of (medical) expertise.
   - Maximize the use of brief sessions.
   - Know when to refer to a mental health professional.
2. Maintain professional boundaries. It has been said that we must remember, "the patient is the one with the disease." We do not attempt to solve the patient's problems.
3. Concentrate on the feeling and not the details of the issue at hand. Sometimes we have to interrupt the patient who insists on giving all of the details of an event in real time.
4. Stay in the here and now. When the patient says, "All my problems are because of the way my mother treated me as a child," a response might be, "What is it about your relationship to your mother *now* that is bothering you today?"
5. Recognize that grief is the exception to the here-and-now focus. The grieving patient needs to talk about the lost person at length to friends, family, clergy, and sometimes to one's physician, and this often involves talking about the distant past.
6. Avoid giving direct advice. Rare exceptions include advising patients to consult legal counsel if they disclose legal problems or illegal behavior.
7. Absolve guilt whenever reasonable and possible to do so. For example, a patient may come to the physician very anxious and upset after not realizing that a dependent elderly parent has developed a fever, cough, or pneumonia. Just a few words (if true) from the physician, noting that the patient obviously takes excellent care of the parent and that the patient brought the parent to medical attention just as soon as anyone could possibly have done so, can go a long way toward alleviating guilt and discomfort.
8. Stick to the 15-minute time frame as much as possible. It usually takes 6 to 8 weeks to at least partially calm a singular life crisis.
9. Follow up on any "homework" that the patient is given as part of the therapy. Forgetting to ask about the homework at the next visit signals to the patient that the homework and the therapy process are not very important.

10. Undertake therapy only if you have invested in the training and clinical supervision to feel comfortable in practice. If the physician does not have that training and confidence, the patient should be referred to a mental health professional for therapy.

Light Therapy

Patients who suffer recurrent MDD with a pattern of return of symptoms during the fall and winter months (seasonal affective disorder) may benefit from light therapy. The light used is about 200 times brighter than the usual household lighting (2500 lux), and the patient is exposed to the light for 1 to 2 hours per day in the morning. The patient is instructed not to stare at the light but to glance at it occasionally. Improvement in depressive symptoms is often noted after 2 to 4 days of treatment, and patients may relapse after 2 to 4 days of no light treatment. The most common complaints about light therapy are headache, eyestrain, and a feeling of irritability; these are usually manageable with a decrease in the time of light exposure (19).

PATIENT AND FAMILY EDUCATION

When a diagnosis of depressive disorder is established, it is crucial to invest time at the outset in educating the patient and family about the nature of the specific disorder and its treatment (Table 4.23). There is strong social stigma attached to mental illness, and it is very important for the patient and family to understand the cause of the depressive disorders in a context that removes the stigma of blame, character defect, and lack of fortitude.

The patient and family must understand that, with the use of the antidepressant medications, the "bad news" (the side effects) will present itself in the first few days and may make the patient feel worse than before (usually temporarily), whereas the "good news" (resolution of MDD symptoms) may take 10 to 30 days to occur. It takes a lot of faith and confidence in the relationship with the physician to put up with the full spectrum of the initial side effects of SSRIs or TCAs. However, if the patient can tolerate the first 2 weeks, most of the symptoms will decrease or resolve, often just about the

TABLE 4.23. Educational Points to Convey to the Patient and Family

- Depressive illness is a psychobiologic disorder involving altered biochemical states in the brain.
- Depressive episodes, although they may be triggered by stressful life events and the effects of drugs, may also develop spontaneously (2).
- It is important for both the patient and the family to learn as much as possible about depressive disorders and to be vigilant for any future return of symptoms, because it is easier to treat a recurrent episode of major depressive disorder if it is caught early.
- Antidepressant medications may temporarily make the patient feel worse.

time the depression begins to lift. Without patient education, it is unlikely that the patient will comply with the initial days of treatment.

FOLLOW-UP

When a patient is just starting antidepressant therapy, it is helpful to see the patient at weekly intervals for brief visits. The focus of these visits is medication monitoring for compliance and side-effect management. It is very important to be supportive, informative, and reassuring during these early visits, when the patient may be experiencing medication side effects without having experienced beneficial effects (2).

Monitoring for suicidal ideation (which may emerge as the patient begins to improve in a patient who previously denied it) and the initiation of psychotherapy, if the physician is skilled in this procedure, are two additional key matters in the follow-up of the patient with MDD. If the patient has a full therapeutic response, the patient should be seen at least every 1 to 2 months, for medication monitoring alone, during the initial year of antidepressant medication.

REFERENCES

1. American Psychiatric Association. Diagnostic and statistical manual of mental disorders. 4th ed. Washington, DC: American Psychiatric Association, 1994.

2. Judd LL. Mood disorders. In: Isselbacher KJ, Braunwald E, Wilson JD, et al, eds. Harrison's principles of internal medicine. 13th ed. New York: McGraw-Hill, 1994:2400–2408.

3. McCoy DM. Treatment considerations for depression in patients with significant medical comorbidity. J Fam Pract 1996;43(6 suppl):S35–S44.

4. Goodnick PJ. Practical considerations in the treatment of depression in the diabetic patient. Prim Psychiatr 1997;4:37–40.

5. Frasure-Smith N, Lesperance F, Talajic M. Depression following myocardial infarction. Impact on 6-month survival. JAMA 1993;270:1819–1825 [Published erratum JAMA 1994;271:1082].

6. Ruoff GE. Depression in the patient with chronic pain. J Fam Pract 1996;43 (6 suppl):S25–S33.

7. Susman JL. Postpartum depressive disorders. J Fam Pract 1996;43(6 suppl):S17–S24.

8. Gunderson JG, Phillips KA. Personality disorders. In: Kaplan HI, Sadock BJ, eds. Comprehensive textbook of psychiatry/IV. 6th ed. Baltimore: Williams & Wilkins, 1995:1441.

9. Roy A. Suicide. In: Kaplan HI, Sadock BJ, eds. Comprehensive textbook of psychiatry/IV. 6th ed. Baltimore: Williams & Wilkins, 1995:1739–1751.

10. Kreisman JJ, Straus H. I hate you—don't leave me: understanding the borderline personality. New York: Avon Books, 1989.

11. Depression Guideline Panel of the Agency for Health Care Policy and Research (AHCPR). Synopsis of the clinical practice guidelines for diagnosis and treatment of depression in primary care. Arch Fam Med 1994;3:85-92.

12. Bhatia SC, Bhatia SK. Major depression: selecting safe and effective treatment. Am Fam Physician 1997;55:1683-1698.

13. Balon R. The effects of antidepressants on human sexuality: diagnosis and management update 1996. Prim Psychiatr 1997;4:32-44.

14. Rizack MA, ed. The medical letter handbook of adverse drug interactions. New Rochelle, NY: The Medical Letter, 1997.

15. Mills KC. Serotonin syndrome. Am Fam Physician 1995;52:1475-1482.

16. Berga SL, Parry BL. Psychiatry and reproductive medicine. In: Kaplan HI, Sadock, BJ, eds. Comprehensive textbook of psychiatry/IV. 6th ed. Baltimore: Williams & Wilkins, 1995:1700.

17. Hirschfeld RM, Schatzberg AF. Long-term management of depression. Am J Med 1994; 97(6A):33S-38S.

18. Stuart MR, Lieberman JA III. The fifteen minute hour: applied psychotherapy for the primary care physician. 2nd ed. New York: Praeger, 1995.

19. Sadock BJ, Kaplan, HI. Other biological therapies. In: Kaplan, HI, Sadock BJ, eds. Comprehensive textbook of psychiatry/IV. 6th ed. Baltimore: Williams & Wilkins, 1995:2145.

....
Erik Lindbloom

Developmental Delay

The family physician often encounters parents who ask, "Is this normal for a child this age?" This question may be raised during a visit for a well-child examination or when a specific illness is presented. An estimated 5% to 10% of children in a typical practice have some kind of developmental delay (1). It is often the family physician's task to identify and manage such developmental abnormalities; doing so in a timely fashion may help the family address, and sometimes improve, the underlying cause.

CHIEF COMPLAINT

Parents or guardians may express a multitude of concerns, depending on the child's age and the parents' expectations. Motor, language, social, and cognitive development are common areas of concern. Complaints may range from floppy muscle tone in a newborn infant to poor classroom performance in an elementary school student. Other common presenting complaints from parents include lack of interaction, poor feeding, delay in sitting or crawling, and language abnormalities.

HISTORY

Medical (including prenatal and perinatal) history and developmental history are crucial in identifying the underlying etiology.

Medical History

Questioning the parent or reviewing the chart may reveal previously established diagnoses (e.g., meningomyelocele, chronic infections, chromosomal abnormalities). If such diagnoses have not been made, a careful history-taking can identify risk factors for developmental delay (Table 5.1). Identification of risk factors may help determine the role of environmental and social issues in the child's developmental delay (2).

Developmental History

Prior developmental milestones. Ideally, these milestones have been documented in the child's chart. If such documentation is not available, rough

TABLE 5.1. Risk Factors for Pediatric Developmental Delay

SOCIAL/FAMILY
Family history of developmental delay or sensory abnormalities
Poor feeding or growth (may be multifactorial)
Substance abuse in family (before or after birth)
Abuse of any sort
Limited parental support
Other major stressors

INFECTIOUS
Congenital infections
Sepsis
Meningitis
Encephalitis
Recurrent infections (e.g., chronic otitis media or pulmonary infections)
HIV

NEUROLOGIC
Seizures
Hypoxic events
Microcephaly
Myelomeningocele
Intracranial hemorrhage or cerebrovascular accident
Infections

PRENATAL/OBSTETRIC
Prematurity
Low birth weight
Intrauterine growth retardation
Congenital malformations or infections
Intrauterine toxin exposure
Obstetric complications

METABOLIC
Hypoglycemia
Hyperbilirubinemia
Toxin exposure (intrauterine or postpartum)
Hypothyroidism

TABLE 5.2. Developmental Milestones

	Milestone	Age (75% will accomplish)
Gross motor	Head up to 45 degrees	8 weeks
	Rolls over	4 months
	Pulls to sit—no head lag	5 months
	Sits without support	6.5 months
	Stands holding on	8.5 months
	Stands momentarily	12 months
	Walks well	13.5 months
	Climb stairs	21 months
	Jumps in place	2.5 years
	Broad jump	3 years
	Hops on one foot	4 years
Fine motor	Follows to midline	4 weeks
	Follows past midline	2 months
	Grasps rattle	4 months
	Passes cube hand to hand	6.5 months
	Thumb-finger grasp	9.5 months
	Neat pincher grasp	12.5 months
	Stacks 2 cubes	17 months
	Dumps raisin from bottle	2 years
	Picks longer of 2 lines	3.5 years
	Draws man—3 parts	4.7 years
Social	Smiles responsively	6 weeks
	Smiles spontaneously	3 months
	Plays peek-a-boo	7.5 months
	Has stranger anxiety	9.5 months
	Drinks from cup	14 months
	Helps in house	21 months
	Washes and dries hands	2.5 years
	Dresses with supervision	3 years
	Dresses without supervision	4 years
Language	Vocalizes (not crying)	1.5 months
	Laughs	3 months
	Turns head to sound of a voice	6.5 months
	"Dada" or "mama" (nonspecific)	8 months
	3 words (not dada or mama)	15 months
	Points to 1 named body part	21 months
	Uses plurals	2.7 years
	Gives first and last name	3.2 years
	Recognizes colors	3.7 years

Adapted from the Denver Developmental Screening Test.

determinations can be obtained from the parents, but aside from language concerns, that information has proved to be unreliable (3).

Current development (home or school). A current assessment of the child's status is more reliable than parental recollection of past development and may reveal whether parents have realistic expectations regarding anticipated development. Information obtained with a formal developmental screen, such as the Denver Developmental Screening Test (DDST), also provides reliable data to assess current developmental levels. DDST milestones are listed in Table 5.2.

PHYSICAL EXAMINATION

The initial examination should begin with simple growth data, including height, weight, and head circumference. Evaluating vision and hearing (as appropriate for age and developmental level) is also essential, as sensory loss can be devastating to all aspects of a child's development.

In addition to sensory abnormalities, anomalous appearance or integument abnormalities can suggest chromosomal abnormalities (e.g., nail dysplasia in children with trisomy disorders) or neurologic disorders. Neurocutaneous disorders associated with developmental delay are listed in Table 5.3. Cardiac, abdominal, or eye abnormalities also have significance in certain conditions, such as Down's syndrome and inborn errors of metabolism (4).

A thorough neurologic examination should be conducted when developmental delay is suspected. In addition to the usual assessments of muscle tone, deep tendon reflexes, sensation, gait and speech, attention also needs to be paid to posturing and disappearance of primitive reflexes.

DIAGNOSTIC TESTING

Documentation of developmental milestones, such as those listed in Table 5.2, and referral for formal intelligence and cognitive testing can be instru-

TABLE 5.3. Neurocutaneous Disorders Associated With Developmental Delay

Disorder	Physical findings
Neurofibromatosis	Café-au-lait spots
	Neurofibromas
Tuberous sclerosis	Hypopigmented spots
	Adenoma sebacea (cheeks, chin, forehead)
	Shagreen patch (yellow roughness, lumbosacral region)
von Hippel-Lindau syndrome	Retinal angiomata
Sturge-Weber disease	Port-wine stain (facial nevus, usually unilateral)
Linear nevus syndrome	Midline facial nevus

mental in narrowing the differential diagnosis. As in other conditions, testing can often be streamlined depending on the history and exam findings.

- Lead testing—This is especially important information to have in possible developmental delay and may have already been performed in children who are at risk.
- Thyroid function testing—Hypothyroidism is a potentially reversible cause for developmental delay, and thyroid function tests should be strongly considered in all children presenting with developmental delay.
- Metabolic tests—Testing for levels of plasma amino acids, organic acids, and blood lactate, for example, can be done to detect inborn errors of metabolism in patients with motor delay or cognitive dysfunction. Given the extremely low incidence of inborn errors, other symptoms such as vomiting, lethargy, odor, failure to thrive, or family history can further support testing (3).
- Chromosomal analysis—This analysis may be indicated in children with anomalies of appearance.
- Creatine phosphokinase (CPK) or aldolase—This is merited as a screen for muscular dystrophy in patients with abnormal muscle tone.
- Neuroimaging or electroencephalography (EEG)—This form of testing may be considered in children with:
  - Evidence of seizures
  - Abnormal neurologic findings
  - Abnormal head circumference
  - Impaired sensory functions

DIFFERENTIAL DIAGNOSIS

Normal Variation

Screening norms are distributions of age-dependent milestones. By definition, some children who have no underlying developmental abnormality fall outside standard deviations. Many sources list developmental milestones and the corresponding ages at which developmental delay should be considered (with some variation between sources). The clinician should have one of these standard frameworks in mind, such as an expanded version of Table 5.2, when screening for developmental delay (5,6).

Vision or Hearing Abnormalities

Abnormalities in vision or hearing can have profound effects on a child's development, particularly communication, social, and cognitive skills. Rule out sensory impairment before exploring other possible causes. Any abnormalities found when screening visual acuity or hearing thresholds warrant further investigation.

Hypothyroidism

Although newborn screening includes a test for hypothyroidism, it is still important for the clinician to be familiar with the presenting symptoms. Infants with hypothyroidism are lethargic, are late to sit and stand, and have difficulty learning language skills. Facial edema, macroglossia, hypothermia, umbilical hernia, and constipation are findings associated with hypothyroidism in infants. Later in life, the child may exhibit growth retardation, delayed bone and dental maturation, delayed puberty, galactorrhea, thickened skin, and coarse brittle hair.

Lead Poisoning

High serum levels of lead can cause mental retardation and behavior disorders. Vomiting, seizures, anemia, and abdominal pain may be clues to the diagnosis of lead poisoning.

Learning Disabilities

Learning disabilities are the most prevalent developmental disorders diagnosed. They affect 5% of school-aged children and twice as many boys as girls (7). Pathogenesis is unknown. There is no universally accepted definition; diagnosis commonly relies on the difference between educational achievement and intellectual potential. Inadequate school performance reported by the school or parent is usually the presenting complaint.

Learning disabilities include a group of disorders that cause difficulty in the following areas:

- Listening
- Speaking
- Reading
- Writing
- Reasoning
- Mathematical abilities

Language Disorders

Developmental delay is often associated with language disorders. These may range from difficulty articulating words to difficulty understanding language (8). The physician should consider poor hearing or social disadvantage as possible causes of language disorders.

Mental Retardation

The prevalence of mental retardation is 2.5% of the population. Classic criteria include:

- Below-average intellectual functioning on formal intelligence testing (2 standard deviations below the mean).

- Impaired ability to adapt to the environment, which may include limited communication skills and inability to provide self-care or avoid hazards
- Consequence of an injury, disease, or abnormality that existed before the age of 18 (e.g., genetic disorders, hypoxic episodes, neurologic infections)

Mental retardation itself has a differential diagnosis for the underlying cause, including the following:

- Cerebral palsy
- Sensory and communication deficits
- Neuropsychiatric disorders
- Various syndromes (e.g., fragile X syndrome, Down's syndrome, fetal alcohol syndrome) (9)

Cerebral Palsy

Cerebral palsy (CP) is not a specific disease, but rather a collection of motion and posture abnormalities resulting from a central nervous system injury in the first 5 years of life (Table 5.4). CP can coexist with cognitive, sensory, or communication abnormalities. The prevalence of CP is approximately 0.2%.

Inborn Errors of Metabolism

Rare disorders of metabolism, such as galactosemia, maple syrup urine disease, and biotinidase deficiency, should be suspected in cases of developmental delay accompanied by:

- Vomiting
- Seizures
- Odor
- Hepatomegaly
- Renal stones

TABLE 5.4. Causes of Cerebral Palsy

Time of Origin	Percentage of Cases	Insult
Prenatal	40–50	Infections, teratogens, chromosomal abnormalities, placental abnormalities, anatomic abnormalities
Perinatal	~25	Prematurity, preeclampsia, sepsis, asphyxia, other delivery complications
Childhood	~5	Meningitis, traumatic brain injury, toxins
Uncertain	20–25	

Adapted from Hagberg B, Hagberg G. Prenatal and perinatal risk factors in a survey of 681 Swedish cases. In: Stanley F, Alberman E. The epidemiology of the cerebral palsied. Philadelphia: JB Lippincott, 1984, pp 116–134.

Autism

Autism is a pervasive developmental disorder that includes impaired social interaction, impaired communication, and inflexible behavior. The diagnosis is based on clinical criteria; two-thirds of children first show symptoms of indifference and social withdrawal in infancy. Pathogenesis is unknown, but increased risk of autism exists with several genetic syndromes.

Neurocutaneous Syndromes

Children with any of the following syndromes may present with various manifestations of developmental delay:

- Neurofibromatosis
- Tuberous sclerosis
- Sturge-Weber disease
- von Hippel-Lindau disease
- Linear nevus syndrome

A thorough skin exam may be the key to the diagnosis. Table 5.3 lists the common skin findings in those conditions.

Psychosocial Conditions

Many psychiatric diagnoses have a higher prevalence in children with developmental delay. Affective disorders and attention-deficit hyperactivity disorder (see Chapter 2) are two to three times more prevalent in mentally retarded individuals than in the general population (10). Anxiety, psychosis, and aggressive or self-injurious behavior are also considerations in these children, regardless of the underlying cause of developmental delay. Social and environmental deprivation must always be a consideration in developmental delay as well. Children with behavioral abnormalities may benefit from psychiatric intervention (11).

WHEN TO REFER

Some causes of developmental delay, such as hypothyroidism, lead toxicity, and some visual and auditory impairments are readily reversible. Most disorders, however, require long-term behavioral therapy, frequent psychologic reevaluations, or special accommodations at home and school. Referral should be based on an individualized assessment of the available resources to optimize the diagnostic accuracy and the family's satisfaction with the overall situation.

MANAGEMENT

Medication

Treatment for conditions such as hypothyroidism or lead poisoning is well documented in general medical texts. The psychopharmacology in children with developmental delay is discussed less often and may be helpful in symptomatic treatment. A useful review of medications for developmental delay can be found in an article by Mercugliano (12). Antispasticity medications, antidepressants, antipsychotics, and methylphenidate (Ritalin) all have roles in treating associated or coexisting psychiatric and neurologic manifestations.

Other Treatment Modalities

Behavior management is a key issue in children with developmental delay, because the prevalence of behavior disorders in this group is about 50%. Techniques used in children of all abilities such as positive reinforcement and time-outs can be used effectively to modify the child's behavior to a more acceptable standard. Consultation with a behavioral therapist may be helpful in this situation.

In addition, attention must be paid to the rehabilitation potential of the child. Orthotics, wheelchairs, physical therapists, and occupational therapists can assist in providing the optimal physical functioning of a given child.

FOLLOW-UP

Close follow-up is essential not only for the child, but for the family as well. Ongoing psychosocial support for both the child and family is essential to provide the most cohesive environment, and the family physician is generally a key member of the team, providing this continuum of services. Pay close attention for signs of increasing strain in family relationships, particularly between the parents. Regular inquiry and reassessment regarding the child's educational and social environment should be made.

PATIENT EDUCATION

Ideally, a comprehensive continuum of services can be provided to the child and family to optimize the child's health and development.

Involvement with organizations outside the home, such as day care and support groups, may be invaluable. An excellent place to start looking for these resources is by contacting the National Academy for Child Development, P.O. Box 380, Huntsville, UT 84317. 801-621-8606. www.nacd.org. Most larger communities have regional centers that provide multiple services for developmentally disabled individuals.

REFERENCES

1. Simeonsson RJ, Sharp MC. Developmental Delays. In: Hoekelman RA, ed. Primary pediatric care. 2nd ed. St. Louis: Mosby-Year Book, 1992.

2. Allen MC. The high-risk infant. Pediatr Clin North Am 1993;40:479–490.

3. McCune YD, Richardson MM, Powell JA. Psychosocial health issues in pediatric practices: parents' knowledge and concerns. Pediatrics 1984;74:183.

4. Levy SE, Hyman SL. Pediatric assessment of the child with developmental delay. Pediatr Clin North Am 1993;40:465–477.

5. First LR, Palfrey JS. The infant or young child with developmental delay. N Engl J Med 1994;330:478–483.

6. Levine MD, Carey WB, Crocker AC, eds. Developmental-behavioral pediatrics. 2nd ed. Philadelphia: WB Saunders, 1992.

7. Shapiro BK, Gallico RP. Learning disabilities. Pediatr Clin North Am 1993;40:491–505.

8. Newton RW, Wraith JE. Investigation of developmental delay. Arch Dis Child 1995;72:460–465.

9. Batshaw ML. Mental retardation. Pediatr Clin North Am 1993;40:507–521.

10. Gillberg C, Persson E, Grufman M, et al: Psychiatric disorders in mildly and severely mentally retarded urban children and adolescents: epidemiological aspects. Br J Psychiatry 1986;149:68–74.

11. Mauk JE. Autism and pervasive development disorders. Pediatr Clin North Am 1993;40:537–551.

12. Mercugliano M. Psychopharmacology in children with developmental disabilities. Pediatr Clin North Am 1993;40:593–616.

CHAPTER 6

···

Margaret E. McCahill

Fibromyalgia Syndrome

Any discussion of fibromyalgia syndrome (FS) must first acknowledge that there has been considerable controversy about whether the condition really exists (1–3). Although FS may show considerable overlap with the somatoform and depressive disorders, there are times when the diagnosis of FS is the best explanation for the patient's symptoms. Establishing the diagnosis when appropriate can benefit patients, perhaps by making them feel that their symptoms are understood. In this way, they can develop a strong therapeutic alliance with the physician (Table 6.1) (4). Helping patients understand and cope with their condition can be most rewarding.

CHIEF COMPLAINT

Patients with FS typically complain of diffuse musculoskeletal pain, stiffness, sleep disturbance, exaggerated tenderness at specific sites, and easy fatigability. A relatively high percentage (67%) of patients report "pain all over" (3,5).

HISTORY

A thorough medical history must be obtained. Patients with FS may have a history of the following:

- Generalized aching of the trunk, hips, and shoulders. Stiffness may be worse in the morning and improve during the day, or it may persist all day (10).
- Fatigue and "nonrestorative sleep." Patients with FS may wake up tired and complain of exhaustion. They may not complain of sleep disturbance symptoms even though they may be awakening often during the night and falling sleep again.
- Other common complaints such as paresthesias, anxiety, headaches, irritable bowel symptoms, urinary urgency, dysmenorrhea, sicca symptoms, and Reynaud's phenomenon (3).

Patients with FS often report that their symptoms are aggravated by cold or humid weather, nonrestorative sleep, physical or mental fatigue, too much

73

TABLE 6.1.   Diagnostic Criteria for Fibromyalgia

1. History of widespread pain of at least 3 months' duration.
2. Pain in at least 11 of 18 paired tender points on digital palpation (see physical examination for listing of tender points).

Adapted from references 1, 3, and 10.

EPIDEMIOLOGIC CONSIDERATIONS

FS is seen almost exclusively in women. Studies have examined the prevalence of fibromyalgia in the general population. These studies used the 1990 American College of Rheumatology criteria for diagnosis (6–9); the data suggest that at a given point, 3% to 6% of the population (including children) meet criteria for FS. This figure is probably a conservative estimate.

or too little physical activity, and anxiety or stress. Conversely, they may report that symptoms improve with warm, dry weather, hot showers or baths, restful sleep, moderate activity, stretching exercises, and massage (5).

The overlap of FS symptoms with the symptoms of somatoform (Chapter 10) and depressive disorders (Chapter 4) should prompt careful assessment of the patient for the presence of any mental illness. Symptoms primarily due to those mental illnesses should improve with treatment of the primary problem.

The history of a patient with FS is often similar to that of a patient with chronic fatigue (Chapter 3) and myofascial pain. The physical examination can help distinguish FS from these other disorders.

PHYSICAL EXAMINATION

A complete medical history and complete physical examination, including comprehensive exam of joints and nervous system and several diagnostic tests (see following text) are required to ensure that other medical explanations for symptoms of FS are not overlooked.

The characteristic physical finding of FS is demonstration on examination of tenderness at specific sites. The American College of Rheumatology has specified 18 sites to be tested by the examining physician; for a diagnosis of FS, the patient must have pain in at least 11 of the 18 sites (1,3,5,10). The following are the nine bilateral pairs:

- The suboccipital muscle insertions
- The anterior aspects of the intertransverse process spaces at C5–C7
- The midpoint of the upper border of the trapezius muscles

- Above the scapular spine and near the medial border of the scapula
- The second costochondral junctions, just lateral to the junctions on the upper surfaces
- The lateral epicondyles
- The upper, outer quadrants of the buttocks
- The posterior aspect of the trochanteric prominence
- The medial fat pad of the knees proximal to the joint line (3,5,10)

Examination of tender sites is usually done with the thumb or second and third fingers, with an approximate pressure of 4 kg. A rolling motion is helpful in eliciting tenderness (3). The patient with FS has generalized pain, with at least 11 specific tender points on exam. The patient with myofascial pain syndrome, in contrast, has a more focal pain with the primary feature of the "trigger point" on exam (1). Pressure over trigger points causes pain to be referred to a nearby site. (Pressure over tender sites causes pain only at that site [1,10].)

DIAGNOSTIC TESTING

All diagnostic test data are normal in patients with fibromyalgia syndrome, although 10% of FS patients may have an unexplained positive antinuclear antibody (ANA) test (5). No clinical, biochemical, serologic, inflammatory, immunologic, or structural pathologic findings have been consistently

IS FS AN INDEPENDENT ENTITY?

FS may be associated with tender point sites on examination because affected patients have a lower tolerance for pain than controls; this lower pain tolerance has been ascribed to a state of altered pain modulation and pain amplification (3). In one study, however, many normal controls also complained of pain with the application of 4 kg of point pressure (1). Although the American College of Rheumatology diagnostic scheme for FS relies almost exclusively on the presence of the tender point sites, some studies have shown that the tender point counts are associated with measures of depression, fatigue, and poor sleep—independent of pain status (2). The nocturnal encephalogram findings thought to be characteristic of FS have also been found in more than 30% of controls (1).

A study by Croft, Schollum, and Silman showed that most people with widespread pain did not have high tender point counts, and most people with high tender point counts did not have chronic widespread pain; in addition, tender points were associated with measures of distress such as depression, fatigue, and sleep disturbance. The researchers concluded that fibromyalgia does not seem to be a distinct entity in the general population (2).

TABLE 6.2. Initial Laboratory Evaluation for FS Patients

FOR ALL PATIENTS
Complete blood count (CBC) with differential
Chemistry panel (glucose, electrolytes, renal and liver panels)
Erythrocyte sedimentation rate (ESR)
Muscle enzymes
Thyroid-stimulating hormone (TSH)

FOR SELECTED PATIENTS (BASED ON HISTORY AND EXAM)
Rheumatoid factor
Antinuclear antibody (ANA)
Radiological studies
Electromyographic studies

implicated in FS (5). Because FS is a diagnosis of exclusion, other causes for the patient's symptoms must be ruled out. Useful tests are listed in the Table 6.2.

WHEN TO REFER

If the diagnosis of FS is in doubt, referral to a rheumatologist may be appropriate. With a clear diagnosis of FS established, whether the physician uses that term or sees it as one of the somatoform disorders, the family physician is the ideal person to provide long-term follow-up for the patient.

MANAGEMENT

Patients who suffer from FS typically have a chronic relapsing course, and the approach to management is similar to that with patients with somatoform disorder and chronic pain (Chapter 10).

Medications

Medication decisions should be individualized to the patient's comorbid diagnoses and primary symptoms.

- Salicylates and other nonsteroidal anti-inflammatory medications or acetaminophen may help with symptomatic relief of the widespread pain.
- Tricyclic antidepressants in low doses have been found helpful for patients with FS in controlled studies (10,11). Amitriptyline (Elavil) and doxepin (Sinequan) have been considered to be more helpful than other tricyclic agents in patients with FS because they are more serotonergic. (If this result is substantiated, it may be that newer antidepressants such as selective serotonin reuptake inhibitors may be helpful in FS.) Note that the doses of

amitriptyline, doxepin, and cyclobenzaprine (Flexeril) (a skeletal muscle relaxant structurally related to the tricylics, not generally used as an antidepressant) are much lower than the doses used to treat major depression (Table 6.3). In addition, it may take up to 9 weeks to see treatment response (11).

- Glucocorticoids are of little benefit and should not be used in patients with FS (10).
- Injection of tender point sites (with corticosteroids or lidocaine) may provide only temporary relief or none at all and should be discouraged (10).

Physical and Environmental Measures

Patients with FS report that their symptoms are improved with warm baths or showers, massage, and the proper balance of rest and exercise (5). Patients should be advised to avoid extremes of activity and inactivity. Work or exercise to the point of exhaustion is harmful. Total rest is also harmful, leading to further deconditioning, increased fatigue, disturbed sleep patterns, and worsened self-image.

Patients should also be advised to eat a balanced diet, avoiding fads and eccentricities (e.g., avoid "protein diet," "grapefruit diet"). Vitamin supplements have no proven benefit and megadose vitamins should be avoided, but a multivitamin supplement (1 tablet/day) is permissible if the patient desires.

Patients should also be encouraged to make the following lifestyle modifications:

- Minimal or no alcohol
- No recreational drugs
- No smoking

Aerobic Exercise Program

Low-impact aerobic exercise has been shown to be of some benefit for patients with FS (10). Patients may need to begin exercising at a very low level (5 minutes every other day is helpful at first) and gradually increase the length and frequency of exercise to at least 20 to 30 minutes at least four times per week.

T ABLE 6.3. Tricyclic Agents in Fibromyalgia Syndrome

Agent	Dosage
Amitriptyline (Elavil)	10–25 mg at bedtime
Doxepin (Sinequan)	10–25 mg at bedtime
Cyclobenzaprine (Flexeril)[a]	10–20 mg at bedtime

[a]A skeletal muscle relaxant structurally related to the tricylics.

Alternative Therapies

Patients who seek information about FS via computer should be cautioned that much of the medical information on the internet has not been screened and may not be accurate. Gently and with understanding, guide patients away from alternatives that are toxic, expensive, or unreasonable.

PATIENT EDUCATION

Patients with FS need reassurance that although they have a chronic, possibly relapsing, condition, it is not crippling or deforming, is not a degenerative process, and does not shorten longevity (10). Unless evidence exists to the contrary, reassure patients that they are not mentally ill. Also, there is no firm evidence that FS is inherited.

As in the management of pain disorder, the patient needs to understand that the goal of treatment is not necessarily to be completely pain-free, but to be as functional as possible. This shift in focus may assist the patient in working toward improved health.

FAMILY AND COMMUNITY INVOLVEMENT

It is helpful for family members to understand that the patient's complaints are not "all in his head" and that the patient experiences very real distress.

Support groups for patients with FS are often combined with groups for chronic fatigue syndrome (CFS); a list of several groups is provided at the end of the chapter on CFS (see Chapter 3).

FOLLOW-UP

Monitoring of FS is identical with that of pain disorder (p. 130). The cornerstone of therapy involves brief, regularly scheduled visits with the family physician to monitor over time for the development of new signs suggestive of new illnesses. In the follow-up of patients with FS, the goal is not "curing" but "caring" for and about these patients. It is important to help patients shift their focus from eliminating pain to living as healthy a life as possible.

REFERENCES

1. Bohr TW. Fibromyalgia syndrome and myofascial pain syndrome: do they exist? Neurol Clin 1995;13:365-384.
2. Croft P, Schollum J, Silman A. Population study of tender point counts and pain as evidence of fibromyalgia. BMJ 1994;309:696-699.
3. Wolfe F. When to diagnose fibromyalgia. Rheum Dis Clin North Am 1994;20: 485-501.

4. McCahill ME. Somatoform and related disorders: delivery of diagnosis as first step. Am Fam Physician 1995;52:193-204.

5. Hench PK. Evaluation and differential diagnosis of fibromyalgia: approach to diagnosis and management. Rheum Dis Clin North Am 1989;15:19-29.

6. Wolfe F, et al. The prevalence and characteristics of fibromyalgia in the general population [Abstract]. Arthritis Rheum 1993;136(suppl):48.

7. Silman A, et al. The epidemiology of tender points counts in the general population [Abstract]. Arthritis Rheum 1993;36(suppl):48.

8. Forseth KO, et al. The prevalence of fibromyalgia among women aged 2-49 years in Arendal, Norway. Scand J Rheumatol 1992;21:74-78.

9. Buskila D, et al. Assessment of nonarticular tenderness and prevalence of fibromyalgia in children. J Rheumatol 1993;20:368-370.

10. Gilliland BC. Relapsing polychondritis and miscellaneous arthritides. In: Isselbacher KJ, Braunwald E, Wilson JD, et al, eds. Harrison's textbook of internal medicine. 13th ed. New York: McGraw-Hill, 1994:1706-1707.

11. Goodnick PJ, Sandoval R. Psychotropic treatment of chronic fatigue syndrome and related disorders. J Clin Psychiatr 1993;54:13-20.

Margaret E. McCahill

Headache

Nearly every person experiences a headache at one time or another. Severe, disabling headache reportedly occurs a minimum of once a year in at least 40% of persons worldwide (1). Headache is such a common symptom that the occasional headache can be considered a normal aspect of living. The physician typically is called on only when the character of a headache is such that the patient or family is concerned that it goes beyond the norm.

Historically, problematic headaches were categorized as "migraine" if they were thought to be of vascular origin and were accompanied by a particular constellation of symptoms. They were thought to be "tension" headaches if they were thought to have a muscular genesis with emotional factors contributing to their onset. More recently, the terminology has changed. It has become recognized that there is a continuum of "normal" headaches and headaches that have both muscular and vascular contributing factors.

When evaluating the patient with headache, the task facing the physician is as follows:

1. Decide whether the headache is indicative of a medically emergent or urgent condition, such as meningitis, subarachnoid hemorrhage, or temporal arteritis.
2. Determine whether the headache is less acutely threatening, but in a special treatment category.
3. Determine whether the headache is one of the more chronic conditions that need ongoing management, such as tension and migraine headaches (Table 7.1).

CHIEF COMPLAINT

Patients of any age, sex, ethnicity, educational level, or occupation may present with headache as a complaint. In addition to the complaint of headache, the patient may have other associated symptoms.

HISTORY

Because the physical examination is most often normal in a person with headache, the history is the primary diagnostic tool. Although pain intensity

TABLE 7.1. Types of Headaches

EMERGENCY TREATMENT REQUIRED
Meningitis
Subarachnoid hemorrhage
Giant cell (temporal) arteritis

SPECIAL TREATMENT CATEGORY
Brain tumor
Postconcussion headache
Ophthalmologic headache
Sinus headache

HEADACHE TYPES SEEN MORE OFTEN IN MEN
Cluster headache
Coital headache
Cough headache

CHRONIC/RECURRENT HEADACHE SYNDROMES
Classic migraine headache
Common migraine
Tension headache
"Tension-vascular" headache continuum

is of great therapeutic importance and makes an impact on the degree of impairment from headache, this information rarely assists with the differential diagnosis of headache (1). Carefully review these aspects of the headache:

- Quality
- Location
- Duration
- Time course
- Factors that precipitate the headache
- Factors that relieve the headache
- Any accompanying symptoms

The history for common headache syndromes is described in the following text (Table 7.2). Management of the more benign headache syndromes is discussed in the treatment section of this chapter.

Headaches Indicating Emergent, Potentially Life-Threatening Conditions

Meningitis
The headache in meningitis is just one symptom in a patient who generally appears very ill. Whenever headache occurs along with fever and nuchal

T ABLE 7.2. Comparative Features of Headache Syndromes

Type of Headache	Demographics	Quality of Pain	Location of Pain	Duration/Time Course	Treatment Approach
Brain tumor	Any age, sex	Nondescript, dull aching	Variable, diffuse	Worse with change of position; progressively worsening headache; may be preceded by nausea/vomiting	Neuroimaging performed with any neurologic symptoms; neurosurgery consultation
Cluster headache	Men outnumber women >7:1; comes in clusters of 1–3 attacks/day for 4–8 weeks, then period of no headaches; may be provoked by alcohol	Excruciating	Unilateral, periorbital, with red, lacrimating eye, nasal stuffiness, ptosis, nausea	Sudden onset, maximal in 5 minutes, lasts 1/2–2 hours, predictable periodicity, often awakens the patient from sleep	Oxygen inhalation for acute attack; prevention with lithium or prednisone
Coital headache	Men outnumber women 4:1	May be throbbing, aching	Diffuse	Sudden onset at or near time of orgasm; sporadic and usually resolves within a few minutes	Usually resolves before treatment is given; if persistent, or nausea also present, rule out subarachnoid hemorrhage with head CT
Cough headache	Men outnumber women 4:1	Severe	Generalized, but may be localized in 1/3 of patients	Sudden onset with cough, stooping, lifting, bending, sneezing; lasts seconds to a few minutes	Neuroimaging needed to rule out intracranial malformations found in approximately 25% of patients; in benign form, the headache may respond to indomethacin

continued

T A B L E 7 . 2 . *continued* **Comparative Features of Headache Syndrome**

Type of Headache	Demographics	Quality of Pain	Location of Pain	Duration/Time Course	Treatment Approach
Giant cell (temporal) arteritis	65% in women; Age: 50–85 years; often muscle aches, malaise, joint stiffness	Recognized as a new type of headache—dull, boring, episodic sharp pain	Feels superficial, may be unilateral or bilateral; usually tender temporal or occipital arteries	Gradual onset with maximum intensity over hours; full illness may last weeks to months	ESR often over 50 mm/hr; patient started on prednisone immediately to preventblindness; temporal artery biopsy obtained
Classic migraine	Any age, either sex; a female predominance in adults; often positive family history	Severe, throbbing, often with nausea, vomiting, and photophobic; may develop neurologic signs, e.g., dysphasia, transient eye symptoms	Unilateral with one side more often affected; often felt as more anterior	Preceded by aura, which may be visual, sensory, or motor; often scintillating scotoma precedes headache by 20–25 min.; may last a few hours to two days	Aspirin, acetaminophen, nonsteroidal anti-inflammatory drugs (NSAIDs), ergotamine, or ergotamine-caffeine combinations; dihydroergot, sumatriptan. Prevention: a variety of medications used
Common migraine headache	As in classic migraine	Severe throbbing or pounding; may or may not have nausea/emesis	Frequently bilateral	No aura, no neurologic disturbances; may last a few hours to 2 days; recurrent	As in classic migraine
Tension headache	All ages; female predominance	Tightness around head; may be throbbing, pressing, squeezing, heavy	Bilateral, generalized	Gradual onset, long duration, recurrent; may worsen as the day progresses	Aspirin, acetaminophen, NSAIDs—mainstay of treatment; lifestyle changes possibly helpful

rigidity, meningitis must be excluded before any other considerations are pursued. Particularly in acute bacterial meningitis, the patient can become critically ill in a matter of minutes to hours, so time should not be invested in other diagnostic considerations. If meningitis is suspected, a lumbar puncture should be performed emergently and antibiotic therapy started immediately.

Subarachnoid Hemorrhage

Patients may report to the emergency department or physician's office complaining of "the worst headache of my life." Despite the fact that most patients with such a complaint ultimately receive a diagnosis of migraine headache (1), it is imperative to consider the possibility of subarachnoid hemorrhage.

Onset is typically sudden, reaches maximum intensity within a few minutes, and is sometimes described as a "thunderclap headache." The headache may occur at any time of day and during activity or rest.

There may be subtle neurologic signs, nuchal rigidity, or brief loss of consciousness at the onset of the hemorrhage and headache (2). If the patient presents several days after the hemorrhage, the headache may have settled into a more constant pattern.

It is imperative to establish the presence of subarachnoid hemorrhage promptly because delay in diagnosis reduces the accuracy of diagnosis and leaves the patient at risk for repeat and possibly more severe hemorrhage. A computed tomographic (CT) scan of the head is 95% sensitive in diagnosing subarachnoid hemorrhage within the first 72 hours, but decreases to only 50% at 1 week and 30% at 2 weeks after the insult (3). Up to 50% of patients with undiagnosed subarachnoid hemorrhage rebleed with 2 weeks, and mortality risk increases.

In general, if the patient presents with sudden onset of severe headache along with stiff neck and fever, he or she needs an immediate lumbar puncture to rule out meningitis, and if the patient has the acute onset of severe headache with stiff neck but with no fever, he or she needs an immediate CT scan of the head and possibly a lumbar puncture to rule out subarachnoid hemorrhage. If suspicion of subarachnoid hemorrhage is confirmed or heightened, a neurosurgical consultation is indicated immediately.

Giant Cell (Temporal) Arteritis

The average age of onset of giant cell arteritis is 70 years, with an age range of 50 to 85. Women represent 65% of cases (1). The affected patient presents with a complaint of a new type of headache, which may be accompanied by malaise and muscle aches.

The head pain may be unilateral or bilateral and appears gradually, taking a few hours to reach maximum intensity. The pain is usually described as dull and boring, with episodic sharp pains. Patients often recognize that their headache has a superficial origin. They may report such scalp tenderness that it is painful to rest their head on a pillow or comb their hair.

The headache may be worse at night or with exposure to cold. The presence of jaw claudication is considered a pathognomonic symptom for temporal arteritis (1,2). There is usually tenderness of the temporal or, occasionally, occipital arteries.

Occasionally, but not reliably, induration may be palpable on examination. The erythrocyte sedimentation rate (ESR) is usually elevated to 50 mm per hour or more. A normal ESR does not exclude the diagnosis of temporal arteritis if clinical suspicion is high (1). The diagnosis is usually confirmed by temporal artery biopsy.

If temporal arteritis is strongly suspected, the patient is started on corticosteroid therapy immediately (e.g., prednisone, 80 mg/day for the first 4 to 6 weeks), and temporal artery biopsy is done within 5 days of initiation of corticosteroid therapy. If corticosteroid therapy is not promptly initiated, 50% of patients may progress to blindness. The ischemic optic neuropathy induced by temporal arteritis is the major cause of rapidly developing bilateral blindness in the patient over 60 years of age (1).

Headaches Seen More Often in Men

Cluster Headaches

Previously called Raeder's syndrome, histamine cephalalgia, and sphenopalatine neuralgia, cluster headache is seen almost exclusively in men, with a 7–8:1 male-to-female ratio. The cluster headache is typically episodic, with one to three brief attacks per day for 4 to 8 weeks, followed by headache-free periods of 1 year or more. The headache may wake the patient from sleep. The unilateral, excruciating periorbital pain begins suddenly, reaching maximum intensity in about 5 minutes and typically lasting 30 minutes to 2 hours. On the side of the headache, there may be lacrimation and reddening of the eye, nasal stuffiness, and lid ptosis. Nausea may be another accompanying symptom.

A history of the distinct pattern of symptoms in cluster headache generally makes the diagnosis clear. The response to treatment is usually most gratifying. Treatment to prevent cluster headache may include lithium, 600 to 900 mg per day, or prednisone, 60 mg per day for 7 days to start with rapid tapering (1). After a cluster headache has begun, oxygen inhalation is very effective at attenuating the attack. The patient may use 9 L per minute via tight mask, and inhalation of 100% oxygen for 15 minutes may be necessary to stop the headache (1).

Coital Headache

More common in men, with a 4:1 male-to-female ratio, the coital headache occurs abruptly, is usually brief, and occurs at or near the time of orgasm. Coital headache is sporadic and fairly brief in duration. If it is prolonged or accompanied by nausea, subarachnoid hemorrhage should be considered, and a CT scan obtained (1,2).

Cough Headache

More common in men, with a 4:1 male-to-female ratio, the cough headache is transient and brief (a few seconds to a few minutes). Affected patients give a history of onset of a new type of headache upon coughing, bending, sneezing, stooping, or lifting. The headache is usually generalized, but may be localized in one third of patients.

Patients may report first onset with a respiratory illness in which coughing was a prominent symptom or on the initiation of a strenuous weight-lifting program. The benign form of this disorder may respond very well to treatment with indomethacin (Indocin) (1).

It is important to recognize cough headache because about 25% of patients have comorbid intracranial structural anomalies (1). One of the most common anomalies is the Arnold-Chiari malformation, a caudal displacement of the medulla and cerebellar tissue through the foramen magnum. It may cause some herniation at the cervicomedullary junction, and patients often do not present with symptoms until adolescence or adulthood. Most patients with cough headache should have evaluation including magnetic resonance imaging (MRI) of the brain to rule out intracranial structural abnormalities (1).

Headaches of Specific Etiology

Brain Tumor

Approximately 20% to 30% of patients with brain tumor present with a chief complaint of headache (1,2), and 70% eventually have headaches. Brain tumor headaches can occur at any age (1). The pain is usually an intermittent, moderate, dull ache, nondescript in quality and location, and worsened by change in position or by physical exertion. Associated nausea and vomiting are common.

The headache of brain tumor is so nondescript that history of headache alone cannot be considered sufficient reason to perform imaging studies of the brain. If the patient has abnormal neurologic signs and other neurologic symptoms, then imaging studies (head CT or MRI) are warranted immediately (2).

Postconcussion Headaches

Approximately 1.4 million people in the United States suffer a head injury each year, and 30% to 50% have postconcussion headaches (4,5). The headache may be accompanied by dizziness, irritability, fatigue, insomnia, anxiety, impaired concentration, and memory difficulties (2). Most posttraumatic headaches are brief and self-limiting (6), but can last up to 18 months after the injury. They are rarely a recurrent problem of very long duration. Postconcussion headaches are not associated with an anatomic brain lesion and may occur after a relatively minor injury. Treatment consists of reassurance that recovery is the rule, and symptomatic treatment is provided in the interim.

Ophthalmologic Headache (Eyestrain)

Astigmatism and refractive errors do not cause headache (7), but prolonged work at a computer screen or reading may cause a dull, bilateral frontal headache, possibly related to cervical muscle tension (2). In spite of the fact that headache from eye disorders is rare, it may be helpful to schedule a routine visit to the ophthalmologist or optometrist for examination and tonometry, if the patient has not had such an examination recently. This provides routine eye care and reassures the patient that the headache is not related to an eye problem.

Sinus Headache

Facial pain and headache from sinusitis are generally seen with acute sinusitis and are accompanied by purulent nasal discharge. The headache is often a dull, constant pressure that worsens when the patient bends over and is very pronounced with percussion over the sinuses.

True sinus headaches are thought not to occur in chronic sinusitis, unless it is relapsing into an acute phase (2). Many chronic sinus headaches may more properly be considered tension headaches or common migraine headaches.

Treatment of the headache accompanying acute sinusitis consists of treatment of the sinus infection and symptomatic treatment for pain.

Chronic/Recurrent Headache Syndromes

Classic Migraine

The classic migraine (migraine with aura) may occur in a person of any age, with the highest incidence in children and young adults. There is a female preponderance in adults. Patients typically give a history of recurring headache with premonitory symptoms (aura) interspersed with pain-free periods. The most common auras are visual, with about one third of migraine sufferers experiencing scotomata or visual hallucinations in the center of the visual fields. The scintillating lights may form an arc or "C" shape that may slowly move out of the field of vision over 20 to 25 minutes, followed by onset throbbing, hemicranial pain. Headache may be accompanied by nausea, vomiting, and photophobia. Sometimes, focal neurologic disturbances or scintillating scotomata may occur without a headache or vomiting. This is called *migraine equivalent* (1).

Common Migraine

The common migraine is also called migraine without aura and is the most common type of headache reported by patients. The common migraine now refers to headaches previously called periodic tension headache (1). The common migraine may occur in a person of any age; the highest incidence is in children and young adults. There is a female preponderance in adults. The headache is severe, is not preceded by an aura, and has no accompanying neurologic disturbances. The pain may be throbbing or pounding and is often bilateral. Nausea and vomiting may or may not occur.

Tension Headache

Tension headache can be seen in people of all ages; there is a female preponderance. This headache has a more gradual onset and is often described as "throbbing." The pain is bilateral and may last from a few hours to 1 or 2 days. The headache is sometimes described as a fullness, pressure, or tightness in the occipital and nuchal area or frontal areas; hence, the description by some patients of a tight band around the head and down the neck (1).

PHYSICAL EXAMINATION

The physical findings to be noted in patients suffering headaches indicative of an emergent, life-threatening condition, or special categories of headaches are described in the above discussion of those particular headaches.

Patients with classic migraine may show varied, usually transient neurologic abnormalities on examination; rarely, such impairment is permanent (1). The physical examination is most often within normal limits for patients with classic migraine, common migraine, and tension headache.

DIAGNOSTIC TESTING

In the headache patient with a completely normal neurologic examination and no history of head trauma, neuroimaging is only rarely indicated, and the diagnosis is usually established entirely based on the medical history. The following are some signs that might indicate a need for radiologic or laboratory investigations:

- Fever, stiff neck, acutely ill appearance—Lumbar puncture and cerebrospinal fluid examination

---

TENSION-MIGRAINE CONTINUUM

Tension headaches sometimes occur during times of psychological stress. However, no evidence supports the older hypothesis that the pain has its origin in tightness of the muscles of the head. There is some evidence that tension headaches can be precipitated by the administration of a vasodilator or by histamine administration, suggesting a link between tension headaches and vascular, migraine headaches (1).

Although regional cerebral blood flow studies have shown mild hypoperfusion during classic migraine attacks, no such changes have been noted in common migraine or tension headache (1).

Nevertheless, the current etiologic theories place both types of migraine and tension headache on a continuum. Thus, the initial treatment approach is similar for all three (1,2). There is often a strong family history in both classical and common migraine headache, and it has been suggested that migraine may be a hereditary perturbation of serotonergic neurotransmission (1).

- Abnormal neurologic examination—Neuroimaging
- Acute onset of "the worst headache of my life"—Neuroimaging to rule out subarachnoid hemorrhage
- Headache with cough, physical exertion—Neuroimaging to rule out Arnold-Chiari or other malformation or intracranial mass
- Headache in patient over 50 years of age, usually with tender temporal artery—Erythrocyte sedimentation rate (ESR) and consideration of temporal artery biopsy
- Patient over 40 years with onset of a persistent, new type of headache—Consideration of neuroimaging (2)

WHEN TO REFER

Emergency

Patients with any of the emergent or potentially life-threatening illnesses heralded by headache (meningitis, subarachnoid hemorrhage, or giant cell [temporal] arteritis) should be referred to the hospital emergency department or, in some instances, treated in the physician's office emergently.

Neurologic/Neurosurgical

Prompt referral to a neurosurgeon is important in patients with headaches indicative of intracranial masses or lesions. Referral to a neurologist should be considered in patients with abnormal neurologic findings on examination.

No Referral Necessary

Patients with clearly established classic migraine without neurologic sequelae, those with common migraine, and those with tension headache can be managed by the family physician.

MANAGEMENT

The management of the emergent and potentially life-threatening or otherwise specific types of headache is covered in the History section earlier in this chapter. Common migraine, tension headache, and classical migraine are considered together here as a continuum. Table 7.3 lists commonly used medications.

Initial Treatment

Aspirin or acetaminophen should be tried initially. If these are not successul, then ibuprofen (Motrin) or naproxen (Naprosyn) can be tried (1). Naproxen may be particularly helpful for headaches considered "tension-vascular."

Acute Migraine

During an acute migraine headache (classic and common), ergotamine (Ergostat) or ergotamine-caffeine preparations (oral or suppository) are often helpful. If they do not help, parenteral dihydroergotamine (DHE 45) or subcutaneous or oral sumatriptan (Imitrex) can be used.

TABLE 7.3.   Medications Used in Common Headache Syndomes

Agent	Pediatric Dose*a* (All not to exceed adult dose)	Usual Adult Dose*a*
Acetaminophen	10–15 mg/kg/4 hr	650 mg/4 hr
Aspirin	Not recommended	650 mg/4 hr
Ibuprofen (Motrin)	5–10 mg/kg/6 hr	200–400 mg/4 hr or 600–800 mg/ 8 hr short term; max: 3200 mg/day
Naproxen (Naprosyn)	5–10 mg/kg/12 hr (over 2 years old)	250–375–500 mg/8–12 hr; max: 1000 mg/day
Ergotamine (Ergostat)	Not recommended	2 mg sublingual; repeat every 30 min. as needed; max: 6 mg/24hr or 10 mg/wk
Ergotamine— caffeine tabs: ergotamine 1 mg/ caffeine 100 mg	Not recommended	2 tabs at start of headache, then 1/30 min; max: 6/24 hr or 10/wk
Suppository: ergotamine 2 mg/ caffeine 100 mg		1 at start of headache, then 1 in 1 hour; not to exceed 2/24 hrs and 5/wk
Dihydroergotamine (DHE 45)	Not recommended	1 mg/1 mL parenteral 1 mL intramuscularly at start of headache, then 1 mL in 1 hr; max: 3 mL/24 hr and 6 mL/wk
Sumatriptan (Imitrex)	Not recommended	6 mg subcutaneously; repeat once in 1 hr if needed
Midrin (fixed combination isometheptene, dichloralphenazone, acetaminophen)	Not recommended	2 at onset of headache then 1/60 min; not to exceed 5/12 hr or 8caps/day
Narcotic analgesics	Not recommended	Codeine or meperidine sometimes needed to abort severe headaches; to preserve efficacy, avoid daily use

*a*All doses are according to the patient's needs.

Migraine Prophylaxis

In patients with at least two or three migraine headaches per month, prophylaxis should be considered. Agents used for migraine prophylaxis include the following (1):

- Propranolol (Inderal)
- Antidepressants
- Amitriptyline (Elavil)
- Phenelzine (Nardil), a monoamine oxidase inhibitor
- Nortriptyline (Nortriptyline), the preferred antidepressant
- Verapamil (Calan)
- Valproic acid (Depakene)
- Methysergide (Sansert)

The probability of successful treatment with each of the antimigraine medications is 60% to 75% (1). Trying several medicines sequentially until one medicine proves successful results in relief for nearly all tension-vascular headache sufferers. If the patient complains of chronic, daily headaches, use of narcotic analgesics should be minimized to no more than 2 days out of 7 (1).

Other Treatment Modalities

Rigorously controlled trials have shown that nonpharmacologic treatments for migraine headaches have not been successful without the use of medications specific for migraine (1). This is not to say that certain lifestyle changes (see Patient Education) are not helpful and indicated.

FOLLOW-UP

The patient who suffers chronic, recurrent headaches should be seen at intervals agreed upon by the patient and physician to monitor the course of this chronic problem. The task in the follow-up visits is to monitor for any change in the type of headaches and for the development of any neurologic signs or other signs of illness.

PATIENT EDUCATION

Teaching the patient and family about the nature of the tension-migraine continuum of common and chronic headaches greatly assists the patient in coping with recurrent headaches. In addition, a patient and family members are often concerned that the headache may indicate the presence of a brain tumor or other catastrophe; thus, evaluation by the physician and reassurance that this does not appear to be the case can assist the patient in managing their headaches.

Lifestyle Changes

Exposure to occupational toxins (e.g., carbon monoxide, lead, or nitrates) may increase vulnerability to headache and should be avoided (6). Some patients are able to identify certain exacerbating factors, such as the consumption of red wine, hunger, lack of sleep, and menses, and may choose to avoid precipitating factors as much as possible.

REFERENCES

1. Raskin NH. Headache. In: Isselbacher KJ, Braunwald E, Wilson JD, et al, eds. Harrison's textbook of internal medicine. 13th ed. New York: McGraw-Hill, 1994: 65-71.

2. Coutin IB, Glass SF. Recognizing uncommon headache syndromes. Am Fam Physician 1996;54(7):2247-2252.

3. van Gijn J, van Dongen KJ. The time course of aneurysmal haemorrhage on computed tomograms. Neuroradiology 1982; 23(3): 153-156.

4. Ham LP, Andrasik F, Packard RC, Bundrick CM. Psychopathology in individuals with post-traumatic headache and other pain types. Cephalalgia 1994;14(2): 118-126.

5. Packard RC. Posttraumatic headache: permanency and relationship to legal settlement. Headache 1992;32(10):496-500.

6. Duman S, Ginsburg SH. Headaches and facial pain. In: Friedman HH, ed. Problem-oriented medical diagnosis. 6th ed. Boston: Little, Brown and Company, 1996: 398-400.

7. Headache Classification Committee of the International Headache Society. Classification and diagnostic criteria for headache disorders, cranial neuralgias and facial pain. Cephalalgia 1988;8(suppl 7):1-96.

CHAPTER 8

Margaret E. McCahill

Insomnia

One third of adults in the United States experience occasional or persistent sleep disturbances (1). Therefore, family physicians often see patients with this complaint.

CHIEF COMPLAINT

The patient's complaints may include the following:

- Difficulty falling asleep
- Difficulty staying asleep
- Insufficient amount of sleep, chronic fatigue, or daytime tiredness
- Certain behavior (such as bruxism) occurring during sleep

The complaint of insomnia may be brought to the physician's attention by the patient or by the patient's bed partner or roommate.

HISTORY

Insomnia is a symptom that is often treated without prior diagnosis (2). The history should be directed toward uncovering the cause of insomnia. A careful history is the key to diagnosis, because the most common causes have some consistent features.

The patient history should include an initial assessment of the patient's patterns of activities, work, eating, drinking, drug use, and sleep for at least a 2-week period.

Examine this pattern with the patient for any evidence of features typical of the following disorders, which are the most common causes of insomnia seen in primary care.

Transient Situational Insomnia

Patients with transient situational insomnia report the following:

- They have had difficulty sleeping for one to a few nights.
- They often have difficulty falling asleep (sleep-onset insomnia), and they may awaken frequently during the night.

EPIDEMIOLOGIC CONSIDERATIONS

Most adults sleep 7 to 8 hours per night in one sleep episode.

In some countries and cultures, sleep is customarily broken into two episodes, with one occurring in the afternoon.

As adults get older, daily sleep time may be reduced. The elderly often awaken much earlier in the morning than they did when they were younger. This does not constitute a sleep disorder, but is merely normal maturity.

Adults who routinely sleep fewer than 4 hours or more than 9 hours per night have a higher mortality rate than those who sleep 7 to 8 hours (1).

Narcolepsy occurs at about the same rate in the population as does multiple sclerosis, but awareness of narcolepsy seems much lower than that of multiple sclerosis (2).

Sleep apnea may afflict 5% to 15% of the adult population in the United States (2).

An estimated 2 to 5 million people in the United States stop breathing for 15 to 150 seconds at a time and for a dozen to several hundred times every night (1).

- They may report recent situational stressors, such as the following:
- Job change
- School pressures
- Deadline or examination
- Illness or hospitalization
- Staying in an unfamiliar place or a hotel
- Death of a family member or friend

Insomnia generally improves with the resolution of the change or stress or within 2 to 3 weeks (1).

Inadequate Sleep Hygiene

The patient with inadequate sleep hygiene reports having trouble falling asleep and may report trying to fall asleep in the following circumstances:

- Immediately after coming home from work late at night
- With the television on
- After a large meal
- After vigorous exercise
- After ingesting caffeine, alcohol, or other drugs

Psychophysiologic Insomnia

Patients with psychophysiologic insomnia may report the following:

- Insomnia starting around the time of a stressful event, but persisting after the stress is resolved

- Great difficulty sleeping in their own bed most nights, but easily sleeping at unscheduled times when not trying to do so, on weekends and holidays, and at the home of family or friends
- Preoccupation with insomnia, with their rigorous attempts to sleep resulting in hyperarousal and leading to a learned behavior of insomnia (1,2)

Sleep Apnea Syndrome

Sleep apnea is characterized by the following:

- The syndrome can occur at any age, but the patient is most often an obese man 30 to 60 years old.
- The patient may give a history of daytime tiredness, perhaps falling asleep during daytime activities.
- Patients may give a history of restless sleep.
- The key elements of the history are obtained from the patient's bed partner, who will report that the patient snores loudly and has periods of apnea lasting for more than 10 seconds each and occurring more than 30 times during a 7-hour sleep period (1-3).

Periodic Limb Movement Disorder

The following are characteristics periodic limb movement disorder (previously called nocturnal myoclonus):

- The patient usually complains of nonrefreshing sleep.
- The patient may report experiencing a periodic unilateral or bilateral activity of the leg muscles, which may range from subtle extension of the big toe to kicking of the whole leg.
- If the movement does not awaken the patient, the patient's bed partner may have to provide the history (1,2).
- The disorder is found on sleep studies in 17% of patients with insomnia and may coexist with other causes of insomnia, such as narcolepsy and sleep apnea (1).

Restless Legs Syndrome

Restless legs syndrome is characterized by the following:

- Patients report a creeping or disagreeable sensation in their legs during waking hours, resulting in an irresistible urge to move the legs, which relieves the symptoms for a time. The feeling is usually in the lower legs, but may extend proximally.
- The urge to move the legs is at its worst when the person is lying in bed just before sleep; this interferes with sleep onset.
- The syndrome may begin or worsen during pregnancy (1,2).

Altitude Insomnia

In altitude insomnia, the patient reports an acute onset of insomnia, usually within about 72 hours after moving to an altitude above 4000 feet (1,2). Frequent awakenings and poor-quality sleep are usually accompanied by headaches, anorexia, and fatigue.

Drug- or Alcohol-Dependent Insomnia

Drug-dependent insomnia is a very common cause of insomnia. A careful alcohol and drug history should be obtained in all patients who complain of insomnia. It is important to ask about the history of past use of sedatives for sleep because a common cause of insomnia is "rebound insomnia" due to withdrawal from sedative-hypnotics or habituation to them (2).

Although alcohol may promote drowsiness and shortened sleep latency, it results in frequent awakenings because it interferes with the ability of the brain to maintain sleep (2).

Alcohol significantly exacerbates obstructive sleep apnea syndrome, and the person may have a history of more snoring after alcohol consumption.

The following are selected drugs that can contribute to insomnia:

- Drugs of abuse such as amphetamines and cocaine
- Prescription medications such as fluoxetine (Prozac) and bronchodilators
- Over-the-counter medications, such as pseudoephedrine
- Diphenhydramine (paradoxical response)
- Caffeine in beverages (even in modest quantities)
- Nicotine

Narcolepsy

The patient and his or her family give a history of excessive daytime sleepiness with involuntary sleep episodes. The severity of this disorder varies greatly.

Excessive daytime sleepiness is always present in patients with narcolepsy; the other symptoms are variably present (1,2).

Typically identified in the second decade of life, age of onset of narcolepsy may range from 5 to 50 years (1). A family history should always be pursued if narcolepsy is suspected because there is a strong familial trend (2).

The classic "narcolepsy tetrad" includes the following:

- Excessive daytime sleepiness
- Cataplexy (a sudden weakness or loss of control of muscles), which may be brought on by emotional stress, may be mild and brief, or may be complete paralysis lasting 20 to 30 minutes in rare cases (1)
- Hypnogogic hallucinations
- Sleep paralysis of the voluntary muscles with the onset of sleep

Sleep Disorders Associated With Neurologic Disorders

Insomnia or daytime sleepiness may be seen in patients with the following conditions:

- Migraine
- Seizure disorder
- Parkinson's disease
- Huntington's chorea
- Dementia
- Fatal familial insomnia (very rare) (2)

Sleep Disorders Associated With Other Chronic Medical Conditions

Any pattern of insomnia may occur in patients with chronic disorders such as the following:

- Asthma
- Chronic obstructive pulmonary disease
- Cystic fibrosis
- Chronic pain from rheumatologic disorders
- Congestive heart failure (including paroxysmal nocturnal dyspnea and nocturia)
- Gastroesophageal reflux
- Menopause
- Renal and liver failure
- Thyroid disorders

Shift-Work Sleep Disorder

In patients who work nights and especially those who frequently rotate shifts (e.g., shift changes every 2 weeks), disturbance of the body's circadian rhythm can lead to insomnia. History-taking in a patient complaining of insomnia should always include information about timing of work schedules.

Sleep Disturbance Due to Parasomnias

Parasomnias are episodic disorders of arousal, partial arousal, or sleep-stage transition that may be initiated or worsened by sleep (2). Patients may complain of nonrefreshing sleep. Family members may need to add history about the patient's behavior during sleep. The more common parasomnias include the following:

- Sleepwalking
- Sleep terrors
- Bruxism (grinding the teeth)
- Enuresis

Sleep Disturbance Due to Anxiety or Depressive Disorder

Insomnia and fatigue very often constitute the chief complaint in both anxiety and depressive disorders. The history defines the symptoms and diagnostic criteria for the particular anxiety or depressive disorder (see Chapters 1 and 4).

PHYSICAL EXAMINATION

With most causes of insomnia, the patient's physical examination is normal. Patients with insomnia due to some other medical or neurologic condition have the physical findings to support those diagnoses.

Sleep Apnea Syndrome

The patient with sleep apnea may develop pulmonary hypertension, right-sided heart failure, and systemic hypertension and may have physical findings consistent with those sequelae.

Insomnia Due to Alcohol Use or Dependence

Patients may have the physical stigmata of alcoholism (see Chapter 11).

DIAGNOSTIC TESTING

Laboratory Testing

The laboratory evaluation of a person with insomnia should be individualized according to the history and physical examination (Table 8.1).

- The complete blood count (CBC) may be useful in that patients with sleep apnea syndrome may eventually develop polycythemia, and this can also be seen in altitude insomnia.

TABLE 8.1. Laboratory Evaluation in Insomnia:

IN ALL PATIENTS
Complete blood count (CBC)
Blood chemistry panel
Thyroid-stimulating hormone (TSH)
Urine analysis

IN SELECTED PATIENTS
Vitamin B_{12} level
HLA testing (if narcolepsy is suspected)
Follicle-stimulating hormone (FSH; to confirm menopause, if needed)

- An elevated mean corpuscular volume (MCV) hints that alcoholism may be a factor.
- The chemistry panel (abnormal electrolytes, blood urea nitrogen [BUN], creatine, or glucose) may help explain nocturia that leads to insomnia, and elevated liver function test results may constitute another hint about potential alcoholism.
- Thyroid-stimulating hormone (TSH) should always be checked, because hypothyroidism is in the differential diagnosis of sleep apnea and thyroid disorders in general can contribute to insomnia.
- Human leukocyte antigen (HLA) testing is rarely indicated, but because of the importance to the family as a whole, HLA testing may help confirm a diagnosis of narcolepsy. Most patients with narcolepsy have HLA types HLA-DR2 and HLA-DQwl; this could be explored if the diagnosis is in doubt (4).

Other Diagnostic Tests

The electrocardiogram (ECG) may show evidence of right ventricular hypertrophy and right axis deviation in a patient with cor pulmonale due to sleep apnea syndrome.

The multiple sleep latency test (MSLT) is useful in the evaluation of narcolepsy and other sleep disorders that result in daytime somnolence (1). The time to onset of sleep under standardized conditions during the day after a quantified nocturnal sleep is calculated as an average of four to six tests administered every 2 hours over the test day. Results are interpreted as an objective measure of daytime sleep tendency.

Polysomnography

If insomnia persists despite a clinical and laboratory evaluation and initial treatment of the usual causes of insomnia, consideration should be given to referring the patient to an accredited sleep study laboratory. The standard clinical polysomnogram (an overnight sleep study) usually includes the following:

- Electroencephalogram (EEG)
- Electro-oculogram (EOG), a measure of eye movement activity used to determine stages of sleep
- Surface electromyogram (EMG), which can determine leg or other muscle movement
- ECG, which is important for determining whether cardiac arrhythmia is occurring during periods of sleep apnea
- Measures of respiration, such as respiratory effort, air flow, and oxygen saturation (usually by ear oximetry) (1,3).

Polysomnography helps to identify sleep apnea syndrome, periodic limb movement disorder, and restless legs syndrome.

WHEN TO REFER

The patient who does not respond to the initial evaluation and treatment of the common forms of insomnia should be referred to an accredited sleep evaluation laboratory to assist in establishing the diagnosis. Patients with severe sleep apnea syndrome may need referral to a pulmonary medicine specialist; those with narcolepsy or other neurologic disorders may need referral to a neurologist. If a mental illness is suspected as the underlying cause of insomnia, referral to a psychiatrist may be appropriate.

Many communities have a sleep disorder clinic or center that includes a multidisciplinary team approach to the evaluation of insomnia. Referral to such a center may be helpful if the cause of the insomnia is in doubt or if the insomnia is persistent and is interfering with the patient's life function.

MANAGEMENT

The essential step in the management of a patient with insomnia is to discover the underlying cause and treat it. Insomnia that is a symptom of a primary physical or mental illness should improve or resolve as that illness is treated. "Sleeping pills," often requested by patients, should be a short-term step, if used at all. For all the causes of insomnia, proper sleep hygiene is the first step in treatment (see Patient Education).

Management of Specific Syndromes

Transient Situational Insomnia and Insomnia Due to Inadequate Sleep Hygiene

Insomnia that is situational and insomnia due to inadequate sleep hygiene generally respond to sleep hygiene (instructions follow) and possibly a short course of treatment with hypnotic medication (less than 2 weeks).

Psychophysiologic Insomnia

Patients whose insomnia is psychophysiologic may benefit from a combination of good sleep hygiene and behavioral and relaxation therapy, plus a short course of a hypnotic medication (of less than 2 weeks' duration) at the start of treatment (1).

Shift-Work Sleep Disorder

To minimize insomnia, shift work should take into account circadian rhythm, if at all possible:

- Shift changes should occur in a clockwise direction.
- Patients should reduce the number of consecutive days worked from 7 to 4 or 5.
- Shift changes should occur no more often than once per month (1).
- Sometimes a "doctor's note" is needed to persuade employers of the need

to establish shifts that take into account circadian rhythms. The patient needs to assess the impact of such an approach on his or her relationship with the employer.

Insomnia Due to Anxiety or Depressive Disorders

Management of this very common cause of sleep disorder is treatment of the underlying disorder (see Chapters 1 and 4).

Sleep Apnea Syndrome

Patients with sleep apnea should be encouraged to make the following lifestyle changes:

• Lose weight.
• Avoid alcohol and sedative use.
• Sleep on your side.
• Avoid sleeping in the supine position.

If these measures are not sufficient, oral prostheses may improve airway patency. Another option is the use of the tricyclic antidepressant, protriptyline (Vivactil), 20 to 30 mg, at bedtime. Nasal continuous positive airway pressure (CPAP) (or delivered by mask) is currently the most successful treatment, being well-tolerated and effective in 80% of patients (3,5).

Selected patients with refractory sleep apnea may benefit from uvulopalatopharyngoplasty (3,5). If that fails, tracheostomy provides immediate relief from the airway obstruction and its potential fatal consequences (3,5).

Periodic Limb Movement Disorder

Patients with limb movement disorder can be managed with benzodiazepines, often clonazepam (Klonopin), starting at 0.25 to 0.5 mg as a single dose at bedtime. The benzodiazepines do not necessarily stop the limb movements, but they diminish the arousal generated by the movements and thereby allow more restful sleep (1,2).

Restless Legs Syndrome

Restless legs syndrome is exacerbated by anemia, iron deficiency, renal failure, and pregnancy and may improve when these are resolved (1). Caffeine also exacerbates the syndrome and should be avoided. Restless legs syndrome is often found along with other causes of insomnia, especially periodic limb movement disorder. When this is the case, the treatment should start with the coincident disorder (in this case, with clonazepam). If those treatments are unsuccessful, night-time opiates (such as codeine) may help (2).

Narcolepsy

Medication plays an important role in management of narcolepsy. It can be very dangerous because the patient may suddenly fall asleep while driving or performing some hazardous activity. Methylphenidate (Ritalin) is often given to maintain alertness during the day. To prevent tolerance, patients should take short naps instead of medication sometimes and take "drug holidays" if their situation allows (1). Protriptyline (Vivactil) is sometimes used in the management of cataplexy, but its anticholinergic effects may limit its use (1).

Medications

Medication choices specific to many of the more common diagnoses have been listed previously. If a short-term sedative-hypnotic is desired while awaiting the improvement in the insomnia as the underlying disorder is treated, a benzodiazepine is often chosen for this purpose.

Many physicians suggest over-the-counter (OTC) sleep aids, such as anti-histamines. However, many OTC agents are untested, so some physicians prefer prescription medications, which have been rigorously tested (2).

In any case, the patient should take the sedating medication no more than 2 or 3 nights consecutively and should repeat the cycle no more than two or three times. The long-term use of sedatives is generally not recommended (2). A comparison of sedative-hypnotic medications is listed in Table 8.2.

Other Treatment Modalities

Some patients may benefit from behavioral and relaxation approaches to treatment, particularly those with insomnia in association with chronic pain syndromes (6).

TABLE 8.2.   Sedative-Hypnotic Medications

Drug[a]	Half-life (hours)	Daytime Drowsiness %	Potential Problems	Relative Benefits
Flurazepam (Dalmane)	48–120	24	Confusion, hip fractures, auto accidents, Rx interactions	
Triazolam (Halcion)	2–6	14	Amnesia, confusion, rebound insomnia, Rx interactions	Daytime alertness
Temazepam (Restoril)	8–20	17	Rebound insomnia with discontinuation	Daytime alertness
Zolpidem (Ambien)	3–8	5	Limited use; potential for idiosyncratic side effects; REM sleep suppression in some patients	Daytime alertness—no withdrawal

Adapted from Pagel JF. Treatment of insomnia. Am Fam Physician 1994;49:1417–1421.

[a]Any benzodiazepine can also have sedative-hypnotic usefulness in some patients. Doses of benzodiazepines are listed in Chapter 1.

FOLLOW-UP

The frequency of follow-up varies with the cause of the insomnia. Many patients respond to improvements in sleep hygiene and need no further follow-up. Those with anxiety and depressive disorders need follow-up according to those treatment needs. Those with sleep apnea syndrome need periodic evaluation to assess the continued efficacy of the treatment approach chosen and to monitor for the development of hypertension, cor pulmonale, and right-sided heart failure.

PATIENT EDUCATION

Both the patient and the family need to be educated about the nature of the patient's sleep disorder. This is critically important for the patient with narcolepsy, for example, for whom safety issues may be paramount and other affected family members may need to be identified. The bed partner of a patient with sleep apnea, restless legs syndrome, or periodic limb movement disorder will also appreciate an explanation from the physician about what is going on with their family member and what can be done about it. But even for the more common forms of insomnia, it is helpful if family members understand that the environment needs to be conducive to sleeping. All patients complaining of insomnia should be given the following instructions for improving their sleep hygiene:

- Avoid all drugs of abuse.
- Limit, and preferably stop, the use of caffeine, nicotine, and alcohol. As few as three to five cups of coffee early in the day can result in insomnia in caffeine-sensitive patients (1).
- Have a regular schedule for retiring to bed and getting up in the morning.
- Avoid large meals or vigorous exercise for several hours before sleep.
- Do not watch television or read in bed; use the bed only for sleep and sexual activity.
- Go to bed only when sleepy; if unable to get to sleep in about 20 minutes, get up and do some routine, boring activity. Do not read or do anything that requires intellectual activity. (Folding laundry is an example often given as a fairly nonstimulating task.) Go back to bed when feeling sleepy, and if sleep does not come in another short period, get up again and repeat this sequence.
- Get up for the day at the same time each day, even if not much sleep was obtained during the night. It is important to establish a regular schedule.
- Do not take naps during the day (7).

References

1. Czeisler CA, Richardson GS, Martin JB. Disorders of sleep and circadian rhythms. In: Isselbacher KJ, Braunwald E, Wilson JD, et al, eds. Harrison's textbook of internal medicine. 13th ed. New York: McGraw-Hill, 1994:162-171.

2. Williams RL, Karacan I, Moore CA, Hirschkowitz M. Sleep disorders. In: Kaplan HI, Sadock BJ, eds. Comprehensive textbook of psychiatry/VI. 6th ed. Baltimore: Williams & Wilkins, 1995:1373-1408.

3. Phillipson EA. Disorders of ventilation. In: Isselbacher KJ, Braunwald, E, Wilson JD, et al, eds. Harrison's textbook of internal medicine. 13th ed. New York: McGraw-Hill, 1994:1234-1238.

4. Cox PM Jr, Bokinsky GE. Sleep disorders. In: Friedman HH, ed. Problem oriented medical diagnosis, 6th ed. Boston: Little, Brown, 1996:25-27.

5. Brock ET, Shucard DW. Sleep apnea. Am Fam Physician 1994; 49:385-394.

6. Integration of behavioral and relaxation approaches into the treatment of chronic pain and insomnia. NIH Technol Assess Statement 1995;Oct 16-18:1-34.

7. Pagel JF. Treatment of insomnia. Am Fam Physician 1994; 49:1417-1421.

Memory Concerns

The family physician is often the first person whom patients and their families approach with concerns about memory loss. Through a careful history and evaluation, the family physician can determine the degree of impairment and the relative urgency of diagnosis, and hence can efficiently determine the combination of care and support needed to treat the underlying condition.

CHIEF COMPLAINT

The patient's presentation with memory loss covers a broad range. The patient may complain of slight difficulty remembering names or numbers, or a family member may bring the patient to the physician because of concern over more marked memory loss.

HISTORY

Consider taking a history not only from the patient but also from close friends or family members. Patients' own recollections of impairment have been shown to be less relevant to actual cognitive function compared with family members' assessments (1).

A thorough understanding of the chronologic course should be gained from the patient and family. It is important to inquire about the following:

- Onset and acuity of symptoms
- Gradual decline versus stepwise deterioration
- Perceived baseline mental state
- Personality change or other cognitive deficits (e.g., judgment, language, praxis, constructional ability, abstract thinking)
- Severity of symptoms, particularly the ability to perform activities of daily living (ADLs; Table 9.1) (2); more subtle memory deficits tend to affect instrumental before basic ADLs.

In addition to the specifics of the chief concern and functional status, the patient history should include information about the following:

TABLE 9.1. Activities of Daily Living

BASIC
Feeding
Dressing
Ambulation
Toileting
Bathing
Transfer
Continence
Grooming
Communication

INSTRUMENTAL
Writing
Reading
Cooking
Cleaning
Shopping
Doing laundry
Climbing stairs
Using the telephone
Managing medication
Managing money
Ability to travel

Adapted from Katz S, Ford A, Moskowitz R, et al. The index of ADL: a standardized measure of biological and psychosocial function. JAMA 1963;185:914–919.

- Family and psychosocial details
- Associated symptoms of possible comorbid conditions
- Medication history (preferably, the patient should bring all medications to the office visit)

PHYSICAL EXAMINATION

It is a matter of personal preference whether to begin with the mental status examination before the rest of the physical examination. The cognitive assessment may be better accepted by the patient if a physical exam precedes it, giving the patient more time to become accustomed to the physician. On the other hand, it may be useful to have some idea of the patient's mental status before conducting the physical exam.

Mental Status Examination

Regardless of when it is done, a thorough mental status examination includes evaluation not only of memory but also of general appearance and behavior, awareness and arousal, mood and affect, attention and concentration, insight and judgment, language ability, abstract thinking, calculations, and motor and visuospatial function (3).

The memory examination can be divided into evaluation of immediate, recent, and remote memory.

Immediate Memory

- Have patient repeat a string of numbers presented at half-second intervals; the "digit span" is the longest string the patient can remember, with normal recall being six to seven numbers.
- Alternatively, ask the patient to spell backward a short word such as "world." Remember that immediate memory also reflects the patient's attention.

Recent Memory

- Ask patient to recall three common objects or words 5 minutes after they are first disclosed.
- Alternatively, ask the patient to recall events from the past 2 weeks.

Remote Memory

- Ask the patient dates or names of historical significance.

Note: All components of the memory exam may be contained in a more comprehensive cognitive screen, which is discussed under Diagnostic Testing.

Neurologic Examination

The neurologic exam can identify signs of specific underlying conditions associated with memory loss and dementia.

- Cranial nerve abnormalities suggest focal central nervous system lesions or sensory impairment that may affect the ability to gather information.
- Tremor suggests Parkinson's disease.
- Gait and motor examination may reveal extrapyramidal symptoms, ataxia, or apraxia (discussed under Differential Diagnosis).
- Abnormal sensation may indicate alcohol abuse, vitamin B_{12} deficiency, or diabetes (with its associated vascular risks).
- Reflexes (including the presence of primitive reflexes) can hint at underlying abnormalities such as hypothyroidism, frontal lobe damage, and basal ganglia dysfunction (3).

General Physical Examination

Consider performing a comprehensive exam for the remainder of the physical evaluation, with attention to comorbid conditions. Particularly evaluate the following:

- Cardiovascular status—hypertension, evidence of heart failure
- Thyroid—thyromegaly, nodules, systemic symptoms of thyroid disease
- Evidence of infection (urinary tract infections in particular are a common infectious cause of mental status changes in the elderly)
- Pulmonary status—chronic obstructive pulmonary disease, hypoxia, infection

DIAGNOSTIC TESTING

Objective Measurement of Cognitive Function

Before considering laboratory or imaging studies, obtain some objective measure of cognitive function such as the standardized questionnaires that may be administered by family physicians (e.g., the Mini-Mental State Examination [see Appendix J] or the Blessed Dementia Scale) or a more comprehensive neuropsychological testing battery (4-6). This not only gives a baseline with which to compare future exams, but also indicates other areas of cognition that may be affected.

Laboratory and Imaging Studies

Although there is no standard panel of tests for assessment of dementing illness, many articles have addressed the indications for specific testing (7-9). Most sources recommend the following tests:

- Complete blood count (CBC)
- Glucose (or glycohemoglobin if diabetes is strongly suspected)
- Electrolyte levels
- Calcium levels
- Phosphorus levels
- Serum function tests of kidney, liver, and thyroid
- Vitamin B_{12} levels

In addition, the National Institutes of Health Consensus Conference recommends the following (7), although other authors may reserve these tests for patients with suggestive exam findings:

- Chest x-ray
- Echocardiogram
- Urinalysis
- VDRL (syphilis test)
- Folate levels

The following tests may be indicated in selected cases:

- Computed tomographic (CT) scan of the head (or magnetic resonance imaging [MRI] if posterior fossa lesions are suspected) if the latter clinical evaluation and laboratory tests do not identify a reversible cause (10)

- Erythrocyte sedimentation rate (ESR) may identify comorbid conditions (e.g., vasculitis, underlying infection), but is nonspecific (8,9)
- HIV testing, where clinically indicated
- Toxin screening, where clinically indicated

DIFFERENTIAL DIAGNOSIS

Memory loss can be insidious or abrupt in onset, and the course can wax or wane or relentlessly worsen. Certain diagnoses are supported by a gradual decline and others by a stepwise deterioration. The differential diagnoses listed in the following text represent most of the memory impairments seen in family practice.

Delirium

Delirium is rarely subtle. It is characterized by acute disturbance in the following areas:

- Attention
- Sleep patterns
- Ability to process new information from the environment

Although delirium and severe dementia can sometimes be difficult to distinguish, isolated memory concerns with no other cognitive deficit are inconsistent with delirium.

Benign Senescent Forgetfulness

A minor degree of memory loss can be a normal age-related change, as in benign senescent forgetfulness (also called age-associated memory impairment), which is characterized by the lack of other cognitive deficits and no dysfunction in ADLS. Inability to recall names quickly or repetition of questions are typical of benign senescent forgetfulness.

If the distinction between benign senescent forgetfulness and dementia remains in doubt, the patient should be observed closely for a period of months for evidence of progression or other form of impairment (11).

Amnestic Syndromes

Amnestic syndromes are characterized by transient or chronic memory loss and can be associated with other findings. Korsakoff's syndrome secondary to alcoholism (or nonalcoholic thiamine deficiency) is an example of an amnestic syndrome. Korsakoff's syndrome is characterized by the following:

- Impaired ability to retain recent information despite normal alertness

- Immediate memory usually normal, but recent information poorly retained
- Disorientation, a common result of loss of recent memory

Note: Permanent mental impairment may occur if thiamine is not administered.

Isolated memory loss similar to Korsakoff's syndrome can occur with head trauma, anoxic events, encephalitis, cerebrovascular insufficiency, or early Alzheimer's disease. Complex partial seizures, classic migraine headaches, and drugs (discussed later in this chapter) have been reported to cause memory lapses as well.

Transient global amnesia is a poorly understood phenomenon involving isolated memory loss with complete recovery in 2 to 12 hours. Episodes are sometimes associated with physical or emotional stress or extreme temperatures.

Psychogenic amnesia may follow severe stress with event-specific memory loss and amnestic gaps during the "fugue" state.

Dementia

The remainder of the differential diagnosis includes causes for dementia or progressive memory deficit with at least one other area of cognitive deficit. These deficits must by definition be severe enough to interfere with activities and relationships; however, early dementia can present as an isolated memory concern. The differential diagnosis for dementia is extremely broad; extensive tables are available in other resources (7–9). The causes discussed in the sections that follow are those most commonly seen in the family physician's office.

Alzheimer's Disease

First reported by neuropsychiatrist Alois Alzheimer in 1907, the diagnosis of Alzheimer's disease (AD) was initially applied to dementia of middle age, or "presenile dementia." Interest in the disease increased in the early 1960s as the associated microscopic findings were better studied. By the 1970s, it was clear that AD represented the most common cause of dementia. Estimates vary, but AD is generally reported as the underlying cause of 50% to 70% of all diagnosed dementia. Dementia affects approximately 5% of those over age 65 and 20% of those over age 85 (11, 12).

AD (primary neuronal degeneration) is a progressive mental dementia characterized by the following:

- Gradually worsening memory loss
- Confusion and disorientation
- Hallmark microscopic findings in brain tissue (neurofibrillary tangles and amyloid plaques) (13)

The only definitive diagnostic test for AD is brain biopsy. Therefore, the National Institute of Neurological and Communicative Disorders and Stroke-Alzheimer's Disease and Related Disorders (NINCDS-ADRDA) released clini-

TABLE 9.2. Clinical Criteria for Probable Alzheimer's Disease

- Dementia established by examination and documented by objective testing
- Deficits in two or more cognitive areas
- Progressive worsening of memory and other cognitive functions
- No disturbance of consciousness
- Onset between age 40 and 90 years
- Absence of systemic disorders or other brain diseases that could cause above.

From the National Institute of Neurological and Communicative Disorders and Stroke-Alzheimer's Disease and Related Disorders Association (NINCDS-ADRDA).

cal criteria for "probable Alzheimer's disease" (Table 9.2). Diagnostic accuracy of these clinical criteria has been shown to exceed 85% when correlated with postmortem biopsies (12).

Frontal lobe dementias such as Pick's disease (named for the Pick bodies or Pick cells seen under the microscope) can appear clinically identical with AD and are distinguishable only by biopsy at this time.

Vascular Dementia

Vascular dementia is the second most prevalent cause of dementia after AD (with some overlap), accounting for approximately 15% of cases of dementia in the United States (14,15). It is sometimes divided into two categories: multi-infarct dementia, which involves cortical and subcortical brain tissue (because of difficulty in distinction, this term is often used for the entire spectrum of vascular dementia); and Binswanger's disease, which involves mainly subcortical tissue, with white matter changes secondary to vascular pathology (hypertension or sclerosis). Because these two conditions are often hard to distinguish, the term "multi-infarct dementia" is often used for the entire spectrum of vascular dementia. The following are key points in identifying vascular dementia:

- Vascular dementia is classically a stepwise deterioration, although this is often difficult to determine by history.
- Identification of vascular risk factors (e.g., hypertension, diabetes, and prior stroke) by history and exam is essential.
- A focal neurologic finding (e.g., homonymous hemianopsia associated with posterior cerebral blood flow, speech difficulty, or focal weakness) can help distinguish vascular dementia from other types of dementia (16).

Parkinson's Disease and Lewy Body Variant Dementia

Whether the histopathologic finding of cortical Lewy bodies represents a separate entity from the dementia of Parkinson's disease is still being studied (17–20). The following are key points:

- Both disorders are characterized by dementia with associated extrapyramidal symptoms (rigidity, cogwheeling) or visual hallucinations.
- Twenty-five percent of patients with Parkinson's disease have dementia (20).
- Dementia is typically gradual in onset and is frequently associated with mood disturbances (depression or lability).

Depression

Pseudodementia is a phenomenon of at least partially reversible cognitive impairment secondary to depression (11). A thorough history and mental status exam may produce evidence of depression.

A trial of antidepressant therapy may be warranted if there is any possibility that the patient has depression.

Drugs

Potentially toxic medications and chemicals are listed in Table 9.3.

- Confusion can be caused by intoxication with alcohol or other illicit drugs. Therefore, a toxicology screen is appropriate in patients at high risk for illicit drug use.
- A host of prescription medications can also cause confusion, particularly in the elderly population; thus, it is important to get a complete medicine history.

Mass Lesions and Hydrocephalus

Masses such as neoplasms and hematomas can cause memory loss and confusion. Hydrocephalus can result from these masses as well and may occur spontaneously.

T ABLE 9.3. Toxins and Medications Associated With Confusion and Memory Loss

- Heavy metals (most commonly lead and mercury)
- Organophosphates
- Carbon monoxide
- Alcohol and illicit drugs
- Antidepressants (particularly tricyclics)
- Neuroleptics
- Anxiolytics and sedatives
- Antiparkinsonian agents (levodopa [Larodopa], amantadine [Symmetrel], bromocriptine [Parlodel], antihistamines)
- Anticonvulsants
- Analgesics
- Hypoglycemic agents
- Cimetidine (Tagamet)

- Normal-pressure hydrocephalus may not be associated with any other abnormality, but patients classically present with dementia, urinary incontinence, and gait disorder.
- Normal-pressure hydrocephalus is potentially reversible with shunting.

Human Immunodeficiency Virus

With more patients with human immunodeficiency virus (HIV) living longer, dementia secondary to HIV needs to be considered, with attention to the risk factors in the history. HIV infection is associated with a number of central nervous system abnormalities.

WHEN TO REFER

Because the diagnostic approach to memory loss and dementia can involve many disciplines, comprehensive evaluation clinics have developed in many areas of the country. The family physician may consider using such a center at his or her discretion.

Indications for immediate referral for emergent or inpatient evaluation might include the following:

- Rapid decline (within weeks)
- Significant functional impairment
- Evidence of urgent systemic disease
- Changing focal neurologic signs

MANAGEMENT

Any reversible causes of dementia and memory loss should be treated aggressively. For progressive, nonreversible causes, a combination of pharmacologic and supportive care can be offered.

Medication

Alzheimer's Disease

The anticholinesterases, donepezil (Aricept) and tacrine (Cognex), are the only medications in mid-1998 approved by the US Food and Drug Administration for targeting cognitive impairment in early AD. These medications increase central nervous system levels of acetylcholine, a neurotransmitter associated with cognition. Several studies have also documented improved cognitive assessment scores in patients with mild to moderate AD who are receiving anticholesterinases (21–23). Dosages and side effects are listed in Table 9.4.

Many other agents are being studied for AD, including other anticholinesterases, cholinergic agonists and antagonists, other neurotransmitters, calcium channel blockers, angiotensin-converting enzyme (ACE) in-

TABLE 9.4. Agents for Cognitive Impairment in Early AD

Agent	Date of FDA Approval	Dosage	Complications (%)
Donepezil (Aricept)	1996	5 mg daily; then 10 mg daily after 4–6 weeks	Cardiac conduction abnormalities, nausea, diarrhea, insomnia, anorexia
Tacrine (Cognex)	1993	10 mg 4 x daily, increase every 6 weeks to max of 160 mg daily	Hepatotoxicity (50%); gastrointestinal distress (results in discontinuance in 10–20%)

Adapted from references 7, 8, 10, and 12.

hibitors, monoamine oxidase (MAO) inhibitors, metabolic enhancers, nerve growth factor, estrogen, vitamin E, ginkgo biloba, and gene therapy.

In more advanced dementia, behavioral symptoms (e.g., agitation, anxiety, and sleeping difficulties) occur more frequently. Nonpharmacologic approaches such as maintenance of a stable schedule and environment should be attempted first. If medication is necessary, the following agents may be beneficial for patients with AD.

• Chloral hydrate, rather than benzodiazepines, may be a good first choice for sleep difficulties because of its better safety profile.
• Benzodiazepines are often used for anxiety and agitation, but they can cause paradoxical reactions and further deterioration in cognition.
• Neuroleptic agents are also used in this setting.
• Research is being conducted into the possible use of the following agents for anxiety: buspirone (BuSpar), trazodone (Desyrel), β-blockers, anticonvulsants, lithium, and estrogen.
• Neuroleptics are indicated if delusions or hallucinations are distressing to the patient or family.
• Newer atypical antipsychotics such as risperidone (Risperdal) are gaining popularity in this population, particularly in lewybody variant dementia (21).

Coexisting Depression

A careful trial of agents such as selective serotonin reuptake inhibitors (SSRIs) may be useful in patients with depressive pseudodementia (see Chapter 4). Treatment of concurrent depression involves identifying the target symptoms and choosing the antidepressant by its individual characteristics and side-effects profile.

Other Treatment Modalities

If the diagnosis is a progressive dementia, other care issues include evaluation of the support environment, continued preventive health care (with attention to immunizations and nutrition), and discussion of future care plans.

The support environment includes the patient's family, friends, and other care providers as well as the building in which the patient lives. The primary care team must constantly assess the adequacy of the care situation and the coping abilities of those close to the patient. The emotional burden of dementia often takes as heavy a toll on the family as on the patient. The Alzheimer's Association is a great resource for information about dementia of all etiologies: Alzheimer's Association, 919 N. Michigan Ave., Suite 1000, Chicago, IL 60611-1676; 800-272-3900; www.alz.org. Another resource for families is the lay book, *The 36-Hour Day.*

The physician can provide anticipatory guidance to the patient (as appropriate) and family about the possible progression of the dementia and advise them about environmental (e.g., removal of throw rugs, posting of signs) and behavioral strategies (e.g., keeping a consistent schedule). The physician also has a role in encouraging the patient and family to discuss advance directives early in the course of the dementia while the patient may still be able to clearly express his or her wishes.

FOLLOW-UP

Constantly reassess the patient's environment for appropriateness. If the patient reaches a point at which independent living or assisted care at home is no longer the best environment for overall well-being, the physician should assist the family with the difficult decision of determining the most appropriate care.

REFERENCES

1. Roth M, Tyrn E, Mountjoy CQ, et al. A standardized instrument for the diagnosis of mental disorder in the elderly with special reference to the early detection of dementia. Br J Psychiatry 1986;149:698–709.

2. Katz S, Ford A, Moskowitz R, et al. The index of ADL: a standardized measure of biological and psychosocial function. JAMA 1963;185:914–919.

3. Sevush S. Neurologic examination in aging and dementia. Med Clin North Am 1994;78:774–779.

4. Folstein MF, Folstein SA, McHugh PR. Mini-mental state: a practical method for grading the cognitive state of patients for the clinician. J Psychiatr Res 1975;12:196–198.

5. Blessed G, Tomlinsen BE, Roth M. The association between quantitative measures of dementia and of senile change in the cerebral gray matter of elderly subjects. Br J Psychiatry 1968;114:797–811.

6. Lowenstein DA. Neuropsychological assessment in Alzheimer's Disease. Med Clin North Am 1994;78:789–793.

7. NIH Consensus Conference. Differential diagnosis of dementing diseases. JAMA 1987;258:3411-3416.

8. Larsen EB, Lo B, Williams ME. Evaluation and care of patients with dementia. J Gen Intern Med 1986;1:116.

9. Siu Al. Screening for dementia and investigating its causes. Ann Intern Med 1991;115:122.

10. Cummings JL, Arland D, Jarvik L. Dementia. In: Cassel CD, ed. Geriatric medicine. 3rd ed. New York: Springer-Verlag, 1997.

11. Kane RL, Ouslander JG, Abrass IB. Confusion. In: Essentials of clinical geriatrics. 3rd ed. New York: McGraw-Hill, 1994.

12. Morris JC. Differential diagnosis of Alzheimer's disease. Clin Geriatr Med 1994;10:257-276.

13. Rosenberg RN. A causal role for amyloid in Alzheimer's disease. Neurology 1993;43:851-856.

14. Jellinger K, Danielczyk W, Fischer P, et al. Clinicopathological analysis of dementia disorders in the elderly. J Neurol Sci 1990;95:239-258.

15. Mendez M, Mastri AR, Sung HJ, et al. Clinically diagnosed Alzheimer's disease: neuropathologic findings in 650 cases. Alzheimer Dis Assoc Disord 1992;6:35-43.

16. Cummings JL, Benson DF. Dementia: a clinical approach. 2nd ed. Stoneham, Mass: Butterworth-Heinemann, 1992.

17. Burkhardt CR, Filley CM, Kleinschmidt-DeMasters BK, et al. Diffuse Lewy body disease and progressive dementia. Neurology 1988;38:1520-1528.

18. McKeith IG, Perry RH, Fairbairn AF, et al. Operational criteria for senile dementia of Lewy body type (SDLT). Psychol Med 1992;22:911-922.

19. Weiner MF, Risser RC, Cullum CM, et al. Alzheimer's disease and its Lewy body variant: a clinical analysis of postmortem verified cases. Am J Psychiatry 1996;153:1269-1273.

20. Hughes AJ, Daniel SE, Blankson S, et al. A clinicopathologic study of 100 cases of Parkinson's disease. Arch Neurol 1993;50:140-148.

21. Davis KL, Thal L, Gracon SI, et al. Tacrine in patients with Alzheimer's disease: a double-blind, placebo-controlled multicenter study. N Engl J Med 1992;327:1253-1259.

22. Farlow M, Gracon SI, Hershey LA, et al. A controlled trial of tacrine in Alzheimer's disease. JAMA 1992;268:2523-2529.

23. Rogers SL, Friedhoff LT. The efficacy and safety of Donepezil in patients with Alzheimer's disease. Results of a U.S. multicenter, randomized, double-blind, placebo-controlled trial. Dementia 1996;7:293-303.

24. Corey-Bloom J, Galasko D. Adjunctive therapy in patients with Alzheimer's disease: a practical approach. Drugs Aging 1995;7:79-87.

Margaret E. McCahill

Somatoform Disorders, Factitious Disorders, and Malingering

Somatization disorder alone is the fourth most common problem seen in family practice (1), although it is usually given some other diagnostic label. It has been estimated that patients who come to their physician with somatic presentations of psychosocial problems consume more than 50% of the physician's time (1). If somatizers feel that their complaints are not taken seriously by their physician, they generally "doctor shop," going from one physician to another with their complaints, receiving multiple medical evaluations and possibly surgical procedures. Despite these challenges, it is possible to effectively manage the care of these patients, and the experience can be rewarding.

"Somatizers" are patients who present with physical complaints and symptoms but have no objective findings, or their complaints far exceed the demonstrable physical disease. Patients with somatoform disorders are convinced that they have a definite physical illness. The somatoform disorders comprise seven specific syndromes with diagnostic criteria delineated in the *Diagnostic and Statistical Manual of Mental Disorders,* 4th ed (Table 10.1) (2).

The somatoform disorders should be considered a spectrum of disorders, in which a patient may appear to have one specific disorder at one point in time, a different but related diagnosis at another time, and "subsyndromal somatization" at yet another time. Subsyndromal somatization (diagnosed as undifferentiated somatoform disorder) refers to somatic complaints that cannot be explained by objective findings or by a known medical illness but do not meet the full diagnostic criteria for a specific somatoform disorder. Patients with subsyndromal somatization are nevertheless very incapacitated by their illness and generally benefit from the same management strategy used for several of the other somatoform disorders.

Five of the seven somatoform disorders (the first five listed in Table 10.1) are managed in a similar (not identical) manner. This chapter reviews the di-

TABLE 10.1. Somatoform Disorders

Somatization disorder
Somatization disorder not otherwise specified
Undifferentiated somatoform disorder
Pain disorder
Hypochondriasis
Conversion disorder
Body dysmorphic disorder

IMPACT OF SOMATOFORM DISORDERS

- Patients with somatoform disorders often perceive that they are severely ill; their health care costs have been noted to be about nine times the United States per-capita health care utilization cost (3).
- Patients with somatoform disorders spend twice the number of days annually in the hospital; they spend 4.9 to 7 days in bed per month compared with 1 day or less per month for patients with most medical problems (3–5).
- Eight-two percent of patients with somatoform disorders find it necessary to stop their work because of perceived health problems (6).
- Somatoform disorders often cause major life impairment; however, the mortality rate is equal to that of the general population and much lower than that for patients with major depression (3).

agnostic decision points for the somatoform disorders individually and presents a management approach for the patient with each disorder.

Although factitious disorders and malingering are distinct from the somatoform disorders, they are discussed in this chapter because they are included in the differential diagnosis of patients who present with complaints of physical symptoms out of proportion to their physical findings.

CHIEF COMPLAINT

Patients with somatoform disorders present with physical complaints and symptoms that either have no objective findings or far exceed the demonstrable physical disease. Following are common chief complaints and the possible diagnoses:

- Many unexplained symptoms over time that impair functioning—somatization disorder (SD), SD not otherwise specified, undifferentiated somatoform disorder

- All encompassing focus on pain, which is inexplicably severe or persistent—pain disorder
- Persistent and possibly debilitating fear that he or she has a serious disease in spite of evidence to the contrary—Hypochondriasis
- Sudden onset of symptoms or deficits in voluntary motor or sensory function—Conversion disorder
- Excessive concern, preoccupation or loathing about some aspect of his or her appearance—Body dysmorphic disorder
- Complaints and other physical findings that are self-inflicted—Factitious disorder
- Complaints and possibly physical signs and laboratory findings of medical or psychological illness, with secondary gain usually evident—Malingering

EPIDEMIOLOGIC CONSIDERATIONS

- Somatization disorder occurs in 0.2% to 2% of US women and less than 0.2% of US men.
- Undifferentiated somatoform disorder has been estimated to have a lifetime prevalence of 4% to 11% (7).
- Pain disorder is very common, with 10% to 15% of US adults per year having work disability from back pain alone (2).
- Pain disorder is seen in twice as many women as men, with a peak incidence in the fourth and fifth decades, especially among those in blue collar occupations (7).
- Hypochondriasis has been estimated in 4% to 6% of a general medical population in a given 6-month period and is seen equally in both sexes (7).
- Conversion disorder most often occurs in rural settings in patients of lower economic status who are naive about medical and psychological issues.
- Nearly 64% of patients with conversion disorder had evidence of an organic brain disorder compared with 5% of controls in one study (8).
- Body dysmorphic disorder is seen equally in men and women; some studies have suggested that it is so common that it represents a normal developmental issue in adolescence (9).
- Factitious disorder is seen more commonly in women and more often in health care providers than in those in any other occupation (10).
- Munchausen's syndrome accounts for about 10% of factitious disorder.
- Munchausen's syndrome by proxy has been reported to be responsible for 14% of cases of failure to thrive in children and has a mortality rate of 9% (11).
- Malingering appears more prevalent in certain settings, such as the military, prison, and litigious populations, and in Western men from youth through middle age (12).

HISTORY

A thorough medical history is essential, because the diagnosis of somatoform disorders is largely made on this basis.

Somatization Disorder

The patient with SD has a history of many unexplained physical symptoms over time, which have prompted the patient to seek medical or surgical attention and which impair occupational, social, or other functioning. It is important to note that SD symptoms are not consciously contrived, and the patient truly does experience physical distress.

The DSM-IV diagnostic criteria for SD are listed in Appendix R. Cloninger has proposed an abbreviated four-step screening test (13):

1. Unless there is a (current or past) history of medically unexplained pain in at least four different parts of the body, the diagnosis is excluded.
2. Unless there are at least two gastrointestinal symptoms other than pain (e.g., nausea, vomiting, diarrhea, and food intolerance), the diagnosis is excluded.
3. There must be at least one sexual or reproductive symptom other than pain (e.g., sexual indifference, erectile or ejaculatory dysfunction, irregular menses, excessive menstrual bleeding, or vomiting throughout pregnancy).
4. There must be at least one pseudoneurologic or conversion symptom (see Appendix R for examples), with onset of symptoms before age 30, symptoms unexplainable by another medical or mental illness, and duration of symptoms at least several years.

Manifestations of SD may be influenced by culture. The descriptions and management suggestions in this chapter are derived from studies done in the United States.

Somatization Disorder Not Otherwise Specified

The patient with somatization disorder not otherwise specified (SDNOS) presents with physical complaints with no medical explanation but does not meet the diagnostic criteria for any other somatoform disorder. The patient may present with one or a few medically unexplained complaints of recent onset. For example, pseudocyesis, the false belief of being pregnant, may be listed as SDNOS (2), although sometimes it is considered one of the symptoms of conversion disorder (7).

SDNOS is a category that covers patients who suffer symptoms and seek medical attention but who generally do not meet the 6-month minimum time criterion for other disorders. Often, patients are first given this diagnosis and then later meet the full diagnostic criteria for one of the other somatoform disorders.

Undifferentiated Somatoform Disorder

The patient presents with one or more medically unexplained physical complaints that have persisted 6 months or longer and cause impairment in functioning. Among the most common complaints are the following (2):

• Chronic fatigue
• Loss of appetite
• Gastrointestinal complaints
• Genitourinary complaints

Patients with undifferentiated somatoform disorder have a history similar to that of SD patients but with fewer symptoms and illness of shorter duration (but at least 6 months). Symptoms cause significant distress and impairment in physical, social, or occupational functioning. Symptoms cause the patient to seek medical attention but cannot be explained by any medical illness or diagnostic finding.

Pain Disorder

The patient with pain disorder (PD) has an all-encompassing focus on pain in one or a few locations. If the patient has any other symptoms (e.g., insomnia), he or she attributes them to the pain. The patient's pain is more severe or persistent than can be explained by physical findings. The diagnostic criteria for pain disorder are listed in Appendix S.

The subjective intensity of the pain and its consequent disability are the issues of focus for the patient, which differentiates the patient from those with hypochondriasis (in whom the focus is on the meaning of the symptoms) and those with SD (who have a complex series of symptoms).

Hypochondriasis

The patient with hypochondriasis may initially present with fairly typical pain or other symptom, but, after questioning the patient, it becomes apparent that the central problem is persistent fear of what the symptom means. For example, a patient may believe that the pain means that he or she most certainly has cancer. The patient is impaired by this fear (2) and is not reassured by a normal physical examination or laboratory or diagnostic investigations. The diagnostic criteria for hypochondriasis are listed in Appendix T.

Hypochondriasis may begin at any age, although the most common age of onset is the 20s. No connection is found between hypochondriasis and level of education, marital status, or socioeconomic factors (7).

Conversion Disorder

The patient with conversion disorder (CD) develops symptoms or deficits affecting voluntary motor or sensory function and suggesting a neurologic or other medical condition. The symptoms cannot be explained by a medical condition, the effects of a substance, or culturally sanctioned behavior (2). The diagnostic criteria for conversion disorder are listed in Appendix U.

The onset of symptoms is often sudden and transient. A single episode is usually of short duration, although some may persist. Examples of conversion symptoms include the following:

- Paralysis of an extremity
- Areas of anesthesia
- Pseudoseizures
- Hysterical blindness
- Falling
- Aphonia
- Abnormalities of gait, including "astasia-abasia" (staggering, ataxic gait with gross jerks and thrashing or wild waving of the upper extremities, often with inability to stand) (7)

The patient with CD may have an obvious history of extreme emotional stressor such as acute grief, physical or sexual abuse, or a life-threatening experience; on the other hand, this history may also be notably absent. Psychological factors are judged to be associated with the symptom because the onset or exacerbation of the CD was preceded by some conflict or stress.

Body Dysmorphic Disorder

Patients with body dysmorphic disorder (BDD) present most frequently between 20 and 40 years of age. BDD is seen in men and women with equal frequency. Patients express excessive concern, preoccupation, or loathing about some aspect of their physical appearance; especially common are concerns about hair and facial features. Patients may admit that attending to their perceived abnormality requires excessive time and energy. Patients may spend several hours per day checking their physical appearance in mirrors, applying makeup to cover the defect, removing hair or rearranging it, and engaging in other activities intended to cope with or alter the perceived problem. Preoccupation activities can consume so much time that occupational function and relationships are jeopardized; some individuals become housebound. These patients generally want help in correcting the physical defect rather than in changing their own behavior.

The diagnosis of BDD is made only if the patient's symptoms and disability are not better accounted for by another mental disorder. The diagnostic limits of BDD have been challenged, because some studies have found that 36% of female and 17% of male college students meet the diagnostic criteria (9). This suggests that BDD is so common that it represents a normal developmental issue in adolescence. It is reasonable to consider the diagnosis when the preoccupation with an imaginary or slight physical imperfection causes significant impairment in living.

Factitious Disorders

The patient with factitious disorder intentionally produces the signs and symptoms of illness to get emotional needs met through the assumption of the sick role, either by the patient him- or herself or by the victim of an adult perpetrator in factitious disorder by proxy. There is no apparent secondary gain. This distinguishes factitious disorder from malingering, in which secondary gain is nearly always apparent. The diagnostic criteria of factitious disorder are listed in Appendix V.

Patients with factitious disorder often give dramatic, vague, inconsistent histories, and, if challenged, they usually leave treatment against medical advice, only to present with the same symptoms at another facility soon thereafter. For example, a woman comes to the emergency department complaining of hematuria and pain suggestive of ureterolithiasis. She has hematuria, but when informed that the radiologic tests revealed no findings, she disappears from the ward and reports to the emergency department of a hospital 20 miles away with the same complaint.

In the case of "factitious disorder by proxy," the complaints and physical findings are induced in a child or dependent adult by their caregiver, with the intention of having the caregiver's emotional needs met by the victim's assumption of the sick role. The research criteria for factitious disorder by proxy are listed in Appendix V.

Malingering

The person who is malingering presents with complaints and possibly physical signs and laboratory findings of medical or psychological illness, and secondary gain of some sort is usually evident. Many consider malingering to be deliberate deceptive behavior and not a medical disorder at all and that malingering is not diagnosed, but, rather, detected. Malingering is discussed here because it is in the differential diagnosis when patients present with somatic complaints that are not explainable by their medical diagnoses.

Complaints and findings are as diverse as the individuals themselves. Malingering should be suspected with any combination of the following (2):

- Medicolegal context of presentation
- Marked discrepancy between claimed symptoms and findings
- Lack of cooperation during the evaluation and noncompliance with treatment
- Presence of antisocial personality disorder

PHYSICAL EXAMINATION AND DIAGNOSTIC TEST DATA

For patients with SD, SDNOS, undifferentiated SD, pain disorder, hypochondriasis, CD and BDD, the physical examination and laboratory tests are generally entirely within normal limits. If any variation is found, it is a slight variation from normal, which is insufficient to explain the patient's complaints.

It can be challenging in patients with CD to determine that the physical examination is within normal limits (Table 10.2). On mental status examination, patients with CD may show *la belle indifference* (lack of concern or even jovial affect regarding symptoms); although some patients appear very distressed. The type of testing needed for patients with CD depends on their symptom. For example, an electroencephalogram (EEG) obtained along with simultaneous videotaping of the patient may help in the evaluation of pseudoseizures. An electromyogram (EMG) may assist in the evaluation of paralysis symptoms. An optokinetic drum test might be used in the assessment of CD blindness. Again, all testing is within normal limits.

Patients with FD may have abnormal examination and laboratory findings consistent with their complaints. Common findings include the following:

- Electrolyte abnormalities in patients using large doses of diuretics
- Hypoglycemia in nondiabetic patients using insulin
- Very low thyroid-stimulating hormone (TSH) levels in euthyroid patients taking high-dose thyroid medication
- Hematuria induced by finger-prick contamination of urine sample
- Self-induced bruises

TABLE 10.2. Clues to Uncovering Suspected Conversion Disorder at Examination

Symptom	Suggestive of CD
Paralysis of hand	Hand falls to the side when examiner lifts and drops it over patient's face.
Paralysis of leg	There is pressure on examiner's hand under patient's leg when patient is asked to attempt straight leg raising.
Anesthesia	There is a lack of correspondence to dermatomes.
Aphonia	Ask patient to cough. Normal cough suggests vocal cords are functioning properly.
Astasia-abasia	Suggest to patient that although walking is affected, the ability to dance is not; normal dancing establishes normal functioning.
Pseudoseizures[a]	Frequently occur only in prescence of physician or family members; patient generally does not show postictal confusion or sleepiness.

Adapted from Guggenheim FG, Smith GR. Somatoform disorders. In: Kaplan HI, Sadock BJ, eds. Comprehensive textbook of psychiatry/VI. 6th ed. Baltimore: Williams & Wilkins, 1995:1251–1270.

[a]Pseudoseizures present a particular challenge, because most patients with pseudoseizures also have a neurologic diagnosis, often a seizure disorder.

The most common findings in FD proxy involving children caused by their caretakers include the following (14):

- Bleeding (44%)
- Central nervous system symptoms (seizure, ataxia, impaired consciousness) (about 50%)
- Diarrhea and vomiting (21%)
- Fever (10%)
- Rash (9%)

The physician's suspicion should be heightened when the physical exam and diagnostic tests, although positive, do not fit or follow typical patterns seen in the natural course of illness and when patients do not respond to customary treatment.

Malingering patients may have physical and test findings within normal limits or may have self-induced physical signs and laboratory findings such as those seen in FD. Again, the physician's suspicion should be aroused when physical exam and diagnostic test findings do not fit or follow typical patterns and do not respond to treatment.

WHEN TO REFER

For most disorders in the somatoform spectrum, the family physician is the ideal person to manage the patient's care. The "best medicine" in these cases is the patient-physician relationship. Consultation is generally used as needed to assist the family physician in management.

Somatization Disorder, Somatization Disorder Not Otherwise Specified, and Undifferentiated Somatoform Disorder

Patients generally resist referral to a mental health professional. Sometimes, after years of work with the family physician, a patient agrees to individual or group therapy.

Referral to a mental health professional may be indicated in the following situations:

- Willingness of the patient to go to psychotherapy
- Continued decompensation, as evidenced by disability and impairment in life function (not merely verbalization of complaints during office visits)

Pain Disorder

The family physician should maintain the central role and consistently follow up with the patient, coordinating care given by other team members, who may a include physical therapist, occupational therapist, vocational rehabilitation therapist, and mental health professional.

Hypochondriasis

Referral is indicated only when the patient has new or changing symptoms or findings that are a challenge to the family physician. The family physician should advise a consultant that the patient is followed up regularly for hypochondriasis, but that consultation is now requested because of new or changing symptoms or findings.

Conversion Disorder

When true CD is suspected, a psychiatric consultation should be requested for initial diagnosis and to assist in establishing a more appropriate coping strategy for the patient. If symptoms of CD recur, consideration should be given to referring the patient to a mental health professional for ongoing treatment.

Body Dysmorphic Disorder

Consultation with a mental health professional may be indicated in the following circumstances in a patient with BDD:

- The patient expresses suicidal ideation (urgent or emergent referral).
- The diagnosis is unclear.
- The patient has a combination of mental illnesses with complex treatment needs.
- The patient shows no improvement despite patient education, support from family and physician, and possibly a trial of medication

Factitious Disorder

Nearly all patients with FD require referral to and collaboration with a mental health professional.

Malingering

Consultation with a mental health professional may be indicated in the following circumstances:

- If the patient has a coexisting mental disorder
- If the patient expresses a sincere wish to pursue treatment for antisocial personality disorder (a very rare event; pure malingering is generally not amenable to psychotherapy)

MANAGEMENT

The somatoform disorders should be considered a spectrum, in which the patient may appear to have one disorder at one time and a different disorder at another time. Fortunately, several of the somatoform disorders are managed in a similar manner; these include SD, SDNOS, undifferentiated somatoform disorder, PD, and hypochondriasis. Minor variations in management are described following the general recommendations.

CD and BDD are more distinct members of the continuum and easier to separate from the other five. FD and malingering are not in the somatoform spectrum, and patients are not managed in the same way at all. (These disorders are discussed here briefly because they are considered in the differential diagnosis of somatoform disorders.)

When the physician has a clear plan for patients on the somatoform spectrum, he or she will shift the therapeutic expectations from curing to caring. The physician will be able to apply the most powerful treatment available, which is the physician-patient relationship, applied with continuity and empathy over time. When this is done, somatoform patients and their families are able to realize the maximum health status possible, and their health care will be the most cost-effective possible. In that setting of successful treatment, these patients are very rewarding to manage.

Somatization Disorder, Somatization Disorder Not Otherwise Specified, Undifferentiated Somatoform Disorder, Pain Disorder, and Hypochondriasis

It is essential for the patient to feel that the physician understands the degree of suffering that he or she endures and that the physician takes the patient's complaints seriously and investigates them thoroughly. Therefore, the first step in management is a thorough assessment, including the following:

- Obtaining a thorough medical history
- Performing a complete physical examination
- Obtaining laboratory data as indicated by the history and physical
- Reviewing previous medical records and test results

Table 10.3 describes the increasing probability of a mood disorder or anxiety disorder with the increasing number of symptoms presented by the patient. The physician should evaluate the patient for the presence of other mental disorders and treat any that are found. If the patient still meets the diagnos-

TABLE 10.3. Number of Symptoms and Presence of a Mood or Anxiety Disorder

Number of Physical Symptoms	Prevalence of a Mood Disorder	Prevalence of an Anxiety Disorder
0–1	2%	1%
2–3	12%	7%
4–5	23%	13%
6–8	44%	30%
9 or more	60%	48%

Adapted from Kroenke K, Spitzer RL, et al. Physical symptoms in primary care: predictors of psychiatric disorders and functional impairment. Arch Fam Med 1994;3:774–779.

tic criteria for SD after other mental disorders are treated, then the somatoform disorder becomes the focus of treatment.

The foundation of management is regularly scheduled visits with the physician. It is crucial to schedule somatizing patients for these check-ups on a regular basis. To tell the patient to return as needed is an invitation for the patient to develop new symptoms as a ticket to return to the physician. The interval depends on the degree of activity of the disorder. For instance:

• Patients who are experiencing severe symptoms might require brief, weekly visits.
• Patients may then go to 2-week visits, then monthly.
• Patients may possibly go as long as 3 months when well stabilized.

The focus of the "check-up" is to allow the patient to explain the current status of his or her various complaints, with the physician listening empathically for any significant change that could indicate any new disease process. At least some brief exam is done at each visit, depending on the symptoms. Laboratory investigation is kept to a minimum, as indicated by the physical signs.

Over time, the patient and physician develop a therapeutic alliance in which the patient feels comfortable that the physician understands what is going on and will monitor for the development of any serious problem.

Also over time, the focus of the office visits moves from discussion of physical symptoms to some discussion of how the patient is coping with life issues and problems. The goal is to assist the patient's shift of focus from somatic symptoms to improved coping skills. The physician can assist the patient by exploring how he or she is coping with various challenges and giving the patient positive feedback for healthy coping strategies, while avoiding the giving of direct advice. If the patient is able to see some relation between coping difficulties and somatic symptoms, he or she may be receptive to referral to a mental health professional. Psychotherapy for SD patients has been shown to decrease rates of hospitalization and thus decrease health care costs by up to 50% (10).

Smith, Rost, and Kashner studied the effect of a standardized psychiatric consultation on the health outcomes and costs in somatizing patients (5). Their consultation process assisted the primary care physician by verifying the diagnosis of SD and then providing the physician with treatment guidelines similar to those described previously. This approach resulted in decreased health care costs and improved sense of health outcome for the SD patients studied (5).

The use of medications should be minimized to those clearly indicated by objective findings.

Pain Disorder

The best management of patients with PD is prevention by providing proximate treatment of the acute injury aimed at prompt restoration of normal function. A patient and family who have already made chronic pain their life-way will have a poorer prognosis.

A thorough assessment is necessary to rule out treatable disorders such as comorbid mental disorders, especially mood and anxiety disorders, and substance abuse and dependence. After this assessment, the patient can be credibly reassured that the physician has taken his or her distress seriously and has diligently excluded any untreated physical ailments.

Patients with chronic pain are a heterogeneous group, and no single approach works for all patients. An individualized treatment plan should be formulated for each patient and may include the following:

- Physical therapy and other somatic modalities
- Minimizing the use of controlled substances
- Biofeedback
- Pain control programs and clinics
- Possibly psychotherapy (individual, group, or family)

The focus of management should be on restoring normal function as quickly as possible. The liability issues surrounding medication use—specifically narcotics—for chronic pain are beyond the scope of this chapter, but are discussed at length in other sources.

The patient with PD should be seen in regularly scheduled visits with the family physician in a manner similar to that described previously for SD. Optimal management uses a multidisciplinary team approach, with the goal of maximizing functional potential. The family physician should maintain the central role and consistently follow up with the patient, coordinating care given by other team members, who may include a physical therapist, occupational therapist, vocational rehabilitation therapist, and mental health professional. Psychotherapy may include individual or group psychotherapy, as well as family therapy to assist the patient in productive coping strategies.

Hypochondriasis

Patients with hypochondriasis are generally managed in a similar fashion to SD, as already described. The following points are helpful in the management of patients with hypochondriasis:

- Bear in mind that the patient's experience is real and not consciously contrived.
- Pay careful attention to the evaluation for other mental illness, because a high rate of psychiatric comorbidity is found in patients with hypochondriasis. Treatment of a coexisting anxiety or depression disorder may greatly improve the hypochondriacal symptoms.
- The patient's fear of a serious disease may wax and wane over time and may become chronic, but one third to one half of patients improve significantly (10).

Continuity of care with the family physician, with regularly scheduled visits, is key to successful management. Hopping from one subspecialist to another does not help hypochondriacal patients and may worsen their condition. If the patient agrees to see a mental health professional, psychotherapy may assist the patient and family physician in managing hypochondriasis.

Conversion Disorder

Most CD symptoms resolve with supportive treatment and with the suggestion that the symptoms should resolve quickly. In fact, 90% of CD patients without comorbid medical, neurologic, or mental illness recover by the time of hospital discharge (7).

Medication is generally not recommended. The most helpful treatment for CD includes the following:

• Appropriate evaluation and testing based on symptoms and exam
• Supportive care and assurance that symptoms will resolve
• As much as possible, assistance finding a more appropriate way to satisfy the patient's emotional needs

It is important to evaluate and treat patients for coexisting psychological problems, because 25% to 50% of CD patients have a significant mood disorder or schizophrenia and personality disorders are common (7).

If the precipitating cause of the CD symptoms can be identified and a constructive coping strategy can be implemented, then the family physician may follow up the patient as indicated by the primary problem or stressor. In other cases, referral to a mental health professional may be warranted.

Body Dysmorphic Disorder

BDD is generally a chronic disorder, with patients presenting to surgical subspecialists, dermatologists, dentists, and other medical specialists seeking repair of their perceived defect. The first step in management is to acknowledge the patient's distress (not the "disfigurement") and offer assistance to help cope. Very few patients improve merely with reassurance that their appearance is normal.

Many patients with BDD have another psychiatric diagnosis as well; the most common include major depression, psychotic disorders, social phobia, substance abuse disorders, and obsessive-compulsive disorder. (The preoccupation with the imagined or slight defect, with frequent checking behaviors and intrusive thinking, and the favorable response to antiobsessional medications, have led many to consider true BDD as a variant of obsessive-compulsive disorder [9]). Pharmacotherapy of coexisting mental disorders often significantly improves BDD symptoms.

Cosmetic surgery should generally be discouraged, because patients with

BDD who undergo cosmetic surgery often experience more severe psychopathology later (7).

Selective serotonin receptor inhibitors (SSRIs) have been effective in reducing BDD symptoms by at least 50% (10). Relapse of symptoms is common when medication is stopped (7). Antidepressants often used in the treatment of BDD are those with antiobsessional qualities:

- The tricyclic antidepressant clomipramine (Anafranil)
- Selective serotonin reuptake inhibitors (e.g., fluoxetine [Prozac], paroxetine [Paxil], sertraline [Zoloft])

Patients on medication require weekly visits initially for 2 to 4 weeks to enhance compliance with medication and manage side effects. The benefits of the SSRIs are often not seen for 2 to 4 weeks (or longer in the elderly), whereas the side effects generally begin promptly, but are sometimes transient if the patient can be encouraged to continue with treatment. For example, nausea and loose stools may resolve in 7 to 10 days with continued treatment. If the physician monitors the patient closely through the initial problems until some benefit is seen, the patient is often compliant with treatment thereafter. If the patient improves on SSRI treatment, monthly visits may be sufficient for several months. After that, if the patient is stable, visits may be only every 4 months for medication management.

Factitious Disorder

Many approaches have been tried for patients with FD, but no single approach has shown overwhelming success over the others. Referral to a mental health professional for psychotherapy is preferred, but patients rarely accept it. Direct confrontation is rarely successful, but exceptions can occur if this is done in a very supportive environment, which allows the patient to "save face" and agree to a combination of medical and psychotherapeutic treatments.

Patients who must be confronted in an environment that causes them great embarrassment should then be evaluated for possible psychiatric hospitalization, because such a confrontation may challenge and fracture the patient's core identity as a sick person and increase the risk that the patient will become acutely suicidal or psychotic (15).

Another method of management is "treatment without confrontation," which involves the following (16):

- Giving the patient a partial explanation of the illness in medical terms, but stopping short of actually calling the behavior factitious (e.g., suggesting that that the patient's feelings about the major area of conflict in his or her life—marriage, job, etc—might be adversely affecting the healing of the large, deep, chronic wound, which the physician knows is self-inflicted)
- Letting the patient know that you are aware of what is going on, but avoiding confrontation and allowing the patient to save face

The treatment goal is to assist the patient in finding more productive and healthy ways of meeting emotional needs. Follow-up with the family physician may help the patient in coping without the need to develop new signs and symptoms to receive medical attention. Consultation with a mental health professional is almost always needed to establish on an individual basis the frequency and treatment goals for the visits to the family physician.

Factitious Disorder by Proxy

The victim's safety takes first priority, including notifying local authorities responsible for intervention in child or elder abuse and possibly hospitalizing of the victim for safety until those authorities can determine a safe course of action in this disorder, which has a 9% mortality rate (11).

Malingering

It is important to diagnose and treat any coexistent medical or psychiatric disorders. Beyond that, there is no known treatment for malingering itself. Malingering will persist as long as the malingerer considers it beneficial. In some highly structured settings, such as the military or prison environment, the malingerer can be deprived of the usual benefits of the sick role (e.g., the use of radio, television, visitors, and liberty privileges), and this may result in prompt resolution of symptoms (17).

The malingerer should be informed only indirectly that the physician is aware of the deception. The physician might imply to the malingerer that he or she just cannot account for the patient's signs and symptoms, but fortunately they do not seem to indicate a serious disease and the patient can therefore be discharged from medical treatment at this time (18). The malingerer should be told this in a safe environment and should not be labeled a malingerer directly. Very rarely, a malingerer who is so confronted may become violent (19).

Follow-up is uncommon outside the highly structured environments of the military and prisons. In the community, malingerers who are confronted indirectly either go to another physician or stop the behavior if they feel it no longer serves their purpose. If the malingerer has another medical or psychiatric disorder, he or she will need follow-up and treatment for that disorder.

PATIENT EDUCATION

Somatization Disorder, Somatization Disorder Not Otherwise Specified, and Undifferentiated Somatization Disorder

It is important that patients feel that you have taken their complaints and symptoms seriously, investigated them thoroughly, and will "be there" consistently to assess problems in the future. The following are key points to convey to patients:

- The disorder may tend to run in families.
- Medical science does not know the cause.
- Although the disorder causes people to feel distressing symptoms in many areas of the body, it does not threaten longevity.
- The disorder can be managed over time, with some improvement expected over the years.
- It is important to attend the regularly scheduled check-ups to monitor the health status over time and maximize health in spite of multiple, sometimes confusing symptoms.

Family Involvement

The familial consequences and contributions to SD in an individual are very significant. When the physician identifies SD in one patient, the family consequences should be considered and addressed as much as possible. Families with SD may have more illness, use illness more for stress reduction, have more criminal behavior and substance abuse, and generally appear more dysfunctional than control families (20). Children in families with somatizing children have more emergency department visits, more suicidal behavior, and more disability (21). Children in families with somatizing adults had eleven times more emergency department visits and missed school nearly nine times more than children with less somatizing parents (21). Somatization in a child or adolescent may be associated with abuse and may be predicted by parental somatization, substance abuse, or antisocial symptoms (21).

Pain Disorder

The patient with PD should be assured that you have investigated the pain thoroughly and will follow up regularly with the patient. Explain that the goal of treatment is the return to normal function (as much as possible, including coping with chronic pain) and not necessarily complete eradication of pain.

Family Involvement

The chronic pain of one family member may be a central theme for the entire family. For example, a child may feel he or she cannot leave home because of the need to care for the ailing parent. PD also affects families in other ways. The incidence of PD is higher among family members of PD patients, and depression and chemical dependency is more common in those families (7). The most successful treatment of PD includes family assessment and treatment as indicated.

Hypochondriasis

Although the patient is not reassured by a normal physical examination and laboratory findings, it is important to establish that you have performed these steps. The patient may disagree with the diagnosis but still be able to coop-

TABLE 10.4. Summary Table

Disorder	Description	Selected Features	Giving the Diagnosis	Key Treatment Strategies
Somatization disorder (SD)	See Appendix R; evaluate for depression and anxiety disorders	Specific constellation of symptoms with duration of several years; onset before age 30; "illness as a way of life" to get emotional needs met	A "real" medical disorder that runs in families and causes real suffering; it does not reduce longevity; it is not curable but can be safely managed with regularly scheduled follow-up visits	Diagnostic label needed to tie together and validate patient's experience; patients need to feel sure their physician really listens. Regular visits monitoring for the development of new signs or symptoms is key to management
Pain disorder (PD)	See Appendix S; evaluate for depression and anxiety disorders	The patient's focus is on the intensity of the pain itself; can often become chronic; early intervention with expectation of prompt recovery is the most helpful approach	Perhaps accompanied by other conditions; ensure the patient that thorough medical evaluation has been done and that it is understood that the patient suffers pain	Treatment goal is the restoration of as close to normal function as possible in spite of pain—goal is not to be pain-free, although it is hoped for with time; regular follow-up is key
Hypochondriasis	See Appendix T; evaluate for depression and anxiety disorders	Fear of having a serious disease is primary focus; patient not reassured by a normal medical evaluation; needs a label/diagnosis that helps to feel validated	Patient should know that some people have neurologic amplification of bodily sensations; what they feel is real. Because there is no known way to turn down this amplification, it is important to schedule regular checkups to medically monitor their status	As in SD and PD, regularly scheduled follow-up is key; after initial thorough evaluation, further tests prompted only by new objective signs or symptoms

continued

T ABLE 10.4. *continued* Summary Table

Disorder	Description	Selected Features	Giving the Diagnosis	Key Treatment Strategies
Conversion disorder	See Appendix U; most patients are found to have some organic pathology to at least partially explain their symptoms	Neurologic deficit or other symptom, unintentionally produced to meet some psychologic need; most are resolved by the time of hospital discharge	This diagnosis should rarely, if ever, be given	Be aware of the possibility of another explanation for symptoms; encourage the patient to find healthier ways to meet psychologic needs
Factitious disorders	See Appendix V; may be more common among health care workers; often chronic, with presentations dramatic and vague	Sick role intentionally produced in patient (or patient's child/elder) to try to meet some usually unknown psychologic need	Presenting the diagnosis without confrontation by the use of therapeutic double bind allows the patient to save face	Avoidance of confrontation preferable, but at times cannot be avoided; secure the safety of victims of factitious disorder by proxy
Malingering	Not a medical diagnosis; suspect when there is clear secondary gain; be certain that other medical conditions do not coexist	Intentional deceptive behavior with clear goals	Best to avoid stating the diagnosis of malingering to the patient; if it must be told, it should be done in a safe environment with others present	Let the person know indirectly that what's going on is known to prevent facilitation of the deception; avoid direct confrontation; (Physicians have been seriously harmed by direct confrontation.)

Adapted from McCahill ME. Somatoform and related disorders: delivery of diagnosis as first step. Am Fam Physician 1995;52:193–204.

erate with the follow-up plan. The following are key points to convey to the patient:

- The patient has a syndrome that amplifies normal bodily sensations and that the sensations themselves do not threaten the patient's longevity.
- Management of this syndrome consists of frequent, regularly scheduled visits with the physician, during which the symptoms will be reviewed to monitor the patient's health over time.

Family Involvement

Family relationships are often strained by hypochondriasis in one or more of its members. It may be helpful to explain to close family members, with the patient's permission and preferably in the presence of the patient, that the problem is a syndrome of unknown cause that amplifies bodily sensations and which can feel very frightening. The family can be of great assistance in day-to-day management of symptoms and compliance with regular follow-up visits.

Conversion Disorder

It is not helpful to explain to the patient that there is no physiologic basis for his or her problem, because the patient with true CD generally has no insight and is unlikely to develop it in the acute setting. If possible, it is beneficial to encourage the patient to find more appropriate ways of satisfying his or her emotional needs.

Family Involvement

Family members are essential in establishing the precipitating event or events for the CD symptoms and in helping the patient develop a new approach to coping with the overwhelming stressor.

Body Dysmorphic Disorder

It is important to acknowledge the BDD patients' distress and concern over appearance, despite the normal physical examination. Explain that although medication will not change their physical appearance, it may relieve some of their symptoms of distress.

Family Involvement

Involving the family is generally beneficial but must be carefully planned. The physician must take care to avoid any tendency for family members to inadvertently worsen patients' symptoms and strain their interpersonal relationships. For example, a family member who hears the physician's reassurance that the patient's appearance is normal but does not fully understand the nature of BDD may tell the patient, "The doctor said you're normal, so just stop it!" The patient cannot stop.

The physician may, with the patient's permission, talk individually with family members, explaining the nature of BDD as an illness requiring understanding and support from those close to them and possibly requiring medication and follow-up care.

Factitious Disorder

Gentle, indirect confrontation of the patient with the fact that the physician is aware of the factitious nature of the illness may be as much as the patient can be expected to absorb. If the patient is successfully referred to a psychotherapist, he or she may be able to develop more insight over time into the psychological nature of FD.

Family Involvement

Some have advocated that the indirect confrontation of the patient with FD may, in some cases, be best done in the presence of very supportive family members (16).

Consultation with a psychiatrist or psychologist with expertise in the management of FD before proceeding with such a family intervention would be helpful.

If FD by proxy is discovered, obtain psychiatric consultation as well as involve child protective agencies as the parents are told of the diagnosis and treatment.

Malingering

Because of the nature of malingering, patient education does not apply in the usual sense. As Mills and Lipian have noted, "Malingerers do not wish to be treated. The last thing they desire is to have their condition diagnosed. They are consciously gaming the system, manipulating in the hopes of achieving personal gain of some kind" (12).

Family Involvement

Only rarely are family members available in an active malingering, and little is known about them.

SUMMARY

A quick overview of somatoform and factitious disorders and malingering is included in Table 10.4.

REFERENCES

1. Rasmussen NH, Avant RF. Somatization disorder in family practice. Am Fam Physician 1989; 40:206–214.
2. American Psychiatric Association. Diagnostic and statistical manual of mental disorders. 4th ed. (DSM-IV) Washington, DC: American Psychiatric Association, 1994:445–475; 683;725–727.

3. Smith GR. The course of somatization and its effects on utilization of health care resources. Psychosomatics 1994;35:263-267.

4. Smith GR. Toward more effective recognition and management of somatization disorder. J Fam Pract 1987;25:551-552.

5. Smith GR, Rost K, Kashner TM. A trial of the effect of a standardized psychiatric consultation on health outcomes and costs in somatizing patients. Arch Gen Psychiatry 1995;52:238-243.

6. Smith GR, Monson RA, Ray DC. Patients with multiple unexplained symptoms: their characteristics, functional health, and health care utilization. Arch Intern Med 1986;146:69-72.

7. Guggenheim FG, Smith GR. Somatoform disorders. In: Kaplan HI, Sadock BJ, eds. Comprehensive textbook of psychiatry/VI. 6th ed. Baltimore: Williams & Wilkins, 1995:1251-1270.

8. Ford CV, Folks DG. Conversion disorders: an overview. Psychosomatics 1985;26: 371-383.

9. Ford CV. Dimensions of somatization and hypochondriasis. Neurol Clin 1995;13:241-253.

10. Kaplan HI, Sadock BJ, Grebb JA, eds. Kaplan and Sadock's synopsis of psychiatry: behavioral sciences, clinical psychiatry. 7th ed. Baltimore: Williams & Wilkins, 1994:628.

11. Rosenberg DA. Web of deceit: a literature review of Munchausen syndrome by proxy. Child Abuse Neglect 1987;11:547-563.

12. Mills MJ, Lipian MS. Malingering. In: Kaplan HI, Sadock BJ, eds. Comprehensive textbook of psychiatry/VI. 6th ed. Baltimore: Williams & Wilkins, 1995:1614-1622.

13. Cloninger CR. Somatoform and dissociative disorders. In: Winokur G, Clayton PJ, eds. The medical basis of psychiatry. 2nd ed. Philadelphia: WB Saunders, 1994:169-192.

14. Taylor S, Hyler SE. Update on factitious disorders. Int J Psychiatr Med 1993; 23:81-94.

15. Jones RM. Factitious disorders. In: Kaplan HI, Sadock BJ, eds. Comprehensive textbook of psychiatry/VI. 6th ed. Baltimore: Williams & Wilkins, 1995:1271-1279.

16. Eisendrath SJ. Factitious physical disorders: treatment without confrontation. Psychosomatics 1989;30:383-387.

17. Ford CV. The somatizing disorders: illness as a way of life. New York: Elsevier, 1983.

18. Purcell TB. The somatic patient. Emerg Med Clin North Am 1991;9:137-159.

19. Gorman WF. Legal neurology and malingering: cases and techniques. St. Louis: Warren Green, Inc, 1993:139-169.

20. deGruy FV, Dickinson P, Dickinson L, et al. The families of patients with somatization disorder. Fam Med 1989; 21: 438-442.

21. Livingston R, Witt A, Smith GR. Families who somatize. J Dev Behav Pediatr 1995;16:42-46.

CHAPTER 11

Margaret E. McCahill

Substance Use Disorders

On a tombstone at Winchester Cathedral:

Here lies a Hampshire Grenadier
Who caught his death
Drinking cold small beer.
A good soldier is ne'er forgot
Whether he dieth by musket
Or by pot.

From "Bill's Story" in *Alcoholics Anonymous, The Big Book*

The impact of the substance use disorders on the lives of those who suffer them and their families is enormous. The substance use disorders are the most common cause of preventable morbidity and mortality. The annual economic cost of alcohol and drug abuse in the United States was an estimated $114 billion in 1985, and this figure excluded costs related to tobacco use (1).

CHIEF COMPLAINT

Patients with a substance use disorder only rarely come to the physician stating that they have a problem with substance use, abuse, or dependence. Most often, the patient complains of some symptom resulting from the substance use (Table 11.1). Alternatively, a family member may alert the physician to the patient's substance use disorder, whether directly or indirectly. Thus, a chief complaint of any sort may lead to an ultimate diagnosis of a substance use disorder.

The most common presentation for the patient with alcoholism is a neatly dressed, employed person with an intact family who comes to the physician with no signs of either alcohol use or withdrawal. This is also the case for most of the other drugs of abuse. The stereotypic "skid row" alcoholic represents only 5% of those with alcohol abuse and dependence (6). The physician must have a high index of suspicion and look for problems related to substance abuse in virtually all patients.

EPIDEMIOLOGIC CONSIDERATIONS

The National Institutes of Mental Health Epidemiologic Catchment Area Study conducted in the early 1980s found that 16.7% of the US population ages 18 and older met diagnostic criteria for a lifetime diagnosis of either abuse or dependence on some substance, with 13.8% meeting the criteria for an alcohol-related disorder and 6.2% meeting the criteria for substance abuse or dependence on substances other than alcohol or tobacco (1).

In 1978 to 1979, 10% of high school seniors were using cannabis (marijuana or hashish) on a daily basis; this declined to 5% by 1984 and 2% by 1991 (1). Prevalent cocaine use began in the United States in the 1970s. Estimates now put current use of cocaine (within the last 30 days) at 0.6% of the population (1). Nearly 2% of high school students reported using lysergic acid diethylamide (LSD) within the last 30 days in the 1991 High School Survey (2). Phencyclidine (PCP) use is sporadic but has been increasing in some high school populations (2).

At some time during their lives, 90% of the population of the United States drinks alcohol, with most people starting in their early to mid-teens (3). At least 25% of all hospitalized patients have a significant alcohol problem, regardless of the admitting diagnosis, and 20% of patients seen in a primary care physician's office have an alcohol problem (4).

The combination of nicotine addiction and cigarette smoking has been called the principal cause of preventable disease, disability, and premature death in the United States (5). Men who smoke cigarettes have a 70% higher death rate compared with that of nonsmoking men. Cigarette smoking is responsible for 390,000 premature deaths in the United States each year (5).

History

In the history of a patient with substance use disorder, clues to a substance use disorder fall into one or more of the following areas listed in Table 11.2.

If a patient has problems in any *one* of the four categories in Table 11.2 and is aware of the problem but continues to use the substance anyway, the patient has a substance use disorder (6,7).

Keep in mind that the amount of the substance used is not the determining factor; it is the fact that drinking or using continues in spite of deleterious consequences and impairment. Thus, the patient who says that he or she could not possibly be alcoholic, because "I only drink beer" or wine, needs help understanding that the amount or type of alcohol consumed is not the determining factor.

The essential feature of dependence is a cluster of cognitive, behavioral, and physiologic symptoms indicating that the person is continuing substance use despite significant substance-related problems (7).

TABLE 1 1 . 1 .   Common Complaints by Substance Type

ALCOHOL
Insomnia
Gastrointestinal symptoms
Memory and cognitive problems
Symptoms of a mood disorder
Anxiety
Sexual dysfunction (acutely, alcohol consumption may increase libido, but even modest use may interfere with erectile function in men, and long-term alcoholism will cause impotence [2])
Alcoholic stigmata

SNORTED OR SMOKED DRUGS
Nose bleeds
Respiratory symptoms

OPIATES
Chronic pain, most often in the back, joints, or muscles
Migraine
Chronic constipation
Anorexia
Nausea
Vomiting

COCAINE, AMPHETAMINE, OR OTHER STIMULANTS
Fatigue and depression as a consequence of "coming down" off the drug
Insomnia
Mood changes, psychosis, other psychiatric symptoms

Screening

Every physician should screen every patient for substance use disorders. Whether a physician uses the CAGE questions (Table 11.3) or another questionnaire or style of inquiry, the important thing is to have a regular format and routine for screening every single patient.

In addition to screening for alcohol use, all patients should be asked about the following:

- Smoking—tobacco, marijuana, or any other substance
- Use of any other recreational drugs and, if so, the method of administration
- Intravenous drug use—now or at any time in the past

TABLE 11.2. Clues to Substance Abuse in the History

PROBLEMS AT WORK OR SCHOOL
Decline in level of performance
Absenteeism
Erratic behavior (e.g., returning to work late from the lunch hour, a change in mood or irritability)
Neglecting duties or assignments

LEGAL COMPLICATIONS
More than one DUI (driving under the influence of alcohol) charge
Any DUI for illegal substances
Arrests for disorderly conduct or assaults while under the influence of a substance
Legal consequences for possession of illegal substances

DETERIORATION OF RELATIONSHIPS
Estrangement from friends and family members as attachment to the substance grows
Family members suffer the effects of the person spending progressively more time in obtaining the substance and recovering from its use.
Economic hardship as more and more of the family's funds are spent on substance use.

DETERIORATION IN HEALTH
Alcoholic hepatitis or any of the many physical complications of alcoholism
Chronic obstructive lung disease in a cigarette smoker
Mood disorder or other mental illness in a patient who uses cocaine or amphetamine

TABLE 11.3. The CAGE Questionnaire

1. Have you ever thought about **C**utting down?
2. Have you ever felt **A**nnoyed when others criticize your drinking?
3. Have you ever felt **G**uilty about your drinking?
4. Have you ever used alcohol as an **E**ye opener?
Score one point for each positive answer; a score of 2 or 3 suggests alcohol problems (3).

Adolescents and at-risk children need to be asked screening questions without their parents present to allow them to speak honestly without fear of consequences. For the same reason, it may also be important to ask adults about their substance use without other family members present. However, if a patient (child or adult) denies substance use but you suspect it from the history and physical findings, it may be necessary to ask family members.

All patients should be asked these questions about the full spectrum of substance use at:

- The first visit
- All health maintenance visits
- Any acute visit during which the physician wonders if substance use could be a factor

PHYSICAL EXAMINATION

In most cases, the physical examination provides no information about substance use until the stigmata of complications develop. Ideally, patients should be treated for substance use disorders before these complications occur. Be aware of multiple drug use problems, because multiple drug use is common.

Alcohol Abuse or Dependence

Patients with alcohol abuse or dependence may have many physical findings; alcoholism has been called "the great mimicker" of numerous physical and psychiatric illnesses (6). Although not always present, findings may include the following (6):

- Gastritis
- Ulcer disease
- Ascites
- Enlarged liver
- Very small cirrhotic liver
- Pancreatitis
- Splenomegaly
- Palmar erythema
- Testicular atrophy
- Elevated blood pressure
- Alcoholic cardiomyopathy (in advanced disease)
- Peripheral neuropathy (possibly in 5% to 15% of chronic alcoholics)
- Wernicke's syndrome (sixth-nerve palsy and ataxia)
- Korsakoff's syndrome (profound inability to learn new information along with retrograde amnesia and impairment in visuospatial and conceptual reasoning, but with normal intelligence)
- Cerebellar degeneration (in perhaps 1% of chronic alcoholics)

Alcoholic patients may develop severe cognitive difficulties with recent and remote memory, which may last for weeks after binge drinking. An increase in the size of the brain ventricles and sulci is seen in alcoholic patients, but this is due to loss of white matter in the brain and not necessarily to neuronal loss (8). Although the loss of white matter may help explain some of the functional impairment in chronic alcoholism, the structural changes are somewhat reversible, with restoration of white matter if the patient can maintain sobriety (6,8).

Alcohol levels and resulting impairment are listed in Table 11.4.

Alcohol Withdrawal

The patient who is admitted to the hospital for any medical problem may begin to show signs and symptoms of physical withdrawal from alcohol within hours of abstinence. Alcohol withdrawal signs and symptoms may include the following (9):

- Tremor
- Insomnia
- Anxiety
- Craving for alcohol
- Anorexia
- Nausea
- Vomiting
- Diaphoresis
- Hypertension
- Tachycardia
- Agitation
- Irritability

TABLE 11.4.   Impairment at Different Blood Alcohol Levels

Blood Alcohol Concentration	Likely Impairment
20–30 mg/dL(i.e., after 1 or 2 drinks)	Slowed motor performance and thinking ability
30–80 mg/dL	Increases in motor and cognitive problems
80–200 mg/dL	Incoordination problems and judgement errors, labile mood, deterioration in cognition
200–300 mg/dL	Nystagmus, marked slurring of speech, "blackouts"
>300 mg/dL	Respiratory arrest, impaired vital signs, death

Reprinted with permission from Schuckit MA. Alcohol-related disorders. In: Kaplan HI, Sadock BJ, eds. Comprehensive textbook of psychiatry/VI. 6th ed. Baltimore: Williams & Wilkins, 1995:775–791. Note: Tolerance can occur; patients can be seen alert and talking coherently with blood alcohol levels higher than 400 mg/dL, but these patients are still at risk of respiratory arrest and death at that level of intoxication.

Withdrawal symptoms may start within hours of decreased intake of alcohol and usually resolve within 2 days. One or two generalized seizures may occur, usually within 24 to 48 hours after decreased alcohol intake. Some patients develop a more severe withdrawal syndrome including hallucinosis with or without delirium tremens (9).

Depressant Withdrawal

It is important to note that a similar withdrawal syndrome can develop in patients dependent on other central nervous system (CNS) depressants, such as benzodiazepines and meprobamate.

It is important to promptly recognize the withdrawal syndrome due to alcohol or other CNS depressants, assess its severity, and quickly determine whether the withdrawal can be managed on an out-patient basis (low risk, mild symptoms) or whether hospitalization will be required.

Opioid Abuse

The patient with opioid abuse or dependence may show the following on physical examination:

- Needle marks (tracks) from intravenous injections
- Heart murmur (suggesting bacterial endocarditis as a complication)
- Signs of intoxication

A patient examined at the time of opioid use may demonstrate (10):

- Hypotension
- Decreased respiratory drive
- Vomiting
- Constricted pupils
- Mental status changes

Amphetamines

The patient examined while under the influence of amphetamines may have the following:

- Euphoria
- Mood elevation
- High sense of energy
- Paranoia
- Delusions
- Psychosis
- Tachycardia
- Elevated blood pressure
- Pupillary dilatation

Physical complications such as the following may occur (7):

• Intracranial hemorrhage
• Cardiac arrhythmia
• Acute heart failure

Cocaine

Cocaine use may produce a picture similar to that of amphetamine on clinical examination (11). Cocaine is taken orally, intranasally, intravenously, sometimes combined with heroin (speedballing), and via smoking or subcutaneous injection (popping). Cocaine use produces euphoria and a clinical picture of sympathetic nervous system stimulation, which users often try to modulate with alcohol. The use of alcohol and cocaine together results in a compound called *ethylcocaine,* which has cardiovascular effects similar to cocaine alone. The toxic consequences can be additive when ethylcocaine and cocaine are present together (2). Physical findings vary by mode of cocaine use and may include the following:

• Irritation, ulceration, or perforation of the nasal septum (from snorting)
• Tracks (from intravenous use)
• Pulmonary findings, cardiac arrhythmias, stroke, or heart failure (from smoking "free-base" [crack])

It is important to recognize the physical signs of acute cocaine intoxication or overdose, because this is a true medical emergency and the patient should be managed in the intensive care unit (2).

Marijuana

Patients who use marijuana may show the following on physical examination:

• Conjunctival injection
• Tachycardia (tolerance for the tachycardia develops in daily users)
• Pulmonary disease and chronic bronchial irritation (may develop in some)

Lysergic Acid Diethylamide

The physical examination of the patient who has used even very small doses of LSD will show the following:

• Tachycardia
• Hypertension
• Pupillary dilatation
• Tremor
• Hyperpyrexia
• Mental status changes
• Spasm of cerebral arteries (in some patients)

Phencyclidine

PCP can be taken orally, by smoking, or intravenously. The patient who has taken PCP will have the following (2):

- Excitement
- Agitation
- Dysarthria
- Impaired motor coordination

Possible additional findings may include:

- Nystagmus
- Flushing
- Diaphoresis
- Hyperacusis
- Mental status changes

Following are possible advanced sequelae:

- Hypersalivation
- Vomiting
- Myoclonus
- Fever
- Stupor
- Coma
- Spasm of cerebral arteries

It is important to recognize the physical finding suggestive of PCP intoxication and overdose, because management of the coma, seizures, and respiratory depression that can complicate this intoxication requires admission to an intensive care unit (2).

Nicotine Addiction

Findings on physical examination vary according to the extent of tobacco use. The most obvious physical findings in smokers are pulmonary:

- Chronic obstructive pulmonary disease (COPD)
- Dyspnea
- Tachypnea
- Chronic cough
- Breathlessness
- Wheezing
- Distant breath sound on stethoscopic auscultation
- Cyanosis (severe COPD)

Findings may also include oral lesions, which need investigation to rule out carcinoma, esophageal disease, gastritis, ulcers, and cancer, for which smoking increases the risk (9).

Smoking is also a major contributor to premature coronary heart disease, and the patient may have arteriosclerosis and signs of peripheral vascular disease as well (5).

DIAGNOSTIC TESTING

All patients with suspected or confirmed substance use disorders should have the following performed:

Complete blood count (CBC) with differential and red cell indices. Patients with alcoholism often have an elevated mean corpuscular volume (MCV) and may have anemia.

A chemistry panel. Patients with alcoholism may have disturbances in glucose level and electrolytes, elevated uric acid level, and elevated triglycerides. Patients with alcoholism and many other substance use disorders may have elevated liver transaminases.

Gamma-glutamyl transferase (GGT). GGT should be tested if alcoholism is suspected; elevations are 80% sensitive and specific for alcoholism (10).

Vitamin B_{12} level. This level should be checked, especially if the MCV is elevated, because folate treatment can mask vitamin B_{12} deficiency until after neurologic complications develop.

Thyroid-stimulating hormone (TSH). TSH may be indicated in many patients, as well as serologic tests for syphilis (RPR or VDRL).

Amylase, lipase, and coagulation studies. These tests may be indicated in some patients with alcoholism.

Human immunodeficiency virus (HIV). HIV testing should be performed in all patients with a history of intravenous drug use and those who have had sexual relations with intravenous drug users or who have engaged in behavior that is high-risk for HIV.

Urine drug testing. Urine drug testing should be performed in many patients in whom substance use disorders are suspected, with the exception of those with nicotine dependence alone or in the event of a reasonable certainty of alcoholism alone. For example, the patient using amphetamines may be indistinguishable from a patient with schizophrenia on clinical examination. It is crucial to obtain a urine drug screen (UDS) during an acute episode to establish the correct diagnosis. Polydrug use is so common that even if the physician is aware of one drug of abuse, there may be other drugs that need attention in the acute management of the very ill patient. The UDS may be essential in establishing such a diagnosis.

Electrocardiogram (ECG). ECG should be performed in most patients.

Pulmonary function testing. Testing may be indicated in some patients with nicotine dependence.

Ultrasound of the abdomen and a computed tomographic scan of the head. These studies may be indicated in many patients with alcoholism.

Additional diagnostic tests. Additional tests may be indicated, depending on the combination of substances used, the sequelae suspected at the time of examination, and the presence of other medical conditions.

WHEN TO REFER

Referral to a substance abuse treatment program and to Alcoholics Anonymous (AA) or Narcotics Anonymous (NA) is one of the essential steps of management of the patient with a substance use disorder. In addition, patients with a dual diagnosis (those with both substance abuse and another mental disorder) may need referral to a mental health provider because the combination makes treatment of both disorders more challenging.

The patient with complications of substance use may also benefit from referral. (For example, the intravenous drug user with hepatitis C may need referral to a special center for the latest therapy.)

Even if the patient has a need for referral, the family physician should stay involved with the patient in support of his or her recovery.

MANAGEMENT

The management of the substance use disorders by the family physician consists of five essential steps:

1. Identification of the alcoholism or substance use disorder and empathetically confronting the patient so that he or she can acknowledge the illness
2. Treating the medical and psychiatric complications of the alcoholism or substance use disorder
3. Providing detoxification, if needed
4. Referring the patient to rehabilitation programs
5. Counseling the patient in an inpatient or outpatient setting (follow-up)

Identification and Confrontation

Identification of the problem requires thoroughness on the part of the physician to pursue a comprehensive substance use history and medical work up. Confronting the patient is often necessary to overcome the patient's typical denial. It is important to realize that the process of educational confrontation is rarely effective in a single visit. Nevertheless, it is important to acknowledge the patient's problem and begin the process.

Even fairly brief statements by the physician to a "problem drinker" consistently result in significant reductions in alcohol use, even if the patient does continue to drink (12,13). One study showed that problem drinkers who receive 10 to 15 minutes of counseling about alcohol use have decreased health care utilization (fewer emergency department visits and inpatient hospital days) along with their decreased alcohol use (13).

Confrontation Strategy

1. Gather all of the history, physical findings, and laboratory evidence.
2. Meet with the patient and one or more family members.
3. Present the medical evidence that the substance use is impairing health. The family member can provide the evidence of impairment in job or school, relationships, or legal problems.
4. Present the evidence and your concern in a caring, nonjudgmental (nonblaming) way.
5. Sometimes it is helpful to have present at the meeting a clergyperson selected by the family, or a substance abuse specialist.
6. To help the patient understand the seriousness and scope of the problem, it may be helpful to use imagery such as calling alcohol the "universal solvent"—it dissolves stomachs, livers, brains, jobs, families, bank accounts, credit ratings, drivers' licenses, and the future hopes and dreams of those with alcoholism. Imagery such as this, presented in an empathetic way, may help the patient agree to substance abuse treatment, which can be lifesaving.
7. After presenting the evidence and expressing concern (the physician's and family member's), ask the patient to agree to the following:

   • Stop all substance use immediately.
   • Go through a detoxification protocol, if needed.
   • Get into a substance abuse treatment program.

Tobacco Confrontation

A similar confrontation meeting may be appropriate for the patient with nicotine addiction, but more often the physician can simply bring up the topic of smoking cessation in the course of a typical acute office visit for sinusitis, bronchitis, or any cigarette-related problem. The physician points out that these problems are "evidence" of the health consequences of smoking and advises the patient to quit. It is helpful for the physician to give the patient a personalized message and to set a formal quit date (5).

For the patient who firmly refuses to quit smoking, an example of a personalized message is to explain that although we almost never "guarantee" anything in medicine, we can make an exception with smokers. The physician then gives the patient a note on a prescription form (see box below) that describes the health consequences of smoking. The guarantee should be signed and given to the patient to take home, perhaps for placement on the bathroom mirror or refrigerator, as a "transitional object" from the physician and a way to deliver the message repeatedly. Patients may come in weeks to years later to say they have gotten this message and really intend to quit smoking.

Treatment

Therapy for the medical and psychiatric consequences of substance use disorders should be individualized for each patient's combination of substances and medical problems.

Detoxification

The task of providing detoxification is most serious with withdrawal from alcohol or other CNS depressant use.

Alcohol Withdrawal

If the patient is withdrawing from alcohol and has minimal symptoms and a low-risk profile for seizures, DTs, and other life-threatening complications, detoxification could be accomplished in an out-patient setting. Many approaches have been developed to manage alcohol withdrawal.

Some of the most mild withdrawal symptoms are managed with close supervision of a reliable person who will provide emotional support and bring the patient to emergent medical attention if symptoms escalate. This can be provided in a "social detox program," which is often staffed by other recovering persons.

If the patient is having some physical symptoms that need treatment but still is considered low risk, an out-patient medication regimen can be established with daily physician follow-up, using either a fixed-schedule dose, "front-loading" schedule, or symptom-triggered therapy with benzodiazepines (9).

Hospitalization for detoxification from alcohol may be indicated in a patient with any of the following risk factors (9):

PRESCRIPTION FOR SURVIVAL

Mr/Ms Smoking Patient (name); date (today's); in the Rx space:

"I guarantee you emphysema and a life of gasping for breath attached to an oxygen tank. You may also get lung cancer, but you will definitely get COPD, emphysema, and heart problems, if the cancer doesn't get you first. This guarantee is only good if you continue to smoke. You could stop smoking *now* and void this guarantee. I hope you will stop smoking."

- Long duration or large amount of alcohol intake
- Intense alcohol craving
- Prior history of detoxification or seizures or delirium tremens
- Severe withdrawal symptoms on initial examination
- Comorbid medical illness

Management of severe withdrawal syndromes and detoxification is beyond the scope of this chapter. Once the acute detoxification period is over (usually in less than 1 week), benzodiazepines or other sedative-hypnotic agents should not generally be used for patients with alcoholism (6).

Opioid Withdrawal

Detoxification of patients with opioid dependence is usually best done by placing the patient on a long-acting opioid, such as methadone, and rapidly tapering the patient off of the medication. Most patients require between 10 to 25 mg of methadone orally given twice on day 1. After a few days of stabilized symptoms, the dose is reduced by 10 to 20% of the original day 1 dose each day until the methadone is stopped (10).

Nicotine Withdrawal

Patients with nicotine addition will sometimes request nicotine replacement therapy to help them stop smoking. Some of these preparations (e.g., nicotine chewing gum and nicotine patches) are available without prescription. Generally, it is advisable for patients to be actively participating in a smoking cessation support group if they choose to use nicotine replacement therapy. Without such support to assist the patient in truly stopping their smoking altogether, what often happens is that the patient uses the nicotine gum or patch and continues to smoke, making the addition and potential consequences worse. For those who are motivated and willing to participate in a full program, however, nicotine replacement may be very helpful.

Rehabilitation Programs

Referral to a rehabilitation program is a key point in the management of substance abuse disorders. Only about 20% of alcoholic patients will achieve permanent abstinence without participation in a formal treatment program (3). For the rest of those who suffer other forms of substance use disorders, a treatment program is essential to maintain their motivation for abstinence and to reorganize their lives with friends and goals that are substance-free.

There are many types of successful programs; patients must choose an approach that seems best suited to their personal needs. It is important for the physician to convey to the patient and family that substance abuse treatment in general, and alcohol abuse treatment in particular, really works.

Physicians should be familiar with the programs in their local area and have the phone numbers available to give to patients for whom they are appropriate.

Alcoholics Anonymous

AA is one of the most successful rehabilitation programs. There are no fees or dues to join AA, and the only requirement is an honest desire to stop drinking. AA is based on a 12-step approach, and although a deity or "higher power" is mentioned in several of the AA steps, there are atheist AA groups and agnostic AA groups. In fact, there is an AA group that addresses nearly every religious or philosophical variation. AA meetings are also available in many languages; they can be found in every location in the United States (check the local telephone book).

Although some AA meetings are closed to the public, guests are welcome at "open" AA meetings; the interested physician can personally attend an AA meeting and thus tell patients, "I've visited an AA meeting myself." Even if the patient goes to an in-patient substance abuse treatment program, it is likely that he or she will be advised as part of a discharge plan to go to regular meetings of AA.

AA Equivalents

There is a corresponding group called Narcotics Anonymous (NA) for opiate and other drug abusers. Many areas have local program for patients recovering from other specific forms of substance abuse or dependence.

Support for Family Members

Family members may benefit from attending Alanon or Ala-teen, which are 12-step recovery programs for family members or teens of those who have alcoholism. Alanon and Ala-teen can also help the family members of an alcoholic who continues to drink to cope with the pain of ongoing alcoholism in their family.

Community Treatment

Many patients with substance use disorders other than alcohol or nicotine need in-patient treatment followed by living in a drug-free program or halfway house, which uses a therapeutic community approach for up to 1 year to ensure abstinence (10).

Medications

Medication management of nicotine addition and detoxification of other substances has already been discussed, and medications are generally not indicated for other substance use disorders.

Alcohol. Patients with alcoholism should be advised to take a general multiple vitamin supplement (including folate) every day, plus thiamine, 100 mg orally per day, for at least 1 to 4 weeks as they begin their recovery program (6). Disulfiram (Antabuse) has very limited usefulness and is not routinely prescribed (6).

Cocaine. Some studies have suggested that the tricyclic antidepressant desipramine may be helpful in decreasing the craving for cocaine, even when depressive symptoms are not present (2).

PCP. It is important to avoid the use of phenothiazines when treating the acute psychosis and potentially violent manifestations of PCP abuse and intoxication. These drugs can potentiate PCP's adverse effects. Monitor for and treat hypoglycemia, a common sequela. Treatment for PCP abuse is a supportive, quiet environment, and haloperidol (Haldol) and possibly lorazepam (Ativan) are used to sedate the patient with acute PCP psychosis and agitation (2). Doses are individualized, depending on body mass, severity of symptoms, other medical conditions, and potential drug interactions.

FOLLOW-UP

Follow-up is the essential fifth step of the management program. Patients require frequent follow-up visits for at least 1 full year of the patient's recovery from substance use and dependence. During these visits, the physician provides counseling and support because the patient may struggle to maintain his or her resolve to remain abstinent. The following are possible issues for the patient (6):

- Organizing life without alcohol or other substances
- Dealing with free time without substances
- Dealing with friends who drink or use substances
- Dealing with certain jobs in which drinking is expected
- Dealing with the physical adjustments that occur in the recovery process

Recovery Symptoms
Symptoms commonly encountered in the early weeks of recovery include sleep disturbances and mood shifts. These resolve with proper sleep hygiene, nutrition, and rest. If patients do not have someone to assist them in understanding these symptoms, relapse might be more likely.

Relapses
It is important to help patients understand that relapses, if they occur, are to be discussed and then put to rest. For some patients, successful recovery is defined as longer and longer periods of sobriety; they should be counseled against viewing anything except strict abstinence as a failure.

Continuing Users
In the follow-up of patients who continue active substance abuse or dependence, it is important to present the evidence of the illness and need for treat-

ment in a nonjudgmental way at each therapeutic opportunity. House officers often say, "Why should I waste my time talking to him about alcoholism again today? He knows and he continues to drink anyway—why bother?" The saddest mistake physicians sometimes make is to just give up on a person with a substance use disorder. It may be that for the advice to register with this patient, so that he or she acknowledges the problem and enters recovery, the patient needs to hear about it 3000 times; today we are on number 2150. This is not wasted effort—we need to keep on working with the patient and present our intervention with each opportunity.

PATIENT AND FAMILY EDUCATION

There are few areas in medicine in which patient and family education are as important as in the treatment of substance use disorders. Most of the management previously described is aimed at educating the patient and family about the nature of their disorder and the need for abstinence. However, this

IS ALCOHOLISM GENETIC?

All substance use, including alcohol use, is behavior maintained by its consequences—both the positive reinforcement of how one feels under the influence, and the negative consequences when drug use is interrupted. Alcohol use is influenced by cultural and religious factors, but the evidence also supports a genetic vulnerability to alcoholism (3). Some of the data supporting genetic influences in alcoholism include:
- Close family members of an alcoholic have a fourfold increased risk of alcoholism
- The identical twin of an alcoholic has a higher risk of alcoholism than a fraternal twin
- Adopted-away children of an alcoholic have a fourfold increased risk of alcoholism (3).

A large 15-year study of 227 sons of alcoholic fathers compared with 227 matched control subjects revealed an important marker regarding vulnerability for alcoholism in the future (12). The study found that some subjects did not realize just how much they were impaired or affected by the amount of alcohol in their system. The individuals who had a lower sensitivity to modest doses of alcohol had a significant increase in the risk of future alcoholism, perhaps because they drink more heavily and more often to get the same effect as those with normal sensitivity.

The alcohol-naive young man who does not perceive the effect of his elevated blood alcohol level is at risk for developing alcoholism and should be so warned (14). Future research may clarify this issue for women.

process of educational confrontation is rarely effective in a single visit. Often patients negotiate and want to just cut down their use of alcohol or other drugs. It is important to realize that the patient is the one who must decide to abstain from substance use, and the physician should strive to provide education and "keep the door open" to future therapeutic opportunities.

AA and Alanon can provide patients and families with many excellent educational materials regarding substance abuse and dependence.

Risk reduction and health promotion

Most of the substance use disorders begin in childhood, adolescence, or young adulthood. Physicians can educate parents to be vigilant about the peer group their children choose to associate with. Young people should be encouraged to "hang out" with academic teams, supervised team sports, scouts, church groups, and family groups, all of which are likely to discourage or openly forbid substance use.

Children and adolescents should be taught by their family about the norms and appropriateness of alcohol use. Teenagers and young adults should be advised about any family history of substance use disorders, just as they should be about a family history of diseases such as diabetes, hypertension, and cancer.

We should advise adolescents and young adults that if they have a parent with alcoholism, they have a fourfold increased risk of developing it themselves and that they need to consider that fact in their own decision of whether or not to drink and how to monitor how much they drink. When we see a young man or woman who "holds his/her liquor well," that is, seems to be able to drink and not show it or not realize it, we should advise that person that research shows that this trait may suggest a vulnerability to developing alcoholism later and that he or she will need to be extra cautious about alcohol use.

We are, as a society, bringing about regulations that will reduce the availability of cigarettes to children and restrict the advertisement of cigarettes as a glamorous or "sophisticated" product. The American Academy of Family Physicians is a resource for the program TAR WARS for physicians to obtain and use in their practice to aid in the prevention of nicotine addiction.

These are just a few examples of how physicians can take steps to prevent substance use disorders.

Additional and individualized steps in primary prevention will become apparent in each medical practice if physicians keep a very high awareness of the prevalence and impact of substance use disorders and an awareness of the opportunity that the physician has to have a very large impact on this problem.

REFERENCES

1. Jaffe JH. Amphetamine (or amphetamine-like) related disorders. In: Kaplan HI, Sadock BJ, eds. Comprehensive textbook of psychiatry/VI. 6th ed. Baltimore: Williams & Wilkins, 1995:791-799.

2. Schuckit MA, Segal DS. Opioid drug use. In: Isselbacher KJ, Braunwald E, Wilson JD, et al, eds. Harrison's textbook of internal medicine. 13th ed. New York: McGraw-Hill, 1994:2425-2429.

3. Jensen GB, Pakkenberg B. Do alcoholics drink their neurons away? Lancet 1993;342:1201-1204.

4. Mendelson JH, Mello NK. Cocaine and other commonly abused drugs. In: Isselbacher KJ, Braunwald E, Wilson JD, et al, eds. Harrison's textbook of internal medicine. 13th ed. New York: McGraw-Hill, 1994:2429-2433.

5. Holbrook JH. Nicotine addiction. In: Isselbacher KJ, Braunwald E, Wilson JD, et al, eds. Harrison's textbook of internal medicine. 13th ed. New York: McGraw-Hill, 1994:2433-2437.

6. Schuckit MA. Alcohol-related disorders. In: Kaplan HI, Sadock BJ, eds. Comprehensive textbook of psychiatry/VI. 6th ed. Baltimore: Williams & Wilkins, 1995:775-791.

7. Jaffe JH. Substance-related disorders: introduction and overview. In: Kaplan HI, Sadock BJ, eds. Comprehensive textbook of psychiatry/VI. 6th ed. Baltimore: Williams & Wilkins, 1995:755-774.

8. Schuckit MA. Alcohol and alcoholism. In: Isselbacher KJ, Braunwald E, Wilson JD, et al, eds. Harrison's textbook of internal medicine. 13th ed. New York: McGraw-Hill, 1994:2420-2425.

9. Saitz R. Recognition and management of occult alcohol withdrawal. Hosp Pract 1995;(June 15):49-58.

10. Kinney J, ed. The busy physician's five-minute guide to the management of alcohol problems. Chicago: American Medical Association, 1989.

11. American Psychiatric Association. Diagnostic and statistical manual of mental disorders. 4th ed. (DSM-IV) Washington, DC: American Psychiatric Association, 1994:175-272.

12. Fleming MF, Barry KL, Manwell LB, et al. Brief physician advice for problem alcohol drinkers: a randomized controlled trial in community-based primary care practices. JAMA 1997;277:1039-1045.

13. Schuckit MA. Low level of response to alcohol as a predictor of future alcoholism. Am J Psychiatry 1994;151:184-189.

14. Wallace P, Cutler S, Haines A. Randomised controlled trial of general practitioner intervention in patients with excessive alcohol consumption. BMJ 1988;297:663-668.

CHAPTER 12

Systemic Lupus Erythematosus

Systemic lupus erythematosus (SLE) is an autoimmune disease that can affect nearly every system in the body. Incidence in America is about 4 per 10,000, and SLE may affect up to 1 in 1000 young women (1,2). Because of its varying degrees of severity and its multitude of possible effects, SLE often poses a diagnostic and management quandary for physicians. Family physicians can make a difference in the lives of their patients with early recognition; 10-year survival rate for patients with SLE approaches 90%, which is twice what it was 40 years ago (3-7).

CHIEF COMPLAINT

Patients may present with a wide range of symptoms. SLE symptoms can develop in any organ system at any time during the course of the disease; severity can wax and wane. Diagnostic criteria for SLE are listed in Table 12.1. The most common initial concerns include the following:

* Polyarthritis
* Arthralgias
* Dermatitis

Other possible presentations include the following:

* Hematologic disturbances (clotting abnormalities)
* Kidney dysfunction (proteinuria, glomerulonephritis, and renal failure)
* Cardiac complications (pericarditis, arrhythmias, and heart failure)
* Psychiatric problems (mental status changes, psychosis)
* Neurologic disorders (headache, seizures)

HISTORY

Given the wide spectrum of SLE manifestations, the family physician must be aware of the interrelated symptoms and findings that lead to the diagnosis.

TABLE 12.1. Criteria for Systemic Lupus Erythematosus

Formal diagnosis requires that a patient have four of these 11 criteria, in any order or simultaneously:
Malar rash
Discoid rash
Photosensitivity
Oral ulcers
Arthritis
Serositis (pleuritis or pericarditis)
Renal disorder (3+ proteinuria, 0.5 grams urinary protein / day, or cellular casts)
Neurologic disorder (seizures or psychosis)
Hematologic disorder (hemolytic anemia, leukopenia, lymphopenia, or thrombocytopenia)
Antinuclear antibody
Immunologic disorder, including any of the following:
• Positive LE cell preparation
• Anti-DNA antibody
• Anti-Sm antibody
• False-positive test for syphilis (positive for 6 months, confirmed by treponemal study)

Adapted from Tan EM, Cohen AS, Fries JF, et al. The 1982 revised criteria for the classification of systemic lupus erythematosus. Arthritis Rheum 1982;25:1271–1277.

For example, the combination of joint pains and a rash merits investigation for SLE or another connective tissue disorder. The following are other important clues:

• Unexplained pregnancy losses or premature deliveries
• Frequent infections
• Cardiac disease
• Unexplained fever
• Chronic fatigue
• Cognitive changes
• Family history of SLE (8)

It is also important to gather information on environmental factors and medication use, because many factors can precipitate or exacerbate SLE or similar rheumatologic findings in susceptible persons. Some of these include the following (9):

• Sunlight
• Hair dyes
• Food coloring
• Certain metals (gold, mercury, cadmium)
• Certain amino acids (L-canavanine, L-tryptophan)
• Cocaine

- Pharmaceutical agents
  - Procainamide (Pronestyl)
  - Quinidine
  - Colchicine (Colbenemid)
  - Hydralazine (Apresoline)

PHYSICAL EXAMINATION

Because SLE has such a wide range of possible effects, a complete physical examination should be performed on the patient with possible SLE. If time is limited, focus on the chief complaint and schedule a return visit soon thereafter for the complete exam.

The most common findings in patients with SLE relate to the skin and joints, and there are many possible manifestations in these areas. The malar or "butterfly" rash most commonly associated with SLE, also termed *acute cutaneous lupus erythematosus* (ACLE), occurs in 20% to 60% of patients with SLE (10). It may manifest as follows:

- An erythematous eruption over the cheeks, usually bilateral and sparing the nasolabial folds
- Usually associated with photosensitivity
- May be widespread throughout the body (more often in sunlight-exposed areas)
- May resemble a maculopapular drug eruption
- Oral ulcerations possible

Other subsets of patients may have skin manifestations but relatively few systemic symptoms. Included in this group are patients with subacute cutaneous lupus erythematosus (SCLE) and patients with chronic cutaneous lupus erythematosus (CCLE). Patients with SCLE may exhibit the following:

- Nonscarring papulosquamous or annular lesions over trunk and extremities, with marked photosensitivity
- Peripheral vasculitis and Raynaud's phenomenon
- Anti-Ro or anti-La antibodies common

Patients with CCLE commonly manifest the following:

- Discoid lupus erythematosus—flat or slightly elevated, well-circumscribed, erythematous, scaly macules or papules

There is some overlap among all forms of cutaneous lupus erythematosus. However, only 20% or less of patients with SCLE or CCLE go on to develop SLE (10).

Arthritis

In addition to skin findings, arthritis is the other condition most associated with SLE. One review found arthritis to be 86% sensitive, but only 37% specific for SLE (11). Arthritis in SLE patients may be characterized by the following:

* Usually involves small joints of the knees, wrists, and hands
* Joint fluid less inflammatory than in rheumatoid arthritis (12)
* No spinal involvement
* Tendinitis and tendon rupture possible
* May be deforming, but usually damage confined to soft tissues, with little or no bone erosion

Other Findings

Neurologic examination may reveal subtle cognitive deficits early in the course of the disease, as may focal findings related to cerebrovascular injury. Neuropsychologic testing may prove insightful and suggest targeted therapy, depending on the type of dysfunction (13).

Cardiopulmonary exam may reveal an increased pulse rate, which can be an important identifying factor for an SLE flare-up. It is more sensitive but less specific than laboratory tests (14). A cardiopulmonary exam also should evaluate for the following:

* Pleuritis
* Pericarditis
* Pleural or pericardial effusion
* Infection
* Early congestive heart failure

DIAGNOSTIC TESTING

Serologic Tests

Several serologic tests can help fulfill the diagnostic criteria for SLE:

* Antinuclear antibody (ANA) test—highly sensitive, but not particularly specific
* Anti–double-stranded DNA antibodies, anti-Sm antibodies, lupus erythematosus cells—very specific but less sensitive than the ANA test (11)
* Complete blood count (CBC)—may reveal decreased levels of any cell line listed in Table 12.1
* Complement—low levels associated with SLE, with similar sensitivity as anti-DNA antibody, but not a formal diagnostic criterion and somewhat nonspecific (11,15)

Other Tests Focusing on Specific Organ System

Certain test that focus on specific organs can be helpful in diagnosis of SLE:

- Urinalysis may reveal proteinuria or casts, both of which are part of the diagnostic criteria for SLE.
- Kidney biopsy may be needed for a more specific tissue diagnosis.
- Pregnancy testing is advisable if there is any suspicion of pregnancy, because management in pregnancy is facilitated by early diagnosis (16).
- Chest x-ray and echocardiogram is helpful if involvement of the heart or lungs is suspected (17).
- Liver function tests may indicate early hepatitis before symptoms develop.
- Skin biopsies may be helpful if cutaneous lesions are atypical.
- Joint fluid sampling can help narrow differential diagnosis in patients with arthritis or joint effusions of unclear etiology.
- Lumbar puncture may be indicated to exclude other possibilities, such as infection, in patients with neurologic symptoms.

DIFFERENTIAL DIAGNOSIS

Connective Tissue Disorders

The differential diagnosis for SLE includes many of the connective tissue diseases. Features that distinguish these diseases from SLE are listed in Table 12.2.

Drug-Induced Lupus Erythematosus

Autoantibodies and lupuslike disease have been associated with over 30 medications, most notably procainamide, hydralazine, and quinidine (18). The following are implicated drug classes:

- Antiarrhythmics
- Antihypertensives
- Antipsychotics
- Anticonvulsants
- Antithyroidals
- Anti-inflammatories
- Diuretics
- Antibiotics (specifically isoniazid, nitrofurantoin, and minocycline)

Drug-induced lupus can be distinguished by a lack of antibodies against native DNA and by resolution of symptoms when the drug is discontinued (although resolution may require several months).

Some medications are also implicated in the exacerbation of SLE symptoms; for example, ibuprofen and other nonsteroidal anti-inflammatory med-

TABLE 12.2. Connective Tissue Diseases in Differential Diagnosis of Systemic Lupus Erythematosus (SLE)

Disorder	Distinguishing Features from SLE
Rheumatoid arthritis	Subcutaneous nodules Erosive joint disease Minimal lymphadenopathy ANA-positive in only 25% of cases Rheumatoid factor positive in only one third of SLE patients Minimal central nervous system (CNS), gastrointestinal, or lung involvement (6–12 months of observation may be needed for definitive differentiation)
Mixed connective tissue disease	Anti-RNP antibody present, anti-Sm antibody absent Swollen hands Minimal CNS involvement or hemolytic anemia
Progressive systemic sclerosis (scleroderma)	Men affected in one third of cases Skin findings (tightness, thickening, hyperpigmentation) CREST syndrome[a] Anticentromere antibodies Minimal CNS involvement 50% ANA-negative
Antiphospholipid antibody syndrome	Can coexist with SLE Notable for hypercoagulability, vascular thrombosis, thrombocytopenia, pregnancy loss
Dermatomyositis and polymyositis	Heliotrope rash, Gottron's nodes Minimal arthitis Minimal CNS, cardiopulmonary, hematologic involvement Men affected in one-third of cases

Adapted from references 19 to 24.
[a]CREST = calcinosis, Raynaud's syndrome, esophagitis, sclerodactyly, telangiectasias; ANA = antinuclear antibody.
Note: Secondary Sjögren's syndrome, or dry eyes and mouth from infiltration of the lacrimal and salivary glands, may occur in nearly all of these disorders

ications (NSAIDs) have been reported to induce aseptic meningitis in SLE patients (18).

Somatoform Disorders and Fibromyalgia

The diffuse symptoms seen in somatoform disorders and fibromyalgia (see Chapters 10 and 6) can include diagnostic criteria for SLE. However, the laboratory investigations previously mentioned can usually support or discount SLE in most cases.

Human Immunodeficiency Virus Infection

Symptoms such as fever, rash, lymphadenopathy, arthralgias, renal dysfunction, neurologic symptoms, and hematologic abnormalities can be the first symptoms of both HIV and SLE. HIV testing can help make the diagnosis, although SLE has been reported to cause false-positive Western blot testing for HIV, but not false-positive ELISA tests (25).

Concurrent HIV infection and SLE is unusual, despite the frequency of transfusions for SLE patients with hemolytic anemia in the late 1970s and early 1980s before the blood supply was effectively screened for HIV (19).

Other Systemic Diseases

Rarely, the following diseases may coexist with or mimic SLE (19):
• Vasculitis
• Sarcoidosis
• Amyloidosis
• Spondyloarthropathies
• Porphyria
• Leprosy
• Tuberculosis
• Carcinoma

WHEN TO REFER

Consultation should be considered in the following circumstances:

• To confirm diagnosis in patients who do not fit the classic criteria for SLE
• For patients who do not respond initially to first-line medications
• For pregnant patients
• For patients with neonatal lupus

MANAGEMENT

Medication

Treatment is usually directed toward the specific system manifestations rather than the overall autoimmune process. Table 12.3 lists dosages and potential side effects of drugs given for SLE.

NSAIDs. These drugs are helpful in the management of patients with arthritis, serositis, and constitutional symptoms (1,12). Caution and vigilance are required with their use, however, because the neurologic and renal toxicities of these medications may exacerbate or mask underlying SLE damage to these systems.

TABLE 12.3. Medications for Systemic Lupus Erythematosus (SLE)

Agent	Daily Dose Range	Comments
Nonsteroidal anti-inflammatory drugs (NSAIDs)[a]		Gastrointestinal side effects most common; renal and hepatic insufficiency may occur in combination with SLE. Also reported: tinnitus, confusion, hypersensitivity meingitis, increased bleeding. Prescribe higher doses only after moderate doses prove unsuccessful.
Ibuprofen (Motrin)	1200–3200 mg divided in 3–6 doses	
Indomethacin (Indocin)	50–200 mg divided in 2–4 doses	
Naproxen	250–1500 mg divided in 2 doses	
Salicylates		As above
Aspirin	1000–6000 mg divided in 2–4 doses	
Salsalate (Disalcid)	1500–5000 mg divided in 2–4 doses	
Antimalarials		Multiple toxicities; overdose possibly fatal
Hydroxy-chloroquine (Plaquenil)	400 mg (approx. 5–7 mg/kg/day) divided in 2 doses	Ophthalmologic exam every 6 months
Chloroquine (Aralen)	250–500 mg daily	Ophthalmologic exam every 6 months
Quinacrine (Atabrine)	25–200 mg daily in combination with other antimalarial	
Corticosteroids		Mainstay therapy for severe disease; same side effects with long-term use as in other conditions
Prednisone	5–100 mg daily (lower for children)	Dosage depends on severity and involved systems
Methyl-prednisone	48–80 mg IV daily in 2–4 doses	IV use for critically ill patients

Adapted from Wallace DJ, Hahn BH, eds. Dubois' lupus erythematosus. 5th ed. Baltimore: Williams & Wilkins, 1997.

[a]Other NSAIDs are also effective.

Antimalarial medications. Drugs such as hydroxychloroquine may relieve arthritis and many SLE skin manifestations (12). Ophthalmologic exams every 6 to 12 months are recommended because of the ocular toxicity of these medicines.

Corticosteroids. Moderate- to high-potency topical corticosteroids may be used for dermatologic concerns. Occasionally, systemic corticosteroids may be needed for symptoms in any organ system, but may cause complications including atherosclerosis, osteoporosis, predisposition to infections, and glucose intolerance.

Endocarditis prophylaxis. A high incidence of SLE patients have cardiac valvular abnormalities; therefore, prophylaxis for endocarditis should be considered for those undergoing dental and surgical procedures.

Treatment of Specific Complications
Lupus Nephritis
Optimal therapy for lupus nephritis, a potentially life-threatening complication, is still under investigation. Close pharmacologic control of hypertension is essential.
Current recommendations include the following:

• Combination of high-dose corticosteroids and pulse intravenous cyclophosphamide (12,26). Toxicities with this regimen include corticosteroid side effects plus marrow suppression, hemorrhagic cystitis, malignancy, infection, ovarian failure, and birth defects.
• Alternative therapy involves azathioprine, methotrexate, or cyclosporine.

Central Nervous System Involvement
• Corticosteroids and cyclophosphamide combination therapy may be beneficial, but care must be taken to exclude other neurologic pathology, such as infection or infarction.
• Prophylactic anticoagulation may be beneficial in patients with infarction or when antiphospholipid antibodies are present (12,22).
• Anticonvulsants and corticosteroids may be used for seizures; anticonvulsant therapy is usually maintained for 1 year after a seizure and discontinued if there is no recurrence. Although anticonvulsants are associated with drug-induced lupus, they do not appear to exacerbate preexisting lupus symptoms (12).
• Antidepressants and neuroleptics may be effective for behavioral symptoms.

Pregnancy
SLE in pregnancy poses a challenge to both the patient and the management team; a number of articles have focused on this topic (16,27–31). Fetal loss

and prematurity are more common in mothers with SLE. It is still a matter of debate whether SLE flare-ups occur more often during pregnancy, but several factors appear to be accurate predictors of fewer SLE complications:

- Quiescent disease in the 6 to 12 months before conception
- Complete remission of nephritis
- Normal renal function

Physiologic and pathologic changes in pregnancy can mask certain manifestations of SLE, such as thrombocytopenia, proteinuria, hypertension, anemia, arthralgias, and skin changes. In particular, preeclampsia may mimic the clinical and laboratory findings of a lupus flare-up.

Medication for the pregnant woman with SLE must be used with caution and with consideration of adverse effects to both mother and fetus. Often, the benefits of medication outweigh the risks, and the literature documents use of salicylates, corticosteroids, and even cytotoxic agents during pregnancy.

The presence of antiphospholipid antibodies may further complicate matters, and a standard of care for pregnant patients with these antibodies has not been established. At the very least, extremely close surveillance is needed to monitor for potential adverse events.

Neonatal Lupus

Neonatal lupus will not be discussed here except to note that it is associated with inflammatory cardiac changes leading to complete heart block and that dermatologic, hematologic, and hepatic abnormalities may be present (32).

Contraception and Hormone Replacement Therapy

Much study has revolved around the use of estrogen in women with SLE (33–36). In general, the data suggest that estrogen-containing compounds may increase SLE exacerbations. When contraception is needed, mechanical barriers are the most recommended forms of contraception in women with SLE. If the patient desires hormonal methods, a progestin-only formulation should be used. There is no consensus on the safety of postmenopausal estrogen replacement in the patient with SLE.

Other Treatment Modalities

Preventive health measures should be recommended at every opportunity, including the following:

- Sun avoidance and sun block use (as a result of photosensitivity)
- Smoking cessation
- Hypertension control
- Cholesterol reduction
- Maintenance of immunizations

- Regular Pap smears and mammograms
- Ophthalmologic examinations

As with any chronic underlying disease, improving patients' baseline health status will improve reserve potential when exacerbations occur.

Periodic monitoring of renal and hepatic function and hematologic values is also recommended. Splenectomy may occasionally be needed for refractory thrombocytopenia (1), but it is generally a last resort because it predisposes the patient to bacteremia.

FOLLOW-UP

As previously mentioned, the family physician may be increasingly expected to coordinate care for the patient with SLE. In addition to yearly health maintenance exams, intermediate visits help keep track of new developments, specialist input, and treatment advances. More frequent visits are needed during times of exacerbations, corticosteroid tapering, and other medication changes.

PATIENT EDUCATION

The patient with SLE should be made aware of the disease's potential multisystem involvement and should be instructed on symptoms that may arise in the future. The following are key points to cover with the patient:

- High variability in course and prognosis
- Regular follow-up visits and acute-care appointments early on during a flare-up to help minimize symptom severity
- Family planning discussions
- Advance directives in case neurologic symptoms become severe
- Information about heredity, diet, and exercise

Family and Community Involvement

Family support, regional groups, and national associations can help the patient to cope with this potentially complicated disease. The American Lupus Society can be reached at 800-331-1802, and the Lupus Foundation can be reached at 800-558-0121.

REFERENCES

1. Mills JA. Systemic lupus erythematosus. N Engl J Med 1994;330:1871–1879.
2. Hochberg MC. Systemic lupus erythematosus. Rheum Clin North Am 1990;16:617–39.
3. Pistiner M, Wallace DJ, Nessim S, Metzger AL, Klinenberg JR. Lupus erythematosus in the 1980s: a survey of 570 patients. Semin Arthritis Rheum 1991;21:55–64.

4. Ginzler EM, Schorn K. Outcome and prognosis in systemic lupus erythematosus. Rheum Dis Clin North Am 1988;14:67-78.

5. Miller MH, Urowitz MD, Gladman DD, Killinger DW. Systemic lupus erythematosus in males. Medicine (Baltimore) 1983;62:327-334.

6. Baker SB, Rovira JR, Campion EW, Mills JA. Late onset systemic lupus erythematosus. Am J Med 1979;66:727-732.

7. Barron KS, Silverman ED, Gonzales J, Reveille JD. Clinical, serologic, and immunogenetic studies in childhood-onset systemic lupus erythematosus. Arthritis Rheum 1993;36:348-354.

8. Arnett FC. The genetics of human lupus. In: Wallace DJ, Hahn BH, eds. Dubois' lupus erythematosus. 5th ed. Baltimore: Williams & Wilkins, 1997:77-117.

9. Mongey AB, Hess EV. The role of environment in systemic lupus erythematosus and associated disorders. In: Wallace DJ, Hahn BH, eds. Dubois' lupus erythematosus. 5th ed. Baltimore: Williams & Wilkins, 1997:31-47.

10. Sontheimer RD, Provost TT. Cutaneous manifestations of lupus erythematosus. In: Wallace DJ, Hahn BH, eds. Dubois' lupus erythematosus. 5th ed. Baltimore: Williams & Wilkins, 1997:569-623.

11. Tan EM, Cohen AS, Fries JF, et al. The 1982 revised criteria for the classification of systemic lupus erythematosus. Arthritis Rheum 1982;25:1271-1277.

12. Pisetsky DS, Gilkeson G, St. Clair EW. Systemic lupus erythematosus: diagnosis and treatment. Med Clin North Am 1997; 81:113-128.

13. Shapiro HS. Psychopathology in the patient with lupus. In: Wallace DJ, Hahn BH, eds. Dubois' lupus erythematosus. 5th ed. Baltimore: Williams & Wilkins, 1997: 755-782.

14. Roberts WN. Keys to managing systemic lupus erythematosus. Hospital Practice 1997;:113-126.

15. Schur PH. Complement and systemic lupus erythematosus. In: Wallace DJ, Hahn BH, eds. Dubois' lupus erythematosus. 5th ed. Baltimore: Williams & Wilkins, 1997:245-261.

16. Syrop CH, Varner MW. Systemic lupus erythematosus. Clinical Obstetrics and Gynecology 1983;26:547-557.

17. Roldan CA, Shively BK, Crawford MH. An echocardiographic study of valvular heart disease associated with systemic lupus erythematosus. N Engl J Med 1996;335:1424-1430.

18. Rubin R. Drug-induced lupus. In: Wallace DJ, Hahn BH, eds. Dubois' Lupus Erythematosus, 5th ed. Baltimore: Williams & Wilkins, 1997:871-901.

19. Wallace DJ. Differential diagnosis and disease associations. In: Wallace DJ, Hahn BH, eds. Dubois' lupus erythematosus. 5th ed. Baltimore: Williams & Wilkins, 1997:943-965.

20. Quismorio FP. Other serologic abnormalities in systemic lupus erythematosus. In: Wallace DJ, Hahn BH, eds. Dubois' lupus erythematosus. 5th ed. Baltimore: Williams & Wilkins, 1997:523-543.

21. Anaya JM, Talal N. Head and neck findings in systemic lupus erythematosus:

Sjogren's syndrome and the eye, ear, and larynx. In: Wallace DJ, Hahn BH, eds. Dubois' lupus erythematosus. 5th ed. Baltimore: Williams & Wilkins, 1997: 783–791.

22. Petri M. Pathogenesis and treatment of the antiphospholipid antibody syndrome. Med Clin North Am 1997;81:151–177.

23. Nahass GT. Antiphospholipid antibodies and the antiphospholipid antibody syndrome. J Am Acad Dermatol 1997;36:149–168.

24. Asherson RA, Khamashta MA, Ordi-Ros J, et al. The "primary" antiphospholipid syndrome: major clinical and serologic features. Medicine 1989;68(6):366–374.

25. Soriano V, Ordi J, Grau J. Tests for HIV in lupus [Letter]. N Engl J Med 1994;331:881.

26. Boumpas DT, Austin HA, Fessler BJ, Balow JE, Klippel JH, Lockshin MD. Sytemic lupus erythematosus: emerging concepts. Part 1: renal neuropsychiatric, cardiovascular, pulmonary, and hematologic disease. Ann Intern Med 1995;122: 940–950.

27. Petri M. Hopkins Lupus Pregnancy Center: 1987 to 1996. Rheum Dis Clin North Am 1997;23:1–13.

28. Khamashta MA, Ruiz-Irastorza G, Hughes GRV. Systemic lupus erythematosus flares during pregnancy. Rheum Dis Clin North Am 1997;23:15–30.

29. Mascola MA, Repke JT. Obstetric management of the high-risk lupus pregnancy. Rheum Dis Clin North Am 1997;23:119–132.

30. Wong KL, Chan FY, Lee CP. Outcome of pregnancy in patients with systemic lupus erythematosus: a prospective study. Arch Intern Med 1991;151:269–273.

31. Julkunen H. Pregnancy in systemic lupus erythematosus: contraception, fetal outcome and congenital heart block. Acta Obstet Gynecol Scand 1994;73:517–518.

32. Tseng CE, Buyon JP. Neonatal lupus syndromes. Rheum Dis Clin North Am 1997;23:31–54.

33. Petri M, Robinson C. Oral contraceptives and systemic lupus erythematosus. Arthritis Rheum 1997;40:797–803.

34. Jungers P, Dougados M, Pelissier C, et al. Influence of oral contraceptive therapy on the activity of systemic lupus erythematosus. Arthritis Rheum 1982;25: 618–623.

35. Van Vollenhoven RF, McGuire JL. Estrogen, progesterone, and testosterone: can they be used to treat autoimmune diseases? Cleve Clin J Med 1994;61:276–284.

36. Sanchez-Guerrero J, Liang MH, Karlson EW, Hunter DJ, Colditz GA. Postmenopausal estrogen therapy and the risk for developing systemic lupus erythematosus. Ann Intern Med 1995;122:430–433.

APPENDIX A

Criteria for Panic Attack

Note: A Panic Attack is not a codable disorder. Code the specific diagnosis in which panic attack occurs (e.g., 300.21 Panic Disorder With Agoraphobia).

A discrete period of intense fear or discomfort, in which four (or more) of the following symptoms developed abruptly and reached a peak within 10 minutes:

1. Palpitations, pounding heart, or accelerated heart rate
2. Sweating
2. Trembling or shaking
4. Sensations of shortness of breath or smothering
5. Feeling of choking
6. Chest pain or discomfort
7. Nausea or abdominal distress
8. Feeling dizzy, unsteady, lightheaded or faint
9. Derealization (feelings of unreality) or depersonalization (being detached from oneself)
10. Fear of losing control or going crazy
11. Fear of dying
12. Paresthesias (numbness or tingling sensations)
13. Chills or hot flushes

Reprinted with permission from the *Diagnostic and Statistical Manual of Mental Disorders*. 4th ed. Copyright 1994 American Psychiatric Association.

Diagnostic Criteria for Panic Disorder (300.01 Panic Disorder Without Agoraphobia; 300.21 Panic Disorder With Agoraphobia)

A. Both (1) and (2)

  (1) Recurrent unexpected Panic Attacks (see Appendix A)

  (2) At least one of the attacks has been followed by 1 month or more of one (or more) of the following:

  a. Persistent concern about having additional attacks

  b. Worry about the implications of the attack or its consequences (e.g., losing control, having a heart attack, "going crazy")

  c. A significant change in behavior related to the attacks

B. The presence or absence of Agoraphobia (two different diagnosis codes above).

C. The Panic Attacks are not due to the direct physiologic effects of a substance (e.g., a drug of abuse, a medication) or a general medical condition (e.g., hyperthyroidism).

D. The Panic Attacks are not better accounted for by another mental disorder, such as Social Phobia (e.g., occurring on exposure to feared social situations), Specific Phobia (e.g., on exposure to a specific phobic situation), Obsessive-Compulsive Disorder (e.g., on exposure to dirt in someone with an obsession about contamination), Post-traumatic Stress Disorder (e.g., in response to stimuli associated with a severe stressor), or Separation Anxiety Disorder (e.g., in response to being away from home or close relatives).

APPENDIX C

Diagnostic Criteria for 308.3 Acute Stress Disorder

A. The person has been exposed to a traumatic event in which both of the following were present:
   (1) The person experienced, witnessed, or was confronted with an event or events that involved actual or threatened death or serious injury or a threat to the physical integrity of self or others.
   (2) The person's response involved intense fear, helplessness, or horror.

B. Either while experiencing or after experiencing the distressing event, the person has three or more of the following dissociative symptoms:
   (1) A subjective sense of numbing, detachment, or absence of emotional responsiveness
   (2) A reduction in awareness of his or her surroundings (e.g., "being in a daze")
   (3) Derealization
   (4) Depersonalization
   (5) Dissociative amnesia (i.e., inability to recall an important aspect of the trauma)

C. The traumatic event is persistently reexperienced in at least one of the following ways: recurring images, thoughts, dreams, illusions, flashback episodes, or a sense of reliving the experience; or distress on exposure to reminders of the traumatic event.

D. The person exhibits marked avoidance of stimuli that arouse recollections of the trauma (e.g., thoughts, feelings, conversations, activities, places, people).

E. The person has marked symptoms of anxiety or increased arousal (e.g., difficulty sleeping, irritability, poor concentration, hypervigilance, exaggerated startle response, motor restlessness).

F. The disturbance causes clinically significant distress or impairment in social, occupational, or other important areas of functioning or impairs the individual's ability to pursue some necessary task, such as obtaining necessary assistance or mobilizing personal resources by telling family members about the traumatic experience.

G. The disturbance lasts for a minimum of 2 days and a maximum of 4 weeks and occurs within 4 weeks of the traumatic event.

H. The disturbance is not due to the direct physiologic effects of a substance (e.g., a drug of abuse, a medication) or a general medical condition, is not better accounted for by Brief Psychotic Disorder, and is not merely an exacerbation of a preexisting Axis I or Axis II disorder.

APPENDIX D

Diagnostic Criteria for 309.81 Post-traumatic Stress Disorder

A. The person has been exposed to a traumatic event in which both of the following were present:

  (1) The person experienced, witnessed, or was confronted with an event or events that involved actual or threatened death or serious injury or a threat to the physical integrity of self or others.

  (2) The person's response involved intense fear, helplessness, or horror.
  Note: Children may express this instead by disorganized or agitated behavior.

B. The traumatic event is persistently reexperienced in one or more of the following ways:

  (1) Recurrent and intrusive distressing recollections of the event, including images, thoughts, or perceptions.
  Note: Young children may exhibit repetitive play in which themes or aspects of the trauma are expressed.

  (2) Recurrent distressing dreams of the event.
  Note: Children may have frightening dreams without recognizable content.

  (3) Acting or feeling as if the traumatic event were recurring (includes a sense of reliving the experience, illusions, hallucinations, and dissociative flashback episodes, including those that occur on awakening or when intoxicated).
  Note: In young children, trauma-specific reenactment may occur.

  (4) Intense psychological distress at exposure to internal or external cues that symbolize or resemble an aspect of the traumatic event

  (5) Physiologic reactivity on exposure to internal or external cues that symbolize or resemble an aspect of the traumatic event.

C. Persistent avoidance of stimuli associated with the trauma and numbing of general responsiveness (not present before the trauma), as indicated by three or more of the following:

  (1) Efforts to avoid thoughts, feelings, or conversations associated with the trauma

  (2) Efforts to avoid activities, places, or people that arouse recollection of the trauma

  (3) Inability to recall an important aspect of the trauma

  (4) Markedly diminished interest or participation in significant activities

  (5) Feeling of detachment or estrangement from others

  (6) Restricted range of affect (e.g., inability to have loving feelings)

(7) Sense of foreshortened future (e.g., does not expect to have a career, marriage, children, or a normal life span)

D. Persistent symptoms of increased arousal (not present before the trauma), as indicated by two or more of the following:
   (1) Difficulty falling or staying asleep
   (2) Irritability or outbursts of anger
   (3) Difficulty concentrating
   (4) Hypervigilance
   (5) Exaggerated startle response

E. Duration of the disturbance (symptoms in criteria B, C, and D) is more than 1 month.

F. The disturbance causes clinically significant distress or impairment in social, occupational, or other important areas of functioning.

Specify if
   Acute: if duration of symptoms is less than 3 months

   Chronic: if duration of symptoms is 3 months or more

Specify if
   With Delayed Onset: if onset of symptoms is at least 6 months after the stressor

---

APPENDIX E

Diagnostic Criteria for 300.3 Obsessive-Compulsive Disorder

A. Either obsessions or compulsions
Obsessions as defined by 1, 2, 3, and 4:
   (1) Recurrent and persistent thoughts, impulses, or images that are experienced, at some time during the disturbance, as intrusive and inappropriate and that cause marked anxiety or distress.
   (2) The thoughts, impulses, or images are not simply excessive worries about real-life problems.
   (3) The person attempts to ignore or suppress such thoughts, impulses, or images, or to neutralize them with some other thought or action.
   (4) The person recognizes that the obsessional thoughts, impulses or images are a product of his or her own mind (not imposed from without as in thought insertion).
Compulsions as defined by (1) and (2):
   (1) Repetitive behaviors (e.g., hand washing, ordering, checking) or mental acts (e.g, praying, counting, repeating words silently) that the person feels driven to perform in response to an obsession, or according to rules that must be applied rigidly
   (2) The behaviors or mental acts aimed at preventing or reducing distress or preventing some dreaded event or situation; however, these behaviors or mental acts either are not connected in a realistic way with what they are designed to neutralize or prevent or are clearly excessive

B. At some point during the course of the disorder, the person has recognized that the obsessions or compulsions are excessive or unreasonable.
Note: This does not apply to children.

C. The obsessions or compulsions cause marked distress, are time-consuming (take more than 1 hour a day), or significantly interfere with the person's normal routine, occupational (or academic) functioning, or usual social activities or relationships.

D. If another Axis I disorder is present, the content of the obsessions or compulsions is not restricted to it (e.g., preoccupation with food in the presence of an Eating Disorder; hair pulling in the presence of Trichotillomania; concern with appearance in the presence of Body Dysmorphic Disorder; preoccupation with drugs in the presence of a Substance Use Disorder; preoccupation with having a serious illness in the presence of Hypochondriasis; preoccupation with sexual urges or fantasies in the presence of a Paraphilia; or guilty ruminations in the presence of Major Depressive Disorder).

E. The disturbance is not due to the direct physiologic effects of a substance (e.g., a drug of abuse or a medication) or a general medical condition.

Specify if

With Poor Insight: if, for most of the time during the current episode, the person does not recognize that the obsessions and compulsions are excessive or unreasonable

---

APPENDIX F

Diagnostic Criteria for 300.02 Generalized Anxiety Disorder

A. Excessive anxiety and worry (apprehensive expectation), occurring more days than not for at least 6 months about a number of events or activities (such as work or school performance).

B. The person finds it difficult to control the worry.

C. The anxiety and worry are associated with three or more of the following six symptoms (with at least some symptoms present for more days than not for the past 6 months).
   Note: Only one item is required in children.
   (1) Restlessness or feeling keyed up or on edge
   (2) Being easily fatigued
   (3) Difficulty concentrating or mind going blank
   (4) Irritability
   (5) Muscle tension
   (6) Sleep disturbance (difficulty falling asleep or staying asleep, or restless unsatisfying sleep)

D. The focus of the anxiety and worry is not confined to features of an Axis I disorder; for example, the anxiety or worry is not about having a panic attack (as in Panic Disorder), being embarrassed in public (as in Social Phobia), being contaminated (as in Obsessive-Compulsive Disorder), being away from home or close relatives (as in Separation Anxiety Disorder), gaining weight (as in Anorexia Nervosa), having multiple physical complaints (as in Somatization Disorder), or having a serious illness (as in Hypochondriasis), and the anxiety and worry do not occur exclusively during Post-traumatic Stress Disorder.

E. The anxiety, worry, or physical symptoms cause clinically significant distress or impairment in social, occupational, or other important areas of functioning.

F. The disturbance is not due to the direct physiologic effects of a substance (e.g., a drug of abuse, a medication) or a general medical condition (e.g., hyperthyroidism) and does not occur exclusively during a Mood Disorder, a Psychotic Disorder, or a Pervasive Developmental Disorder.

Reprinted with permission from the *Diagnostic and Statistical Manual of Mental Disorders.* 4th ed. Copyright 1994 American Psychiatric Association.

183

APPENDIX G

Diagnostic Criteria for 309.21 Separation Anxiety Disorder

A. Developmentally inappropriate and excessive anxiety concerning separation from home or from those to whom the individual is attached, as evidenced by three or more of the following:
   (1) Recurrent excessive distress when separation from home or major attachment figures occurs or is anticipated
   (2) Persistent and excessive worry about losing, or about possible harm befalling, major attachment figures
   (3) Persistent and excessive worry that an untoward event will lead to separation from a major attachment figure (e.g., getting lost or being kidnapped)
   (4) Persistent reluctance or refusal to go to school or elsewhere because of fear of separation
   (5) Persistently and excessively fearful or reluctant to be alone or without major attachment figures at home or without significant adults in other settings
   (6) Persistent reluctance or refusal to go to sleep without being near a major attachment figure or to sleep away from home
   (7) Repeated nightmares involving the theme of separation
   (8) Repeated complaints of physical symptoms (such as headaches, stomachaches, nausea, or vomiting) when separation from major attachment figures occurs or is anticipated

B. Duration of the disturbance at least 4 weeks.

C. Onset before age 18 years.

D. The disturbance causes clinically significant distress or impairment in social, academic (occupational), or other important areas of functioning.

E. The disturbance does not occur exclusively during the course of a Pervasive Developmental Disorder, Schizophrenia, or other Psychotic Disorder and, in adolescents and adults, is not better accounted for by Panic Disorder With Agoraphobia.

Specify if
   Early Onset: if onset occurs before age 6 years

A Comparison of Selected Benzodiazepines

Agent	Half-life (hours)	Adult Dose (mg/day)	Geriatric Dose (mg/day)
Alprazolam (Xanax)	12–19	0.25–5.0	0.125–0.5
Chlordiazepoxide (Librium)	12–48	5–100	5–30 or avoid
Clonazepam (Klonopin)	18–28	0.5–5.0	0.25–2 or avoid
Diazepam (Valium)	20–90	2–40	1–10 or avoid
Flurazepam (Dalmane)	24–100	15–30	avoid
Lorazepam (Ativan)	10–20	1–4	0.5–1.5
Oxazepam (Serax)	8–21	10–60	10–30
Temazepam (Restoril)	12–24	15–30	7.5–15
Triazolam (Halcion)	2.5–3.5	0.25–0.50	avoid

Note: Chlordiazepoxide, clonazepam, diazepam, and flurazepam are not recommended in the elderly because these drugs have very long half-lives; triazolam is not recommended because of its association with potential memory impairment.
Approximate equivalents of some benzodiazepines: 24 mg diazepam = 1.0 mg alprazolam = 0.5 mg clonazepam. However, the only drug that can be reliably substituted for alprazolam without potential seizure risk is clonazepam.

Adapted from data in Bernstein JG. Handbook of drug therapy is psychiatry. 2nd ed. Littleton, Mass: Year Book Medical Publishers, 1988:59, 455.

APPENDIX I

The Basic Mental Status Examination

OBSERVATIONS OF THE PATIENT	EXAMPLES
GENERAL	
DRESS AND GROOMING	Appropriate, casual, professional, disheveled, eccentric, poor hygiene, neglect of selected features (e.g., excessively long fingernails), presence of tattoos and body piercing (other than earrings)
DEMEANOR, ATTITUDE	Cooperative, seductive, apathetic, evasive, hostile, demanding
MOTOR BEHAVIOR	Psychomotor slowing, hyperactive, tics, observed compulsions, gait disturbance, movement disorders
SPEECH	Fluency, volume, speed, pressured, slow, stutter, language disturbances
AFFECT	What the physician observes: The patient appears euthymic ("normal") with full range, blunted, constricted, flat, depressed, elated, expansive, irritable, labile, crying (? appropriate to verbal content)
MOOD	What the patient says his/her mood is: "How would you say your mood is today?" The patient may respond, "OK," or depressed, anxious, tired, etc.

OBSERVATIONS OF THE PATIENT	EXAMPLES
THOUGHT CONTENT	Hallucinations (visual, auditory, gustatory, tactile, olfactory), delusions (false beliefs based on incorrect information and held in spite of evidence to the contrary, e.g., paranoid or persecutory delusions) obsessions, depersonalization, flight of ideas, tangential thoughts, perseveration, incoherence, presence of suicidal or homicidal ideation
COGNITIVE SKILLS AND ORIENTATION	Alertness, arousal, attention, orientation (to person, place, time, situation), recent and remote memory, general impression of intellect (normal, bright, slow). The Folstein Mini-Mental State Examination (MMSE) (see Appendix J, question 2) may be done in patients over 55 years of age and in others in whom cognitive impairment is suspected.
INSIGHT	How well does the patient understand his/her illness or impairment? Insight may be good, fair, poor, unrealistic, appropriate for age (child/adolescent).
JUDGMENT	Judgment may be good, fair, poor, severely impaired; may be adequate in most areas of life, but poor regarding continued substance abuse and dependence; may be adequate in most areas of life, but poor regarding compliance with treatment for chronic mental illness (e.g., bipolar disorder).

Note: It is very important in the mental status examination that all observations and findings be considered for appropriateness within the context of the person's culture.

APPENDIX J

Folstein's Mini-Mental State Examination

The Folstein Mini-Mental Status Examination (MMSE) is a widely used, nationally standardized, brief questionnaire that can be used to screen for dementia. It has been shown to be very consistent from one rater to another and can be administered in the office in approximately 10 minutes. The limitations of the MMSE must be recognized, however. To be valid, the MMSE must be administered to an adult who is alert, fully attentive to the task, cooperative, able to understand the language spoken to him or her, and able to hear the questions asked and see the words and drawing when requested. The MMSE may not be valid if the patient is under the influence of substances or depressant medications, or if the patient has delirium or any neurologic disorder that impairs attention. In addition, the MMSE may not be valid if the patient does not have at least some high school education or if the patient belongs to a culture in which the MMSE questions are not relevant or understandable. For example, an 86-year-old Navajo woman was asked (in Navajo) to give the date. She responded, "It is early in the season when the thunder sleeps." This woman would not be considered impaired for her failure to say that it was Tuesday, October 15, 1990. She gave the correct answer for the date in her culture, education level, and lifeway, and the MMSE score will not be useful. Within these limitations, the MMSE is a very good screening tool in the family practice office. It may be particularly helpful for repeated testing over time to follow the progression of treatment of pseudo-dementia of depression, for example.

MINI-MENTAL STATE EXAMINATION (MMSE)

Add points for each correct response.

	Score	Points
Orientation		
1. What is the:		
Year?	____	1
Season?	____	1

Date?	___	1
Day?	___	1
Month?	___	1
2. Where are we?		
State?	___	1
County?	___	1
Town or city?	___	1
Hospital?	___	1
Floor?	___	1
Registration?	___	1
3. Name three objects, taking 1 second to say each. Then ask the patient to repeat all three after you have said them. Give 1 point for each correct answer. Repeat the answers untill patient learns all three.	___	3

Attention and calculation

4. Serial sevens. Give 1 point for each correct answer. Stop   ___   5
   after five answers. Alternate: Spell WORLD backwards.

Recall

5. Ask for names of three objects learned in question 3.   ___   3
   Give 1 point for each correct answer.

Language

6. Point to a pencil and a watch. Have the patient name   ___   2
   as you point.
7. Have the patient repeat "No ifs, ands, or buts."   ___   1
8. Have the patient follow a three-stage command: "Take a   ___   3
   paper in your right hand. Fold the paper in half. Put the
   paper on the floor."
9. Have the patient read and obey the following: "CLOSE   ___   1
   YOUR EYES." (Write it in large letters.)
10. Have the patient write a sentence of his or her choice.   ___   1
    (The sentence should contain a subject and an object and
    should make sense. Ignore spelling errors when scoring.)
11. Have the patient copy this design. Give 1 point if all sides   ___   1
    and angles are preserved and if the intersecting sides form
    a quadrangle.)

                                                          ___ Total = 30

In validation studies using a cut-off score of 23 or below, the MMSE has a sensitivity of 87%, a specificity of 82%, a false-positive ratio of 39.4%, and a false-negative of 4.7%. These ratios refer to the MMSE's capacity to accurately distinguish patients with clinically diagnosed dementia or delirium from patients without these syndromes.

Source: Courtesy of Marshall Folstein, MD. Reprinted with permission.

For additional information on administration and scoring refer to the following references:

1. Anthony JC, LeReschel, Niaz U, et al. Limits of "Mini-Mental State" as a screening test for dementia and delirium among hospital patients. Psych Med 1982;12: 397–408.

2. Folstein MF, Anthony JC, et al. Meaning of cognitive impairment in the elderly. J Am Geriatr Soc 1985;33(4):228–235.

3. Folstein MF, Folstein S, McHugh PR. Mini-Mental State: a practical method for grading the cognitive state of patients for the clinician. J Psych Res 1975;12:189–198.

4. Spenser MP, Folstein MF. The Mini-Mental State Examination. In: Keller PA, Ritt LG. Innovations in clinical practice: a source book. 1985;4:305–310.

Diagnostic Criteria for a Major Depressive Episode

A. At least five of the following symptoms have been present during the same 2-week period and represent a change from previous functioning; at least one of the symptoms is either (1) depressed mood or (2) loss of interest or pleasure. **Note:** Do not include symptoms that are clearly due to a general medical condition, or mood-incongruent delusions or hallucinations.
   (1) Depressed mood most of the day, nearly every day, as indicated by either subjective report (e.g., feels sad or empty) or observation made by others (e.g., appears tearful). **Note:** In children and adolescents, it can be irritable mood.
   (2) Markedly diminished interest or pleasure in all, or almost all, activities most of the day, nearly every day (as indicated by either subjective account or observation made by others).
   (3) Significant weight loss when not dieting, weight gain (e.g., a change of more than 5% of body weight in 1 month), or decrease or increase in appetite nearly every day. **Note:** In children, consider failure to make expected weight gains.
   (4) Insomnia or hypersomnia nearly every day.
   (5) Psychomotor agitation or retardation nearly every day (observable by others, not merely subjective feelings of restlessness or being slowed down).
   (6) Fatigue or loss of energy nearly every day.
   (7) Feelings of worthlessness or excessive or inappropriate guilt (which may be delusional) nearly every day (not merely self-reproach or guilt about being sick).
   (8) Diminished ability to think or concentrate, or indecisiveness, nearly every day (either by subjective account or as observed by others).
   (9) Recurrent thoughts of death (not just fear of dying), recurrent suicidal ideation without a specific plan, or a suicide attempt or a specific plan for committing suicide.

B. The symptoms do not meet criteria for a Mixed Episode (Mixed Mania and Depression).

C. The symptoms cause clinically significant distress or impairment in social, occupational, or other important areas of functioning.

D. The symptoms are not due to the direct physiologic effects of a substance (e.g., a drug of abuse, a medication) or a general medical condition (e.g., hypothyroidism).

191

E. The symptoms are not better accounted for by Bereavement; that is, after the loss of a loved one, the symptoms persist for longer than 2 months or are characterized by marked functional impairment, morbid preoccupation with worthlessness, suicidal ideation, psychotic symptoms, or psychomotor retardation.

Diagnostic Criteria for 296.2x Major Depressive Disorder, Single Episode

A. Presence of a single Major Depressive Episode (criteria above).

B. The Major Depressive Episode is not better accounted for by Schizoaffective Disorder and is not superimposed on Schizophrenia, Schizophreniform Disorder, Delusional Disorder, or Psychotic Disorder Not Otherwise Specified.

C. There has never been a Manic Episode, Mixed Episode, or Hypomanic Episode. **Note:** This exclusion does not apply if all the manic-like, mixed-like, or hypomanic-like episodes are substance- or treatment-induced or are due to the direct physiologic effects of a general medical condition.

Specify (for current or most recent episode)
Severity/Psychotic/Remission Specifiers

Chronic

With Catatonic Features

With Melancholic Features

With Atypical Features

With Postpartum Onset

Diagnostic Criteria for 296. 3x Major Depressive Disorder, Recurrent

A. Presence of two or more Major Depressive Episodes (as defined above).

B. The Major Depressive Episodes are not better accounted for by Schizoaffective Disorder and are not superimposed on Schizophrenia, Schizophreniform Disorder, Delusional Disorder, or Psychotic Disorder Not Otherwise Specified.

C. There has never been a Manic Episode, Mixed Episode, or Hypomanic Episode. **Note:** This exclusion does not apply if all of the manic-like, mixed-like, or hypomanic-like episodes are substance- or treatment-induced or are due to the direct physiologic effects of a general medical condition.

Specify (for current or most recent episode)
Severity/Psychotic/Remission Specifiers

Chronic

With Catatonic Features

With Melancholic Features

With Atypical Features

With Postpartum Onset

Specify

Longitudinal Course Specifiers (With and Without Interepisode Recovery)

With Seasonal Pattern

Reprinted with permission from the *Diagnostic and Statistical Manual of Mental Disorders.* 4th ed. Copyright 1994 American Psychiatric Association.

Diagnostic Criteria for 300.4 Dysthymic Disorder

A. Depressed mood for most of the day, for more days than not, as indicated either by subjective account or observation by others, for at least 2 years. **Note:** In children and adolescents, mood can be irritable and duration must be at least 1 year.

B. Presence, while depressed, of two (or more) of the following:
   (1) Poor appetite or overeating
   (2) Insomnia or hypersomnia
   (3) Low energy or fatigue
   (4) Low self-esteem
   (5) Poor concentration or difficulty making decisions
   (6) Feelings of hopelessness

C. During the 2-year period (1 year for children or adolescents) of the disturbance, the person has never been without the symptoms in Criterion A or B for more than 2 months at a time.

D. No Major Depressive Episode has been present during the first 2 years of the disturbance (1 year for children or adolescents); that is, the disturbance is not better accounted for by chronic Major Depressive Disorder or Major Depressive Disorder, In Partial Remission).
Note: There may have been a previous Major Depressive Episode, provided there was full remission (no significant signs or symptoms for 2 months) before the development of Dysthymic Disorder. In addition, after the initial 2 years (1 year in children or adolescents) of Dysthymic Disorder, there may be superimposed Major Depressive Disorder, in which case both diagnoses may be given when the criteria are met for a Major Depressive Episode.

E. There has never been a Manic Episode, Mixed Episode, or Hypomanic Episode, and criteria have never been met for Cyclothymic Disorder.

F. The disturbance does not occur exclusively during the course of a chronic Psychotic Disorder, such as Schizophrenia or Delusional Disorder.

G. The symptoms are not due to the direct physiologic effects of a substance (e.g., a drug of abuse, a medication) or a general medical condition (e.g., hypothyroidism).

H. The symptoms cause clinically significant distress or impairment in social, occupational, or other important areas of functioning.

Specify if

Early Onset: if onset is before age 21 years

Late Onset: if onset is age 21 years or older

Specify (for most recent 2 years of Dysthymic Disorder)

With Atypical Features

Diagnostic Criteria for the Adjustment Disorders

A. The development of emotional or behavioral symptoms in response to an identifiable stressor(s) occurring within 3 months of the onset of the stressor(s).

B. These symptoms or behaviors are clinically significant as evidenced by either of the following:
   (1) Marked distress that is in excess of what would be expected from exposure to the stressor
   (2) Significant impairment in social or occupational (academic) functioning

C. The stress-related disturbance does not meet the criteria for another specific Axis I disorder and is not merely an exacerbation of a preexisting Axis I or Axis II disorder.

D. The symptoms do not represent bereavement.

E. Once the stressor (or its consequences) has terminated, the symptoms do not persist for more than an additional 6 months.

Specify if

Acute: the disturbance lasts less than 6 months

Chronic: the disturbance lasts 6 months or longer

Adjustment disorders are coded based on subtype, which is selected according to the predominant symptoms. The specific stressor(s) can be specified on Axis IV.

309.0	With Depressed Mood
309.24	With Anxiety
309.28	With Mixed Anxiety and Depressed Mood
309.3	With Disturbance of Conduct
309.4	With Mixed Disturbance of Emotions and Conduct
309.9	Unspecified

APPENDIX N

Diagnostic Criteria for 301.83 Borderline Personality Disorder

A pervasive pattern of instability of interpersonal relationships, self-image and affects, and marked impulsivity beginning by early adulthood and present in a variety of contexts, as indicated by five (or more) of the following:

1. Frantic efforts to avoid real or imagined abandonment. **Note:** Do not include suicidal or self-mutilating behavior covered in Criterion 5.
2. A pattern of unstable and intense interpersonal relationships characterized by alternating between extremes of idealization and devaluation
3. Identity disturbance: markedly and persistently unstable self-image or sense of self
4. Impulsivity in at least two areas that are potentially self-damaging (e.g., spending, sex, substance abuse, reckless driving, binge eating). **Note:** Do not include suicidal or self-mutilating behavior covered in Criterion 5.
5. Recurrent suicidal behavior, gestures or threats, or self-mutilating behavior
6. Affective instability due to a marked reactivity of mood (e.g., intense episodic dysphoria, irritability, or anxiety usually lasting a few hours and only rarely more than a few days)
7. Chronic feelings of emptiness
8. Inappropriate, intense anger or difficulty controlling anger (e.g., frequent displays of temper, constant anger, recurrent physical fights)
9. Transient, stress-related paranoid ideation or severe dissociative symptoms

Overview of Treatment
for Depression

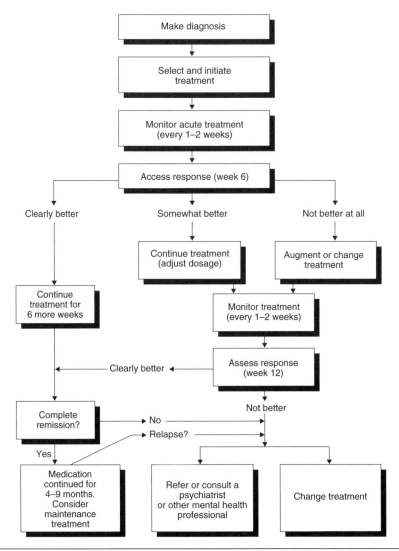

Reprinted from Depression Guideline Panel. Depression in Primary Care: Detection, Diagnosis, and Treatment. Quick Reference Guide for Clinicians, Number 5. Rockville, MD: US Department of Health and Human Services, Public Health Service, Agency for Health Care Policy and Research. AHCPR Publication No. 93–0552. April 1993.

APPENDIX P

Antidepressants Commonly Used in Primary Care

Drug	Adult Dose (mg/day)	Dosage Time	Sedation	Anticholinergic Side Effects
SSRIs				
Fluoxetine (Prozac)	5–80	AM	0	0
Sertraline (Zoloft)	50–200	AM or PM	+/−	0
Paroxetine (Paxil)	20–50	AM or PM	+/−	0
TRICYCLIC ANTIDEPRESSANTS				
Amitriptyline (Elavil)	75–300	Bedtime	++++	+++
Desipramine (Norpramin)	75–300	Bedtime	+	+
Doxepin (Sinequan)	75–300	Bedtime	+++	++
Imipramine (Tofranil)	75–300	Bedtime	++	+++
Nortriptyline (Pamelor)	40–150	Bedtime	++	++
OTHER				
Bupropion (Wellbutrin)	225–480	3–4 x/day	0	++
Nefazodone (Serzone)	200–600	3–4 x/day	+++	0
Trazodone (Desyrel)	50–600	3 x/day	+++	0
Venlafaxine (Effexor)	75–375	3 x/day	+/−	+/−

Adapted from Post RM. Mood disorders: somatic treatment. In: Kaplan HI, Sadock BJ, eds. Comprehensive textbook of psychiatry. 6th ed. Baltimore: Williams & Wilkins, 1995:1160–1161; Bhatia SK. Major depression: selecting safe and effective treatment. Am Fam Physician 1997;55:1683–1698.

APPENDIX Q

Clinical Guidelines from the AHCPR

The Agency for Health Care Policy and Research (AHCPR) has developed Clinical Practice Guidelines to assist practitioner and patient decisions about appropriate health care for specific clinical conditions. Within the field of mental health care, the AHCPR has developed the *Clinical Practice Guideline for Depression in Primary Care: Detection, Diagnosis and Treatment.* The guideline was developed by an independent, multidisciplinary panel of private sector clinicians and other experts which employed an explicit, science-based methodology and expert clinical judgment to develop specific statements on patient assessment and management. The panel's recommendations are primarily based on the published scientific literature. When the literature was incomplete or inconsistent, the recommendations reflect the professional judgment of the panel members and consultants.

The statements from the guidelines which follow are coded according to the strength of the available evidence as interpreted by the AHCPR panel:

A = Good research-based evidence, with some panel opinion, to support the guideline statement

B = Fair research-based evidence, with substantial panel opinion, to support the guideline statement

C = Guideline statement based primarily on panel opinion, with minimal research-based evidence, but significant clinical experience

Some Clinical Guidelines of the AHCPR are reprinted here because they relate directly to the clinical practice issues covered in this text. The complete volumes of the AHCPR guidelines can be obtained from the US Department of Health and Human Services, Public Health Service, as cited in the bibliography.

Diagnosis and Epidemiology of Depression

Guideline: A major depressive episode can occur as part of a primary mood disorder (e.g., major depressive or bipolar disorder), as part of nonmood psychiatric conditions (e.g., eating, panic, or obsessive-compulsive disorders [OCDs]), in cases of drug or alcohol intoxication or withdrawal, as biologic or psychological consequences of various nonpsychiatric general medical conditions, or as consequences of the use of selected prescription medications. Finally, a grief reaction (bereavement) may initially (within the first 2 months) meet the criteria for a major depressive episode. (Strength of the Evidence = A)

Guideline: The point prevalence for major depressive disorder in the western industrialized nations is 2.3% to 3.2% for men and 4.5% to 9.3% for women. The lifetime risk for major depressive disorder is 7% to 12% for men and 20% to 25% for women. Risk factors for major depressive disorder include female gender (especially during the postpartum period), a history of depressive illness in first-degree relatives, and prior episodes of major depression. (Strength of the Evidence = A)

Substance Abuse and Depression

Guideline: Alcoholism and major depressive disorder are distinct clinical entities. They are not different expressions of the same underlying condition. Although alcoholism is rarely a consequence of depression, many alcoholics do develop depressive symptoms or the full syndrome of major depression. (Strength of the Evidence = B)

Guideline: It is recommended that depressed patients with concurrent substance abuse discontinue the abused substance and their condition be reevaluated 4 to 8 weeks later when they are in a drug-free state. If major depressive disorder is still present, it is treated as a primary mood disorder. In certain clinical situations, however, earlier treatment of the depression may be needed. (Strength of the Evidence = B)

Anxiety Disorders and Depression

Guideline: Depressive symptoms or syndromes often accompany anxiety, panic, or phobic disorders. Furthermore, anxiety symptoms are frequent in major depressive episodes. The depression may precede the panic or anxiety disorder, or the anxiety disorder may be the forerunner of and part of the longitudinal course of a mood disorder. The presence of both anxiety/panic and a major depressive disorder results in a more severe disorder with greater impairment than does either disorder alone. When the patient complains of anxiety symptoms, major depressive symptoms should be elicited. (Strength of the Evidence = A)

Guideline: For those depressed patients whose disorder has some obsessive features, the mood disorder is the initial focus of treatment. If full-blown OCD is present with depressive symptoms or manic-depressive disorder, the OCD is usually the initial objective of treatment. Evidence from OCD medication treatment trials suggests that, if the OCD is treated successfully, the depressive symptoms usually abate. (Strength of the Evidence = A)

Somatization and Depression

Guideline: Somatization is defined as the presentation of somatic symptoms by patients with underlying psychiatric illness or psychosocial distress. These somatic symptoms have no, or insufficient, underlying organic cause. Although most depressed patients have medically unexplained somatic complaints, they are rarely of sufficient intensity or frequency to meet the threshold for somatization disorder. (Strength of the Evidence = A)

Guideline: The practitioner is advised to have a high index of suspicion for major depressive or other mood disorders if patients present with two or more unexplained pain complaints. A formal diagnostic evaluation for mood disorders is recommended. (Strength of the Evidence = B)

Personality Disorders and Depression

Guideline: Personality disorders are not uncommon among mood-disordered patients. The presence of a personality disorder does not exclude diagnosis of a mood disorder, if present. When both a major depressive and a personality disorder are present, more frequent and longer major depressive episodes, as well as poorer interepisode recovery (if untreated), may be anticipated. For some with major depression, symptoms that initially appear to be maladaptive personality traits remit once the depressive disorder improves. (Strength of the Evidence = B)

Selected Medical Conditions and Depression

Guideline: The symptomatic expression of depression in patients with diabetes is analogous to that in patients without diabetes. Given the impact of depression on the management of diabetes and the fact that most diabetic patients do not develop major depression, the practitioner is advised to screen, assess fully, and treat major depression when present in these patients. (Strength of the Evidence = A)

Guideline: The relationship between depression and increased morbidity and mortality is well documented in both postmyocardial infarction patients and in coronary artery disease patients without myocardial infarction. Given the higher morbidity and the fact that most of these patients do not develop a major depression, the practitioner is advised to screen, assess fully, and treat major depression when present in these patient groups. (Strength of the Evidence = A)

Guideline: It is essential to separate the symptoms of cancer or its treatment from those of a depressive disorder. A history and clinical interview are needed for a definitive diagnosis. The symptoms of persistent dysphoria, feelings of helplessness and worthlessness, loss of self-esteem, and wishes to die are the most reliable indicators of clinical depression in patients with cancer. Because major depression occurs in approximately 25% of patients with cancer, it should be independently diagnosed and treated. (Strength of the Evidence = B)

Depression and Chronic Fatigue Syndrome and Fibromyalgia

Guideline: Nearly all depressed patients complain of fatigue and low energy. This symptom is associated with a 46% to 75% lifetime rate of major depressive disorder. Complaints of chronic fatigue must be differentiated from the formal chronic fatigue syndrome. (Strength of the Evidence = B)

Guideline: As with other medical conditions, patients with fibromyalgia may or may not have clinical depression. If present, it should be diagnosed and treated as a separate entity. (Strength of the Evidence = B)

Treatment of Depression

Guideline: A depressed outpatient's adherence to treatment can be improved by educating the patient and, in many cases, the family about the treatment, its potential side effects, and its likelihood of success. (Strength of Evidence = A)

Guideline: A 4- to 6-week trial of medication or a 6- to 8-week trial of psychotherapy usually results in at least a partial remission (50% symptom reduction), and a 10- to 12-week trial usually results in a nearly full response (minimal or no symptoms) to treatment. However, full restoration of psychosocial function often takes longer. (Strength of the Evidence = B)

Guideline: If a patient shows a partial response to treatment by 5 to 6 weeks, the same treatment is continued for 5 to 6 more weeks. (Strength of Evidence = A) If the patient does not respond at all by 6 weeks or responds only partially by 12 weeks, it is appropriate to consider other treatment options. (Strength of the Evidence = B)

Guideline: Patients with moderate to severe major depressive disorder are appropriately treated with medication, whether or not formal psychotherapy is also used. Medication is administered in dosages shown to alleviate symptoms. The specific medication choice is based on side-effects profiles, history of prior response, family history of response, type of depression, concurrent general medical or psychiatric illnesses, and concurrently prescribed medications. (Strength of the Evidence = A)

Guideline: Patients with mild to moderate major depression who prefer psychotherapy alone as the initial acute treatment choice may be treated with this option. Psychotherapy alone is not recommended for the acute treatment of patients with severe and/or psychotic major depressive disorders. (Strength of the Evidence = B)

Guideline: Combined treatment (with both medication and psychotherapy) may have an advantage for patients with partial responses to either treatment alone (if adequately administered) and for those with a more chronic history or poor interepisode recovery. However, combined treatment may provide no unique advantage for patients with uncomplicated, nonchronic major depressive disorder. (Strength of the Evidence = B)

Guideline: Electroconvulsive therapy is a first-line treatment option only for patients with more severe or psychotic forms of major depressive disorder, those who have failed to respond to other therapies, those with medical conditions precluding the use of medications, and those with an essential need for rapid response. (Strength of the Evidence = A)

Guideline: No one antidepressant medication is clearly more effective than another. No single medication results in remission for all patients. The selection of a particular medication for a particular patient depends on a variety of factors: short-term and long-term side effects (Strength of the Evidence = A); prior positive/negative response to the medication (Strength of the Evidence = A); history of first-degree relatives responding to a medication (Strength of the Evidence = B); concurrent, nonpsychiatric medical illnesses that may make selected medications more or less risky or noxious (Strength of the Evidence = A); the concomitant use of other nonpsychotropic medications that may alter the metabolism or increase the side effects of the antidepressant medication (Strength of the Evidence = A); likelihood of adherence based on patient's history (Strength of the Evidence = B); type of depression (Strength of the Evidence = B); effectiveness when given once a day (Strength of the Evidence = B); degree of interference in lifestyle expected from treatment (Strength of the Evidence = B); cost of the medication; the practitioner's experience with the agent (Strength of the Evidence = C); patient preference (Strength of the Evidence = C); and other considerations. Although these factors may point toward one or another medication, none is sufficiently predictive to allow selection for treatment with certainty. Therefore, an empirical trial and careful evaluation of outcome, with subsequent revision if response is insufficient, are recommended.

Guideline: If the patient has a concurrent, non-mood psychiatric disorder, then medications that are effective in both depression and the associated psychiatric condition are preferred. (Strength of the Evidence = B)

Guideline: If the patient has not responded at all or has only a minimal symptomatic response to medication by 6 weeks, two steps are needed: (1) reassessment of the adequacy of the diagnosis and (2) reassessment of the adequacy of treatment. (Strength of the Evidence = A)

Guideline: For those with no meaningful symptom response by 6 weeks (or by 4 weeks in the severely ill), there are five possible options (Strength of the Evidence = A):

Continue medication at a corrected dosage.
Discontinue the first medication and begin a second.
Add an adjunctive treatment (augment with a second medication).
Add psychotherapy to the initial medication.
Obtain a consultation/referral.

Guideline: Before changing a patient's treatment, the practitioner is advised to evaluate the adequacy of the medication dosage. (Strength of the Evidence = A)

Guideline: Switching to a new medication is an option after an adequate trial of the first treatment. A general medical principle is that a combination of two drugs should not be used when one drug will suffice. Thus, switching medications is often preferred over augmentation as an initial strategy. (Strength of the Evidence = A)

Guideline: Augmentation of the initial medication with a second one is not advised until the initial trial has been adequate in time and dosage. (Strength of the Evidence = A)

Guideline: For patients with a partial response at week 12 whose residual symptoms are largely psychosocial rather than vegetative, psychotherapy may be added and the medication remain unchanged. If the residual symptoms at 6 or 12 weeks are largely somatic or vegetative, either adjunctive medication or a new, different medication may be indicated. (Strength of the Evidence = C)

Guideline: In any case in which the practitioner feels that he or she lacks sufficient knowledge and/or experience to manage a patient's medication or if two or more attempts at acute-phase medication treatment have failed or resulted in only partial response, the practitioner is advised to seek a consultation from or refer the patient to a psychiatrist well trained in psychopharmacology. In addition, if drug-drug interactions are anticipated (e.g., in patients taking nonpsychotropic medications that may interact with the antidepressants), consultation from a pharmacist or psychiatrist is advisable. (Strength of the Evidence = C)

Guideline: Because psychotherapy alone has produced equivocal results in patients with melancholic (endogenous) symptom features, medication is recommended as the first-line treatment in these patients; medications have clear evidence of efficacy in placebo-controlled trials. (Strength of the Evidence = A)

Guideline: Formal psychotherapy can be used in combination with medication with the objectives of rectifying ongoing psychosocial difficulties that contribute to some depressive symptoms, such as pessimism, low self-esteem, or marital difficulties. (Strength of the Evidence = B)

Guideline: Given the modest advantage for combined treatment and the suggestive evidence that some patients respond better (but others do not) to the combined treatment, clinical judgment remains the basis for deciding when to use combined treatment and which type of psychotherapy to use. (Strength of the Evidence = C)

Geriatric Depression

Guideline: Depression in the elderly should not routinely be ascribed to demoralization or "normal sadness" over financial barriers, medical problems, or other concerns. The general principles for treatment of adults with major depressive disorder apply as well to elderly patients. (Strength of the Evidence = A)

Length of Medication Treatment for Depression

Guideline: The objective of continuation treatment is to decrease the likelihood of relapse (a return of the current episode of depression). If patients respond to acute-phase medication, it is generally continued at the same dosage for 4 to 9 months after return to the clinically well state. (Strength of the Evidence = A)

Guideline: Maintenance treatment is aimed at preventing a new episode of depression. Patients who have had three or more episodes of major depression are potential candidates for long-term maintenance antidepressant medication. Maintenance medications are generally of the same type and dosage found effective in acute-phase treatment. (Strength of the Evidence = A) Maintenance psychotherapy does not appear to be effective in preventing a recurrence, although it may delay the onset of the next episode. (Strength of the Evidence = B)

Guideline: There is very strong evidence that specific medications prevent relapse/recurrence in most patients with recurrent forms of major depressive disorder. Since the episode onset date may not be readily determined, particularly in first-episode patients, most patients should receive the full therapeutic dosage of antidepressant drug for 4 to 9 months (the average duration of a major depressive episode) of continuation therapy after symptom remission is achieved. In those for whom the onset date is known, a somewhat shorter continuation phase may be attempted, but it should not be less than 4 months. For those with episodes of 2 years or more, it may be wise to pursue a continuation period of at least 9 months. Patients who have a recurrence shortly after continuation-therapy withdrawal may require long-term maintenance medication. (Strength of the Evidence = A)

Guideline: Patients who have responded fully in the acute phase of treatment need to be seen only once every 1 to 3 months during the continuation and maintenance phases to evaluate symptoms, efficacy, and side effects and to promote adherence. (Strength of the Evidence = B)

Guideline: Antidepressant medications are generally safe, even with long-term use. However, medications should be discontinued if they are not required. All patients with a single episode of major depressive disorder are advised to discontinue medication after 4 to 9 months of continuation treatment because only 50% will have another episode of major depressive disorder. Even then, the next episode may be years hence. Whenever possible, the decision to discontinue treatment is made collaboratively with the full participation and knowledge of the patient. If the full depressive episode recurs during or shortly after discontinuation, the episode has not "run its course," and the full therapeutic dosage is typically reinstated. (Strength of the Evidence = A)

Guideline: It is advisable to taper all tricyclic antidepressants on discontinuation if the patient has had exposure at therapeutic dosages for 3 months or more. A tapering schedule over 2 to 4 weeks is usually well tolerated. (Strength of the Evidence = A)

Guideline: There is no evidence that bupropion, monamine oxidase inhibitors, fluoxetine, paroxetine, sertraline, or trazodone must be tapered. (Strength of the Evidence = B) [Author note: More recent evidence suggests one should taper the selective serotonin reuptake inhibitors.]

Reprinted from Depression Guideline Panel. *Depression in Primary Care.* Vol 1; *Detection and Diagnosis.* Vol 2; *Treatment of Major Depression.* Clinical Practice Guideline, Number 5. Rockville, MD: US Department of Health and Human Services, Public Health Service, Agency for Health Care Policy and Research. AHCPR Publication No. 93-0550 and 93-0051. April 1993.

APPENDIX R

Diagnostic Criteria for 300.81 Somatization Disorder

A. A history of many physical complaints, beginning before age 30 years, which occur over a period of several years and result in treatment being sought or significant impairment in social, occupational, or other important areas of functioning.

B. Each of the following criteria must have been met, with individual symptoms occurring at any time during the course of the disturbance:
   (1) *Four pain symptoms:* a history of pain related to at least four different sites or functions (e.g., head, abdomen, back, joints, extremities, chest, rectum, during menstruation, during sexual intercourse, or during urination)
   (2) *Two gastrointestinal symptoms:* a history of at least two gastrointestinal symptoms other than pain (e.g., nausea, bloating, vomiting other than during pregnancy, diarrhea, or intolerance of several different foods)
   (3) *One sexual symptom:* a history of at least one sexual or reproductive symptom other than pain (e.g., sexual indifference, erectile or ejaculatory dysfunction, irregular menses, excessive menstrual bleeding, vomiting throughout pregnancy)
   (4) *One pseudoneurologic symptom:* a history of at least one symptom or deficit suggesting a neurologic condition not limited to pain (conversion symptoms such as impaired coordination or balance, paralysis or localized weakness, difficulty swallowing or lump in throat, aphonia, urinary retention, hallucinations, loss of touch or pain sensation, double vision, blindness, deafness, seizures; dissociative symptoms such as amnesia; or loss of consciousness other than fainting)

C. Either (1) or (2):
   (1) After appropriate investigation, each of the symptoms in Criterion B cannot be fully explained by a known general medical condition or the direct effects of a substance (e.g., drug of abuse, a medication).
   (2) When there is a related general medical condition, the physical complaints or resulting social or occupational impairment are in excess of what would be expected from the history, physical examination, or laboratory findings.

D. The symptoms are not intentionally produced or feigned (as in Factitious Disorder or Malingering).

Reprinted with permission from the *Diagnostic and Statistical Manual of Mental Disorders.* 4th ed. Copyright 1994 American Psychiatric Association.

APPENDIX S

Diagnostic Criteria for Pain Disorder

A. Pain in one or more anatomic sites is the predominant focus of the clinical presentation and is of sufficient severity to warrant clinical attention.
B. The pain causes clinically significant distress or impairment in social, occupational, or other important areas of functioning.
C. Psychological factors are judged to have an important role in the onset, severity, exacerbation, or maintenance of the pain.
D. The symptom or deficit is not intentionally produced or feigned (as in Factitious Disorder or Malingering).
E. The pain is not better accounted for by a Mood, Anxiety, or Psychotic Disorder and does not meet criteria for Dyspareunia.

Code as follows
307.80 Pain Disorder Associated With Psychological Factors

307.89 Pain Disorder Associated With Both Psychological Factors and a General Medical Condition

For both of above, specify if
Acute: duration is less than 6 months

Chronic: duration is 6 months or longer

Note: The following is not considered to be a mental disorder and is included here to facilitate differential diagnosis.

Pain Disorder Associated With a General Medical Condition

A general medical condition has a major role in the onset, severity, exacerbation, or maintenance of the pain. (If psychological factors are present, they are not judged to have a major role in the onset, severity, exacerbation, or maintenance of the pain.) The diagnostic code for the pain is selected based on the associated general medical condition if one has been established or on the anatomic location of the pain if the underlying general medical condition is not yet clearly established.

Reprinted with permission from the *Diagnostic and Statistical Manual of Mental Disorders*. 4th ed. Copyright 1994 American Psychiatric Association.

Diagnostic Criteria for 300.7 Hypochondriasis

A. Preoccupation with fears of having, or the idea that one has, a serious disease based on the person's misinterpretations of bodily symptoms.

B. The preoccupation persists despite appropriate medical evaluation and reassurance.

C. The belief in Criterion A is not of delusional intensity (as in Delusional Disorder, Somatic Type) and is not restricted to a circumscribed concern about appearance (as in Body Dysmorphic Disorder).

D. The preoccupation causes clinically significant distress or impairment in social, occupational, or other important areas of functioning.

E. The duration of the disturbance is at least 6 months.

F. The preoccupation is not better accounted for by Generalized Anxiety Disorder, Obsessive-Compulsive Disorder, Panic Disorder, a Major Depressive Episode, Separation Anxiety, or another Somatoform Disorder.

Specify if

With Poor Insight: if, for most of the time during the current episode, the person does not recognize that the concern about having a serious illness is excessive or unreasonable.

Diagnostic Criteria for 300.11 Conversion Disorder

A. One or more symptoms or deficits affecting voluntary motor or sensory function that suggest a neurologic or other general medical condition.

B. Psychological factors are judged to be associated with the symptom or deficit because the initiation or exacerbation of the symptom or deficit is preceded by conflicts or other stressors.

C. The symptom or deficit is not intentionally produced or feigned (as in Factitious Disorder or Malingering).

D. The symptom or deficit cannot, after appropriate investigation, be fully explained by a general medical condition, or by the direct effects of a substance, or as a culturally sanctioned behavior or experience.

E. The symptom or deficit causes clinically significant distress or impairment in social, occupational, or other important areas of functioning or warrants medical evaluation.

F. The symptom or deficit is not limited to pain or sexual dysfunction, does not occur exclusively during the course of Somatization Disorder, and is not better accounted for by another mental disorder.

Specify type of symptom or deficit

With Motor Symptom or Deficit

With Sensory Symptom or Deficit

With Seizures or Convulsions

With Mixed Presentation

Reprinted with permission from the *Diagnostic and Statistical Manual of Mental Disorders*. 4th ed. Copyright 1994 American Psychiatric Association.

PPENDIX V

Diagnostic Criteria for Factitious Disorder

A. There is intentional production or feigning of physical or psychological signs or symptoms.
B. The motivation for the behavior is to assume the sick role.
C. External incentives for the behavior (such as economic gain, avoiding legal responsibility, or improving physical well-being, as in Malingering) are absent.

Code Based on Type

300.16 With Predominantly Psychological Signs and Symptoms
300.19 With Predominantly Physical Signs and Symptoms
300.19 With Combined Psychological and Physical Signs and Symptoms

Research Criteria for Factitious Disorder by Proxy

A. Intentional production or feigning of physical or psychological signs or symptoms in another person who is under the individual's care.
B. The motivation for the perpetrator's behavior is to assume the sick role by proxy.
C. External incentives for the behavior (such as economic gain) are absent.
D. The behavior is not better accounted for by another mental disorder.

Recommended Reading

Some references below are most suited for physicians; others are very helpful for patients and their families. Before recommending any reading material or book to a patient or family, it is very important to read and familiarize yourself with the text to be certain that it is an appropriate and therapeutic tool for that particular patient.

Diagnostic Issues (All Psychiatric Diagnoses)

American Psychiatric Association. Diagnostic and statistical manual of mental disorders. 4th ed. Washington, DC: American Psychiatric Association, 1994.

> *The full* DSM-IV *gives a great deal of epidemiologic and background information, whereas the small, spiral-bound version gives bare-bones lists of criteria.*

Kaplan HI, Sadock BJ, Grebb JA, eds. Kaplan and Sadock's synopsis of psychiatry: behavioral sciences, clinical psychiatry. 7th ed. Baltimore: Williams & Wilkins, 1994.

> *This is an excellent brief text of psychiatry. There is something in this text regarding almost any psychiatric problem that might be seen in a primary care practice.*

Anxiety Disorders

Sheehan DV. The Anxiety disease. New York: Bantam Books, 1986.

> This is a helpful book for patients who suffer panic disorder, agoraphobia, and phobias. Although a bit old in terms of a discussion of medication management, it is a classic. It is important to advise patients that we recommend that they do not follow the instructions in the book for carotid massage and that they do not apply pressure to their eyes as attempts to abort a panic attack. These are old methods that are potentially dangerous.

Depression

Nemeroff CB, ed. Proceedings of a symposium: contemporary issues in the management of depression. Am J Med 1994;97(6A).

> *This supplement to the* American Journal of Medicine *includes seven articles that cover new developments in the treatment of depression.*

Fischer PM, ed. Depression in special patient populations. J Fam Pract Supplement 1996;43(6).

> *These six articles cover the treatment of depressed patients with anxiety, somatic symptoms, chronic pain, medical comorbidity, and postpartum depressive disorders.*

Stuart M, Lieberman, JA. The fifteen minute hour: applied psychotherapy for the primary care physician. 2nd ed. Westport, Conn: Praeger, 1993.

This is an excellent text for primary care physicians.

Burns DD. Feeling good: the new mood therapy. New York: Signet, Penguin Books, 1981.

This is an introductory book for patients on cognitive therapy.

Burns DD. The feeling good handbook: using the new mood therapy in everyday life. New York: William Morrow, 1989.

A sequel and an improvement on the 1981 text, this book is for patients.

Beck AT. Love is never enough: how couples can overcome misunderstandings, resolve conflicts, and solve relationship problems through cognitive therapy. New York: Harper & Row, 1988.

A cognitive therapy approach to marital issues, this book is for patients.

Depression in Primary Care, vol. 1 (AHCPR Publication # 93-0550)

Depression in Primary Care, vol. 2 (AHCPR Publication # 93-0551)

Quick Reference: Depression in Primary Care (AHCPR Publication # 93-0552)

Depression is a Treatable Illness: A Patient's Guide (AHCPR Publication #93-553)

These resources are available from the US Public Health Service, Agency for Health Care Policy and Research, Executive Office Center, 2101 E. Jefferson Street, Suite 501, Rockville, MD 20852; phone: 800-358-9295.

Somatoform Spectrum Disorders

Ford CV. The somatizing disorders: illness as a way of life. New York: Elsevier, 1983.

This text provides comprehensive explanation and coverage of the full somatoform spectrum.

Smith GR. The course of somatization and its effects on utilization of health care resources. Psychosomatics 1994;35(3):263-267.

Smith GR, Rost K, Kashner TM. A trial of the effect of a standardized psychiatric consultation on health outcomes and costs in somatizing patients. Arch Gen Psychiatry 1995;52(3):238-243.

Dr. Smith and his colleagues have written many excellent articles on the somatoform spectrum disorders. The latter two emphasize the effect of somatization on health care costs and what can be done to reduce this impact.

McCahill ME. Somatoform disorders and related syndromes. In: Taylor RB, ed. Family medicine principles and practice. 5th ed. New York: Springer-Verlag, 1998:297-303.

This text chapter provides a clinically practical overview of the somatoform spectrum disorders, factitious disorder, and malingering. The common theme is the patient who presents with multiple somatic complaints and no objective findings.

Substance Abuse

Schuckit MA. Drug and alcohol abuse: clinical guide to diagnosis and treatment. 3rd ed. New York: Plenum Medical Books, 1989.

Schuckit MA. Alcohol and alcoholism. In: Fauci AS, Braunwald E, Isselbacher KJ, et al, eds. Harrison's principles of internal medicine. 14th ed. New York: McGraw-Hill, 1998:2503–2508.

Both of these references provide the physician with comprehensive yet clear information about diagnosis and treatment of substance abuse.

INDEX

Page numbers followed by "t" denote tables.

AA. *See* Alcoholics Anonymous
Acquired immunodeficiency syndrome. *See* Human immunodeficiency virus infection
Activities of daily living (ADLs), 107, 108t
Acute stress disorder (ASD), 1, 5–6
    diagnostic criteria for, 177–178
    management of, 14
    symptoms of, 3t, 5–6
AD. *See* Alzheimer's disease
Adalat. *See* Nifedipine
ADHD. *See* Attention-deficit hyperactivity disorder
Adjustment disorder
    with anxious features, 9
    with depressed mood, 37, 40, 47
    diagnostic criteria for, 196
ADLs. *See* Activities of daily living
Agency for Health Care Policy Research clinical practice guidelines for depression, 200–207
Agoraphobia, 4–5
AIDS. *See* Human immunodeficiency virus infection
Alanon, 155
Ala-teen, 155
Alcohol use/abuse. *See also* Substance use disorders
    chief complaints associated with, 141, 143t
    diagnostic testing for, 150–151
    epidemiology of, 142
    generalized anxiety disorder and, 16
    genetics of, 157
    history taking for, 142, 144t
    impairment related to blood alcohol level, 146t
    insomnia and, 98, 100
    Korsakoff's syndrome and, 111–112
    medication management of, 155
    physical examination for, 145–146
    rehabilitation programs for, 154–155
    screening for, 143–145, 144t
    when to refer for, 151
Alcohol withdrawal
    management of, 153–154
    signs and symptoms of, 146–147
Alcoholics Anonymous (AA), 151, 155
Alprazolam, 12, 13t, 185

Alternative therapies
    for chronic fatigue syndrome, 35
    for fibromyalgia syndrome, 78
Altitude insomnia, 98
Alzheimer's disease (AD), 112–113
    clinical criteria for, 112–113, 113t
    epidemiology of, 112
    medications for, 115–116, 116t
    support group for, 117
Amantadine, 54t
Ambien. *See* Zolpidem
American Lupus Society, 171
Amitriptyline, 53t, 199
    for fibromyalgia syndrome, 76–77, 77t
    for migraine prophylaxis, 92
Amnestic syndromes, 111–112. *See also* Memory concerns
Amoxapine, 53t
Amphetamine
    abuse of, 143t, 147–148
    for attention-deficit hyperactivity disorder, 25, 26t
ANA. *See* Antinuclear antibodies
Anafranil. *See* Clomipramine
Analgesics
    for fibromyalgia syndrome, 76
    for headache, 90–92, 91t
Antabuse. *See* Disulfiram
Antianxiety medications, xxxiv, 13t
    for anxiety due to medical condition, 15
    for generalized anxiety disorder, 16
    for obsessive-compulsive disorder, 14
    for panic disorder, 12–13
    for post-traumatic stress disorder, 14
Antiarrhythmic agents, 52t
Anticholinesterases, 115
Anticonvulsants, 169
Antidepressants, xxxiii, 48–58, 199, 203–207
    for body dysmorphic disorder, 133
    classes of, 50–54 (*See also* specific classes)
        atypical antidepressants, 54, 55t
        monoamine oxidase inhibitors, 52–54, 54t
        selective serotonin reuptake inhibitors, 50–51, 51t, 52t
        tricyclics, 51–52, 53t, 54t
    considerations in selection of, 48–50
    discontinuation of, 207
    dosages of, 199
    drug interactions with, 49

Antidepressants—*Continued*
for dysthymic disorder, 47
efficacy of, 48
for generalized anxiety disorder, 16
length of treatment with, 57-58, 206-207
long-term maintenance therapy with, 58, 58t, 206-207
for major depressive disorder, 47
medical assessment before initiation of, 48-49, 49t
for medically ill patients, 57t
diabetes, 54-55
for migraine prophylaxis, 92
overdose of, 49-50
for panic disorder, 12-13, 13t
patient and family education about, 60-61
for post-traumatic stress disorder, 14
for pregnant or lactating patient, 55-57
side effects of, 49, 199
Antimalarial agents, 168, 168t
Antinuclear antibodies (ANA), xvi, 164
Antiphospholipid antibody syndrome, 166t
Anxiety disorders, xiii-xiv, 1-18
chief complaints in, 1-2
in children, 2
definition of anxiety, 1
depression and, 2, 201
developmental delay and, 70
diagnostic criteria for, 175-184
diagnostic testing for, 11
epidemiology of, 2
follow-up of patients with, 17-18
forms of, 1
history taking for, 2-11, 3t
acute stress disorder, 5-6
anxiety disorder due to medical condition, 8
generalized anxiety disorder, 9
obsessive-compulsive disorder, 7
panic attack, 2-4
panic disorder, 4-5, 5t
post-traumatic stress disorder, 6-7
separation anxiety disorder of childhood/adolescence, 9-11, 10t
specific phobias, 9
substance-induced anxiety, 8t, 8-9
laboratory investigation of, 12t
lifestyle modifications for, 17
management of, 12-17
patient and family education about, 17
physical examination of persons with, 11
sleep disturbance and, 100, 103
somatoform disorders and, 129, 129t
when to refer for, 11-12
Aricept. *See* Donepezil
Arthritis
rheumatoid, 166t
in systemic lupus erythematosus, 164

ASD. *See* Acute stress disorder
Asendin. *See* Amoxapine
Atabrine, 168t
Ativan. *See* Lorazepam
Attention-deficit hyperactivity disorder (ADHD), 19-28
behavioral rating scales for, 21, 22t
behavioral therapy for, 25
chief complaints in, 19
developmental delay and, 70
diagnostic criteria for, 20t
diagnostic testing for, 22-23
differential diagnosis of, 23t, 23-24
follow-up of patients with, 27
history taking for, 19-21
patient education about, 27-28
pharmacotherapy for, 25-27, 26t
complications of, 26
dosing schedule for, 25-26
duration of, 27
patient monitoring during, 26
rate of response to, 25
physical examination in, 22
support groups for, 27t, 27-28
when to refer for, 24-25
Autism, 24, 70. *See also* Developmental delay
Aventyl. *See* Nortriptyline

"Baby blues," 42
BDD. *See* Body dysmorphic disorder
Behavioral rating scales, 21, 22t
Behavioral therapy
for attention-deficit hyperactivity disorder, 25
for chronic fatigue syndrome, 34
for developmental delay, 71
Benign senescent forgetfulness, 111
Benzodiazepines, 185
for anxiety disorders in medically ill patients, 15
dosages of, 185
for generalized anxiety disorder, 16
half-lives of, 185
for insomnia, 104, 104t
for panic disorder, 12-13, 13t
symptoms precipitated by withdrawal from, 9
use in dementia, 116
Bereavement, 6, 41, 41t
management of, 48
Beta-adrenergic blockers, 15t
Binswanger's disease, 113
Biotinidase deficiency, 69
Bipolar disorder, 39t
Blessed Dementia Scale, 110
Blood alcohol level, 146t. *See also* Alcohol use/abuse

Body dysmorphic disorder (BDD), 120t, 121, 124
  family involvement in, 138-139
  management of, 132-133
  patient education about, 138
  when to refer for, 128
Borderline personality disorder (BPD)
  depression and, 37, 40
  diagnostic criteria for, 197
  epidemiology of, 40
  management of, 47-48
Brain tumor, 83t, 87, 114
Breast feeding, antidepressants and, 56-57
Bupropion, 15t, 55t, 199
Buspirone (BuSpar), 15t, 16, 54t

CAGE questionnaire, 143, 144t
Calan. *See* Verapamil
Cannabis, 142, 148
Carbamazepine, 52t
Carbidopa. *See* Levodopa
Cardiovascular disease, 5t
  smoking-related, 150
  systemic lupus erythematosus and, 164
  tricyclic antidepressants for patient with, 49, 51
CBT. *See* Cognitive behavior therapy
CD. *See* Conversion disorder
Cerebral palsy, 69, 69t
CFS. *See* Chronic fatigue syndrome
Children
  anxiety disorders in, 2
    obsessive-compulsive disorder, 7
    separation anxiety disorder, 9-11, 16-17
  attention-deficit hyperactivity disorder in, 19-28
  common normal fears of, 10t
  developmental delay in, 24, 63-71
  differential diagnosis of behavioral problems in, 23t, 23-24
  learning disabilities in, 23, 68
  neonatal lupus, 170
  poor school performance in, xxvii-xxviii
  somatization in, 135
Chlordiazepoxide, 185
Chloroquine, 168t
Chromosomal abnormalities, 66
Chronic fatigue syndrome (CFS), 29-36
  cause of, 29
  chief complaint in, 29
  conditions that do not adequately explain or exclude a diagnosis of, 29, 32t
  conditions that exclude a diagnosis of, 29, 31t
  depression and, 203
  diagnostic criteria for, 30t
  diagnostic testing for, 32-33, 33t
  epidemiology of, 30

  family/community support for patients with, 35-36
  follow-up of patients with, 36
  history taking for, 29-31
  management of, 34-35
    alternative therapies, 35
    cognitive behavior therapy, 34
    medication for symptomatic treatment, 34
    physical and environmental measures, 34-35
  patient education about, 35
  physical examination for, 31-32
  sources of information about, 36t
  when to refer for, 33
Cigarette smoking, 142, 149-150, 152-153
Cimetidine, 53t
Clomipramine, 53t
  for body dysmorphic disorder, 133
  for obsessive-compulsive disorder, 14
Clonazepam, 12, 13t, 185
Cluster headache, 83t, 86
Cocaine use, 142, 143t, 148, 156
Cognex. *See* Tacrine
Cognitive behavior therapy (CBT), for chronic fatigue syndrome, 34
Cognitive enhancers, 115, 116t
Coital headache, 83t, 86
Conduct disorder, 24
Confrontation strategy for patients with substance use disorders, 151-153
Connective tissue diseases, 166t
Conner's Abbreviated Parent-Teacher Questionnaire, 21, 22t
Conversion disorder (CD), 120t, 121, 123-124, 136t-137t
  diagnostic criteria for, 211
  family involvement in, 138
  management of, 131-132
  patient education about, 138
  physical examination and diagnostic testing for, 126, 126t
  when to refer for, 128
Corticosteroids, 168, 168t, 169
Cough headache, 83t, 87
Coumadin. *See* Warfarin
Cyclobenzaprine, 77, 77t
Cyclophosphamide, 169
Cylert. *See* Pemoline
Cyproheptadine, 51

Dalmane. *See* Flurazepam
DDST. *See* Denver Developmental Screening Test
Death of long-term partner, 6, 41, 41t
Delirium, 111
Dementia, 112
  Alzheimer's disease, 112-113, 113t

Dementia—*Continued*
  human immunodeficiency virus infection
    and, 115
  Lewy body variant, 113-114
  Pick's disease, 113
  vascular, 113
Demerol. *See* Meperidine
Denver Developmental Screening Test
    (DDST), 65t, 66
Depakene, Depakote. *See* Valproate
Depressive disorders, xxviii, 37-61
  anxiety disorders and, 2, 201
  atypical, 38
  chief complaints in, 37
  chronic fatigue syndrome and, 203
  developmental delay and, 70
  diagnostic criteria for, 191-197
  diagnostic tests for, 44t, 45, 45t
  "double," 39
  epidemiology of, 201
  fibromyalgia and, 203
  follow-up of patients with, 61
  history taking for, 37-43, 38t
    adjustment disorder with depressed
      mood, 40
    bereavement, 41, 41t
    borderline personality disorder, 40
    depression secondary to substance
      abuse/dependence, 40-41, 201
    dysthymic disorder, 39-40, 40t
    major depressive disorder, 38-39
    medical comorbidity, 41-42, 42t,
      202-203
    medications, 42, 43t
    patients with chronic pain, 42
    postpartum patient, 42
    somatizing patient, 42-43, 43t, 129,
      129t, 202
  management of, 46-60, 198-199, 203-207
    (*See also* Antidepressants)
    adjustment disorder, 47
    Agency for Health Care Policy and Re-
      search clinical practice guidelines for,
      200-207
    algorithm for, 198
    antidepressant medications, 48-58, 199,
      203-207
    approach to, 46-47
    bereavement, 48
    borderline personality disorder, 47-48
    depression secondary to substance
      abuse, 48
    dysthymic disorder, 47
    in elderly patients, 206
    electroconvulsive therapy, 204
    length of medication treatment,
      206-207
    light therapy, 60

  major depressive disorder, 47
  psychotherapy, 58-60, 205-206
  patient and family education about, 60t,
    60-61
  physical examination for, 43, 44t
  pseudodementia and, 114, 116
  with psychotic symptoms, 38
  seasonal, 38
  sleep disturbance and, 100, 103
  suicide risk and, 46, 47t
  when to refer for, 45-46, 46t
Dermatomyositis, 166t
Desensitization therapy, 16
Desipramine, 53t, 199
Desoxyn. *See* Methamphetamine
Desyrel. *See* Trazodone
Detoxification, 153-154. *See also* Substance
    use disorders
  from alcohol, 153-154
  from nicotine, 154
  from opioids, 154
Developmental delay, xiiii, 24, 63-71
  chief complaint in, 63
  diagnostic testing for, 66-67
  differential diagnosis of, 67-70
    autism, 70
    cerebral palsy, 69, 69t
    hypothyroidism, 68
    inborn errors of metabolism, 69
    language disorders, 68
    lead poisoning, 68
    learning disabilities, 68
    mental retardation, 68-69
    neurocutaneous syndromes, 66, 66t, 70
    normal variation, 67
    psychosocial conditions, 70
    vision or hearing abnormalities, 66, 67
  follow-up of patients with, 71
  history taking for, 63-66
    current development, 66
    developmental milestones, 63-66, 65t
    medical history, 63, 64t
  management of, 71
  patient education about, 71
  physical examination for, 66
  prevalence of, 63
  risk factors for, 63, 64t
  support groups for, 71
  when to refer for, 70
Dextroamphetamine (Dexedrine), 26t
Diabetic patients, antidepressants for, 54-55
Diagnostic charts, xiii-xxxii
Diagnostic criteria
  acute stress disorder, 177-178
  adjustment disorder, 196
  anxiety disorders, 175-184
  attention-deficit hyperactivity disorder,
    20t

borderline personality disorder, 197
chronic fatigue syndrome, 30t
conversion disorder, 211
depressive disorders, 191-197
dysthymic disorder, 194-195
factitious disorder, 212
fibromyalgia syndrome, 74t
generalized anxiety disorder, 183
hypochondriasis, 210
major depressive disorder, 191-193
obsessive-compulsive disorder, 181-182
pain disorder, 209
panic disorder, 176
post-traumatic stress disorder, 179-180
separation anxiety disorder of
    childhood/adolescence, 184
somatoform disorders, 208-211
systemic lupus erythematosus, 162t
Diazepam, 16, 185
Diet
    monoamine oxidase inhibitors and, 52
    for patients with fibromyalgia syndrome,
    77
Diffuse complaints, xv
Dihydroergotamine, 91, 91t
Dilantin. See Phenytoin
Disulfiram, 155
"Doctor shopping," 119
Donepezil, 115, 116t
Doxepin, 53t, 199
    for fibromyalgia syndrome, 76-77, 77t
Drug abuse. See Substance use disorders
Drug holidays, 27
Drug interactions with antidepressants, 49
    monoamine oxidase inhibitors, 54, 54t
    selective serotonin reuptake inhibitors, 51,
    52t
    tricyclics, 52, 54t
Drug-induced disorders
    attention deficits, 24
    confusion and memory loss, 114, 114t
    depression, 37, 40-42, 43t, 48, 201
    hyperirritability, 24
    insomnia, 98, 100
    lupus erythematosus, 165-166
    panic attacks, 4
    substance-induced anxiety disorder, 1, 8t,
    8-9, 15
Dysthymic disorder, 37, 39-40
    diagnostic criteria for, 194-195
    "double depression," 39-40
    epidemiology of, 39-40
    vs. major depressive disorder, 39, 40t
    management of, 47

ECG. See Electrocardiogram
Effexor. See Venlafaxine
Elavil. See Amitriptyline

Electrocardiogram (ECG)
    before initiation of tricyclic antidepres-
    sants, 49
    in insomnia, 101
Electroconvulsive therapy, 204
Endocarditis prophylaxis, 169
Endocrine disease, 5t
Ergotamine preparations, 90-91, 91t
Estrogens, 53t
Exercise for patients with fibromyalgia syn-
    drome, 77
Eyestrain, 88

Factitious disorder (FD), 120, 125, 137t. See
    also Malingering
    diagnostic criteria for, 212
    epidemiology of, 121
    family involvement in, 139
    management of, 133-134
    patient education about, 139
    physical examination and diagnostic test-
    ing for, 126-127
    by proxy, 125, 134
    when to refer for, 128
Fatigue, xvi-xviii, xxxiv
    chronic fatigue syndrome, 29-36
FD. See Factitious disorder
Fever, xviii-xx
Fibromyalgia syndrome (FS), 73-78
    chief complaint in, 73
    depression and, 203
    diagnostic criteria for, 74t
    diagnostic tests for, 75-76, 76t
    epidemiology of, 74
    follow-up of patients with, 78
    history taking for, 73-74
    as independent entity, 75
    management of, 76-78
        aerobic exercise, 77
        alternative therapies, 78
        medications, 76-77, 77t
        physical and environmental measures,
        77
    patient education about, 78
    physical examination in, 74-75
    support groups for, 78
    vs. systemic lupus erythematosus, 166
    when to refer for, 76
Flexeril. See Cyclobenzaprine
Fluoxetine, 50-51, 51t, 199
    for body dysmorphic disorder, 133
    for panic disorder, 13
Flurazepam, 104t, 185
Fluvoxamine, 14, 51t
Folstein Mini-Mental State Examination, 110,
    188-190
Forgetfulness. See Memory concerns
FS. See Fibromyalgia syndrome

GAD. *See* Generalized anxiety disorder
Galactosemia, 69
Generalized anxiety disorder (GAD), 1, 9
  vs. adjustment disorder with anxious features, 9
  alcoholism and, 16
  diagnostic criteria for, 183
  management of, 16
  symptoms of, 3t, 9
Geriatric depression, 206
Giant cell arteritis, 84t, 85–86
Grief reaction, 6, 41, 41t
Guanadrel, 54t

Halcion. *See* Triazolam
Haloperidol (Haldol), 116
Hashish, 142
Head injury, 87
Headaches, xxii–xxiv, 81–93
  chief complaint in, 81
  chronic/recurrent, 88–89
    classic migraine, 84t, 88
    common migraine, 84t, 88
    tension headache, 84t, 89
  comparative features of, 83t–84t
  diagnostic testing for, 89–90
  due to emergent, potentially life-threatening conditions, 82–86
    giant cell arteritis, 84t, 85–86
    meningitis, 82, 85
    subarachnoid hemorrhage, 85
  follow-up of patients with, 92
  history taking for, 81–82
  lifestyle changes for, 92–93
  management of, 90–92, 91t
  patient education about, 92
  physical examination for, 89
  prevalence of, 81
  seen more often in men, 86–87
    cluster headaches, 83t, 86
    coital headache, 83t, 86
    cough headache, 83t, 87
  of specific etiology, 87–88
    brain tumor, 83t, 87
    ophthalmologic headache, 88
    postconcussion headache, 87
    sinus headache, 88
  types of, 81, 82t
  when to refer for, 90
Hemorrhage, subarachnoid, 85
Human immunodeficiency virus (HIV) infection
  dementia and, 115
  vs. systemic lupus erythematosus, 166
  testing for, 150
Hydrocephalus, 114
Hydroxychloroquine, 168t
Hylorel. *See* Guanadrel

Hyperactivity. *See* Attention-deficit hyperactivity disorder
Hypochondriasis, 120t, 121, 123, 136t
  diagnostic criteria for, 210
  family involvement in, 138
  management of, 131–132
  patient education about, 135, 138
  when to refer for, 128
Hypothyroidism, 68

Imipramine, 53t, 199
Inattention. *See* Attention-deficit hyperactivity disorder
Inborn errors of metabolism, 69
Inderal. *See* Propranolol
Insomnia, xxv–xxvi, 95–105
  chief complaint in, 95
  diagnostic testing for, 100–101
    electrocardiogram, 101
    laboratory evaluation, 100t, 100–101
    multiple sleep latency test, 101
    polysomnography, 101
  epidemiology of, 96
  follow-up of patients with, 105
  history taking for, 95–100
    altitude insomnia, 98
    drug- or alcohol-dependent insomnia, 98
    inadequate sleep hygiene, 96
    narcolepsy, 98
    parasomnias, 99
    periodic limb movement disorder, 97
    psychophysiologic insomnia, 96–97
    restless legs syndrome, 97
    shift-work sleep disorder, 99
    sleep apnea syndrome, 97
    sleep disorders associated with neurologic disorders, 99
    sleep disorders associated with other chronic medical conditions, 99
    sleep disorders due to anxiety or depressive disorder, 100
    transient situational insomnia, 95–96
  management of, 102–104
    medications, 104, 104t
    other modalities, 104
    specific syndromes, 102–104
  patient education about, 105
  physical examination for, 100
  when to refer for, 102
Instrumental activities of daily living, 107, 108t
Insulin, 54t, 54–55
Isoptin. *See* Verapamil

Klonopin. *See* Clonazepam
Korsakoff's syndrome, 111–112

La belle indifference, 126
Lactation, antidepressants during, 56–57
Language disorders, 68
Lead poisoning, 24, 67, 68
Learning disabilities, 23, 68
Levodopa, 54t
Lewy body variant dementia, 113–114
Librium. See Chlordiazepoxide
Lifestyle modifications
    for anxiety disorders, 17
    for chronic fatigue syndrome, 35
    for headaches, 92–93
Light therapy for depression, 60
Linear nevus syndrome, 66t, 70
Lithium, 52t
Lorazepam, 15, 185
LSD. See Lysergic acid diethylamide
Ludiomil. See Maprotiline
Lupus Foundation, 171
Lupus nephritis, 169
Luvox. See Fluvoxamine
Lymphadenopathy, xxvi–xxvii
Lysergic acid diethylamide (LSD), 142, 148

Major depressive disorder (MDD), 38–39
    diagnostic criteria for, 191–193
    epidemiology of, 39
    management of, 47
    recurrence of, 39
    types of, 38
Malingering, 120, 125, 137t. See also Facti-
        tious disorder
    epidemiology of, 121
    family involvement in, 139
    management of, 134
    patient education about, 139
    physical examination and diagnostic test-
        ing for, 127
    when to refer for, 128
Managed care, xxxiv
Mania, 38, 39t
MAOIs. See Monoamine oxidase inhibitors
Maple syrup urine disease, 69
Maprotiline, 15t, 55t
Marijuana, 142, 148
MDD. See Major depressive disorder
Medical conditions
    antidepressants for patients with, 49
    anxiety disorder due to, 1, 8, 15
    vs. attention-deficit hyperactivity disorder,
        24
    depression and, 41–42, 42t, 202–203
    panic disorder and, 4, 5t
    sleep disorders associated with, 99
Memory concerns, xx–xxii, xxiv–xxv,
        107–117
    affecting activities of daily living, 107, 107t
    chief complaint in, 107

diagnostic testing for, 110–111
    laboratory and imaging studies, 110–111
    objective measurement of cognitive
        function, 110
differential diagnosis of, 111–115
    Alzheimer's disease, 112–113, 113t
    amnestic syndromes, 111–112
    benign senescent forgetfulness, 111
    delirium, 111
    depression, 114
    drugs and toxins, 114, 114t
    human immunodeficiency virus infec-
        tion, 115
    mass lesions and hydrocephalus,
        114–115
    Parkinson's disease and Lewy body vari-
        ant dementia, 113–114
    vascular dementia, 113
follow-up of patients with, 117
history taking for, 107–108
immediate, recent, and remote memory,
        109
management of, 115–117
    medications for Alzheimer's disease,
        115–116, 116t
    medications for coexisting depression,
        116
    other modalities, 116–117
physical examination for, 108–110
    general physical examination, 109–110
    mental status examination, 108–109
    neurologic examination, 109
    when to refer for, 115
Meningitis, 82, 85
Mental retardation, 68–69. See also Develop-
        mental delay
Mental status examination, 108–109,
        186–187
Meperidine, 54t
Metabolic disorders, 69
Methadone maintenance therapy, 154
Methamphetamine, 26t
Methylphenidate, 25, 26t, 71
Methylpredisone, 168t
Methysergide, 92
Migraine, 84t, 88, 89
    acute management of, 90–91, 91t
    prophylaxis for, 91–92
Mini-Mental State Examination (MMSE), 110,
        188–190
Mirtazapine, 55t
Mixed connective tissue disease, 166t
MMSE. See Mini-Mental State Examination
Monoamine oxidase inhibitors (MAOIs),
        52–54
    dietary precautions with, 52
    drug interactions with, 52t, 54, 54t
    hypertensive crisis induced by, 49, 52

Monoamine oxidase inhibitors (MAOIs)—
Continued
  indications for, 52
  for medically ill patients, 49
  overdose of, 49–50
  for panic disorder, 12
  for post-traumatic stress disorder, 14
MSLT. *See* Multiple sleep latency test
Multi-infarct dementia, 113
Multiple sleep latency test (MSLT), 101
Munchausen's syndrome, 121
Munchausen's syndrome by proxy, 121
Muscle pains, diffuse, xv–xvi
  fibromyalgia syndrome, 73–78

NA. *See* Narcotics Anonymous
Narcolepsy, 96, 98, 103–104
Narcotic abuse, 143t, 147. *See also* Substance
  use disorders
Narcotic withdrawal, 154
Narcotics Anonymous (NA), 151, 155
Nardil. *See* Phenelzine
National Academy for Child Development, 71
Nefazodone, 51, 55t, 199
Neonatal lupus, 170
Neurocutaneous syndromes, 66, 66t, 70
Neurofibromatosis, 66t, 70
Neuroleptics, use in dementia, 116
Neurologic disorders, 5t
  vs. attention-deficit hyperactivity disorder,
    24
  cerebral palsy, 69, 69t
  developmental delay and, 66
  memory concerns and, 109
  sleep disorders and, 99
Nicotine addiction, 142, 149–150, 152–153
Nicotine replacement therapy, 154
Nifedipine, 52t
Nonsteroidal anti-inflammatory drugs
  (NSAIDs), 167, 168t
Norpramin. *See* Desipramine
Nortriptyline, 53t, 199
  for migraine prophylaxis, 92
NSAIDs. *See* Nonsteroidal anti-inflammatory
  drugs

Obsessive-compulsive disorder (OCD), 1, 7
  in children, 7
  clinical course of, 7
  diagnostic criteria for, 181–182
  management of, 14–15
  onset of, 7
  pregnancy and, 7
  symptoms of, 3t, 7
Ophthalmologic headache, 88
Opioid abuse, 143t, 147. *See also* Substance
  use disorders
Opioid withdrawal, 154

Oppositional-defiant disorder, 24
Oral contraceptives, 53t
Oral hypoglycemic agents, 54t
Oxazepam, 15, 185

Pain
  depression and, 42
  fibromyalgia syndrome, 73–78
  headache, 81–93
  in somatoform disorders, 121
Pain disorder, 120t, 121, 123, 136t
  diagnostic criteria for, 209
  family involvement in, 135
  management of, 130–131
  patient education about, 135
  when to refer for, 127
Pamelor. *See* Nortriptyline
Panic attack, 1, 2–4
  criteria for, 175
  duration of, 2
  management of, 12
  physical examination during, 11
  provocative chemicals and, 4
  symptoms of, 2–4, 3t
Panic disorder (PD), 1, 4–5, 5t
  agoraphobia with, 4–5
  diagnostic criteria for, 176
  management of, 12–14, 13t
    medications that are not helpful, 15t
  medical conditions in differential diagnosis
    of, 4, 5t
  pregnancy and, 4
  prevalence of, 4
  symptoms of, 3t, 4
Parasomnias, 99
Parkinson's disease, 113–114
Paroxetine, 51, 51t, 199
  for body dysmorphic disorder, 133
  for panic disorder, 13
Patient/family education
  about antidepressants, 60–61
  about anxiety disorders, 17
  about attention-deficit hyperactivity disor-
    der, 27–28
  about chronic fatigue syndrome, 35
  about depression, 60t, 60–61
  about developmental delay, 71
  about fibromyalgia syndrome, 78
  about headaches, 92
  about insomnia, 105
  about somatoform disorders, 134–139
  about substance use disorders, 157–158
  about systemic lupus erythematosus, 171
Paxil. *See* Paroxetine
PCP. *See* Phencyclidine
PD. *See* Panic disorder
Pemoline, 25, 26t
Periodic limb movement disorder, 97, 103

Personality disorders, depression and, 37, 40, 202
Pharmacotherapy
  for Alzheimer's disease, 115-116, 116t
  for attention-deficit hyperactivity disorder, 25-27, 26t
  for chronic fatigue syndrome, 34
  for developmental delay, 71
  for fibromyalgia syndrome, 76-77, 77t
  for generalized anxiety disorder, 16
  for headache, 90-92, 91t
  for insomnia, 104, 104t
  for obsessive-compulsive disorder, 14
  for panic disorder, 12-13, 13t
  for post-traumatic stress disorder, 14
  for separation anxiety disorder of childhood/adolescence, 17
  for social phobia, 16
  for substance use disorders, 155-156
  for systemic lupus erythematosus, 167-169, 168t
Phencyclidine (PCP), 142, 149, 156
Phenelzine, 52
  for migraine prophylaxis, 92
  for social phobia, 16
Phenformin, 54t
Phenytoin, 52t, 53t
Phobia, 1, 9
  common types of, 9
  definition of, 9
  management of, 16
  symptoms of, 3t, 9
Pick's disease, 113
Polymyositis, 166t
Polysomnography, 101
Postconcussion headache, 87
Postpartum patients. *See* Pregnant/postpartum patients
Post-traumatic stress disorder (PTSD), 1, 6-7
  acute vs. chronic, 7
  after death of long-term partner, 6
  diagnostic criteria for, 179-180
  factors affecting development and severity of, 6-7
  management of, 14
  symptoms of, 3t, 6
Prednisone, 168t
Pregnant/postpartum patients
  antidepressants for, 55-57
  depression in, 42
  obsessive-compulsive disorder in, 7
  panic disorder in, 4
  systemic lupus erythematosus in, 169-170
Procardia. *See* Nifedipine
Progressive systemic sclerosis, 166t
Propranolol, 15t, 92
Protriptyline, 103, 104
Prozac. *See* Fluoxetine

Pseudodementia, depressive, 114, 116
Psychotherapy, 130
  for adjustment disorder with depressed mood, 47
  for borderline personality disorder, 48
  for chronic fatigue syndrome, 34
  for depression, 58-60
  for generalized anxiety disorder, 16
  for obsessive-compulsive disorder, 15
  for pain disorder, 131
  for panic disorder, 14
  for post-traumatic stress disorder, 14
  for somatizing patient, 130
PTSD. *See* Post-traumatic stress disorder
Pulmonary disease, 5t, 149, 153

Quinidine, 53t

Remeron. *See* Mirtazapine
Restless legs syndrome, 97, 103
Restoril. *See* Temazepam
Rheumatoid arthritis, 166t
Risk reduction for patients with substance use disorders, 158
Ritalin. *See* Methylphenidate

Sadness, xxviii. *See also* Depressive disorders
Sansert. *See* Methysergide
Schizophrenia in children, 24
Schizotypal personality disorder in children, 24
School phobia, 11, 24
Scleroderma, 166t
Seasonal affective disorder, 38, 60
Sedative-hypnotics, 104, 104t
Seizures, 169
Selective serotonin reuptake inhibitors (SSRIs), 50-51, 51t, 199
  for body dysmorphic disorder, 133
  for depressive pseudodementia, 116
  dosages of, 199
  drug interactions with, 51, 52t
  for generalized anxiety disorder, 16
  for obsessive-compulsive disorder, 14
  overdose of, 49-50
  for panic disorder, 12-13, 13t
  for post-traumatic stress disorder, 14
  side effects of, 50-51, 199
Self-paced exposure therapy, 16
Sensory deficits, 23
  developmental delay and, 66, 67
Sensory neuropathies, xxix-xxx
Separation anxiety disorder of childhood/adolescence, 1, 9-11
  vs. attention-deficit hyperactivity disorder, 24
  diagnostic criteria for, 184
  management of, 16-17

Separation anxiety disorder of
childhood/adolescence—*Continued*
vs. normal fears, 10t
symptoms of, 3t, 9-11
Serax. *See* Oxazepam
Serotonin syndrome, 56
Sertraline, 51t, 199
for body dysmorphic disorder, 133
for panic disorder, 13
Serzone. *See* Nefazodone
Shift-work sleep disorder, 99, 102-103
SIAD. *See* Substance-induced anxiety disorder
Sinemet. *See* Levodopa
Sinequan. *See* Doxepin
Sinus headache, 88
SLE. *See* Systemic lupus erythematosus
Sleep apnea syndrome, 96, 97, 100, 103
Sleep disorders. *See* Insomnia
Smoking, 142, 149-150, 152-153
Social phobia, 16
Somatoform disorders, xxxiii, 119-139
chief complaints in, 120-121
classification of, 119, 120t
comparative features of, 136t-137t
diagnostic criteria for, 208-211
epidemiology of, 121
family involvement in, 135, 138-139
history taking for, 122-124
body dysmorphic disorder, 124
conversion disorder, 123-124, 211
hypochondriasis, 123, 210
pain disorder, 123, 209
somatization disorder, 122, 208
somatization disorder not otherwise
specified, 122
undifferentiated somatoform disorder,
123
impact of, 120
management of, 128-134
mood or anxiety disorders and, 42-43,
129, 129t, 202
patient education about, 134-139
physical examination and diagnostic testing for, 125-127, 126t
subsyndromal somatization, 119
vs. systemic lupus erythematosus, 166
when to refer for, 127-128
Speedballing, 148
SSRIs. *See* Selective serotonin reuptake inhibitors
Stimulants
abuse of, 143t, 147-148
for attention-deficit hyperactivity disorder,
25-27, 26t
Stress
acute stress disorder, 5-6, 14, 177-178
post-traumatic stress disorder, 6-7, 14,
179-180

Sturge-Weber disease, 66t, 70
Subarachnoid hemorrhage, 85
Substance use disorders, 141-158
chief complaints associated with, 141,
143t
depression and, 40-41, 201
diagnostic testing for, 150-151
economic cost of, 141
epidemiology of, 142
follow-up of patients with, 156-157
continuing users, 156-157
duration of, 156
recovery symptoms, 156
relapses, 156
history taking for, 142, 144t
impact of, 141
management of, 151-156
detoxification, 153-154
identification and confrontation,
151-153
medications, 155-156
rehabilitation programs, 154-155
support for family members, 155
treatment, 153
patient and family education about,
157-158
physical examination for, 145-150
alcohol abuse/dependence, 145-146,
146t
alcohol withdrawal, 146-147
amphetamine abuse, 147-148
cocaine, 148
depressant withdrawal, 147
lysergic acid diethylamide, 148
marijuana, 148
nicotine addiction, 149-150
opioid abuse, 147
phencyclidine, 149
risk reduction and health promotion for patients with, 158
screening for, 143-145, 144t
when to refer for, 151
Substance-induced anxiety disorder (SIAD), 1
diagnosis of, 3t, 8-9
management of, 15
medications associated with, 8t
Suicide risk assessment, 46, 47t
Sumatriptan, 91, 91t
Support groups
for Alzheimer's disease, 117
for attention-deficit hyperactivity disorder,
27t, 27-28
for developmental delay, 71
for fibromyalgia syndrome, 78
for substance use disorders, 151
for systemic lupus erythematosus, 171
Symmetrel. *See* Amantadine
Sympathomimetic amines, 53t, 54t